CHRIST-CENTERED

Exposition

NT / COMMENTARY

AUTHOR **Tony Merida**
SERIES EDITORS **David Platt, Daniel L. Akin, and Tony Merida**

CHRIST-CENTERED
Exposition

EXALTING JESUS IN

EPHESIANS

HOLMAN
REFERENCE

NASHVILLE, TENNESSEE

B&H Publishing Group
Nashville, Tennessee
All rights reserved.

ISBN 978-0-8054-9672-7

Dewey Decimal Classification: 220.7
Subject Heading: BIBLE. N.T. EPHESIANS—COMMENTARIES\
JESUS CHRIST

Printed in the United States of America
1 2 3 4 5 6 7 8 9 10 • 18 17 16 15 14
VP

SERIES DEDICATION

Dedicated to Adrian Rogers and John Piper. They have taught us to love the gospel of Jesus Christ, to preach the Bible as the inerrant Word of God, to pastor the church for which our Savior died, and to have a passion to see all nations gladly worship the Lamb.

—David Platt, Tony Merida, and Danny Akin
March 2013

TABLE OF CONTENTS

Acknowledgments   ix
Series Introduction   xi

Ephesians

Introduction to Ephesians   1:1-2   3
Whom Do You Worship?   1:3-14   19
Praying to the Glorious Father   1:15-23   33
But God . . .   2:1-10   43
Our Corporate Identity   2:11-22   54
A Christ-Centered Missionary   3:1-13   69
Praying for Power   3:14-21   81
A Healthy Body   4:1-16   93
A New Set of Clothes   4:17-32   104
Imitate God   5:1-17   117
A Spirit-Filled Marriage   5:18-33   130
Gospel-Centered Families   6:1-4   145
Transferring Masters   6:5-9   156
Life Is War   6:10-24   171

Works Cited   186
Scripture Index   190

ACKNOWLEDGMENTS

I wish to express thanks to the congregations of First Baptist Kenner, Temple Baptist Church, and Imago Dei Church (IDC). I've had the privilege of preaching through the book of Ephesians in each of these contexts. In each case the Lord graciously worked in the lives of His people through His Word. I stand amazed by the fact that I get to expound the Scriptures in the context of the local church; it's an honor beyond words.

In my present context at IDC, a few of our interns helped me edit this manuscript—Manny, Joseph, and Samuel—and I'm supergrateful for their labor. They are wonderful examples of godly young men and will, by God's grace, become faithful pastors in the future. Thank you, brothers.

To the elders at IDC—Matt, Donnie, and Nate—thank you for weekly help in sermon preparation and for your constant evaluation and encouragement. What a joy to labor with you.

I'm also incredibly grateful for Dr. Daniel Akin, who affords me the opportunity to teach at Southeastern Baptist Theological Seminary. SEBTS is a happy place, filled with hungry students and humble professors. I'm honored to be on the team at this Great Commission institution.

To my bride Kimberly, I give God praise for the opportunity we have in living out Ephesians 5:18-33 together. May the Lord grant us many more days to live in happy union and in ministry partnership. And may the Lord's grace be sufficient as we raise five children.

Finally, to the Lord Jesus Christ: the book of Ephesians sparkles with Your glory and dazzles us with Your redeeming grace. May You be glorified by this little commentary. May the readers be equipped and built up, and may those who proclaim Your unsearchable riches be helped and encouraged for the good of Your church and for the glory of Your great name.

Tony Merida

SERIES INTRODUCTION

Augustine said, "Where Scripture speaks, God speaks." The editors of the Christ-Centered Exposition Commentary series believe that where God speaks, the pastor must speak. God speaks through His written Word. We must speak from that Word. We believe the Bible is God breathed, authoritative, inerrant, sufficient, understandable, necessary, and timeless. We also affirm that the Bible is a Christ-centered book; that is, it contains a unified story of redemptive history of which Jesus is the hero. Because of this Christ-centered trajectory that runs from Genesis 1 through Revelation 22, we believe the Bible has a corresponding global-missions thrust. From beginning to end, we see God's mission as one of making worshipers of Christ from every tribe and tongue worked out through this redemptive drama in Scripture. To that end we must preach the Word.

In addition to these distinct convictions, the Christ-Centered Exposition Commentary series has some distinguishing characteristics. First, this series seeks to display exegetical accuracy. What the Bible says is what we want to say. While not every volume in the series will be a verse-by-verse commentary, we nevertheless desire to handle the text carefully and explain it rightly. Those who teach and preach bear the heavy responsibility of saying what God has said in His Word and declaring what God has done in Christ. We desire to handle God's Word faithfully, knowing that we must give an account for how we have fulfilled this holy calling (Jas 3:1).

Second, the Christ-Centered Exposition Commentary series has pastors in view. While we hope others will read this series, such as parents, teachers, small-group leaders, and student ministers, we desire to provide a commentary busy pastors will use for weekly preparation of biblically faithful and gospel-saturated sermons. This series is not academic in nature. Our aim is to present a readable and pastoral style of commentaries. We believe this aim will serve the church of the Lord Jesus Christ.

Third, we want the Christ-Centered Exposition Commentary series to be known for the inclusion of helpful illustrations and theologically driven applications. Many commentaries offer no help in illustrations, and few offer any kind of help in application. Often those that do offer illustrative material and application unfortunately give little serious attention to the text. While giving ourselves primarily to explanation, we also hope to serve readers by providing inspiring and illuminating illustrations coupled with timely and timeless application.

Finally, as the name suggests, the editors seek to exalt Jesus from every book of the Bible. In saying this, we are not commending wild allegory or fanciful typology. We certainly believe we must be constrained to the meaning intended by the divine Author Himself, the Holy Spirit of God. However, we also believe the Bible has a messianic focus, and our hope is that the individual authors will exalt Christ from particular texts. Luke 24:25-27,44-47 and John 5:39,46 inform both our hermeneutics and our homiletics. Not every author will do this the same way or have the same degree of Christ-centered emphasis. That is fine with us. We believe faithful exposition that is Christ centered is not monolithic. We do believe, however, that we must read the whole Bible as Christian Scripture. Therefore, our aim is both to honor the historical particularity of each biblical passage and to highlight its intrinsic connection to the Redeemer.

The editors are indebted to the contributors of each volume. The reader will detect a unique style from each writer, and we celebrate these unique gifts and traits. While distinctive in their approaches, the authors share a common characteristic in that they are pastoral theologians. They love the church, and they regularly preach and teach God's Word to God's people. Further, many of these contributors are younger voices. We think these new, fresh voices can serve the church well, especially among a rising generation that has the task of proclaiming the Word of Christ and the Christ of the Word to the lost world.

We hope and pray this series will serve the body of Christ well in these ways until our Savior returns in glory. If it does, we will have succeeded in our assignment.

David Platt
Daniel L. Akin
Tony Merida
Series Editors
February 2013

Ephesians

Introduction to Ephesians

EPHESIANS 1:1-2

Main Idea: Paul conveys his pastoral heart for the Ephesian believers by writing a letter to them that focuses on who they are in Christ and how they are now to live in light of this new identity.

I. **Why Study Ephesians?**
II. **The Author (1:1a)**
   A. Paul: An apostle of Christ Jesus by the will of God
   B. Be devoted to the apostles' teaching.
III. **The Recipients (1:1b)**
   A. The struggle in Ephesus
   B. The saints in Ephesus
IV. **The Greeting (1:2)**
V. **The Message**
   A. Our position—who we are in Christ (1:3–3:21)
      1. We now have new life in Christ (1:3–2:10).
      2. We now have a new community in Christ (2:11–3:21).
   B. Our practice—how we are to live in Christ (4:1–6:24)
      1. We must now pursue unity and purity in Christ (4:1–5:14).
      2. We must now pursue submissiveness and stability in Christ (5:15–6:24).
VI. **Don't Lose Your First Love.**

Ephesians consists of only six chapters. In my particular copy of the Bible, it is only four pages. It contains only 155 verses. It will take you about 20 minutes to read the whole thing out loud. Yet we find divine beauty and power in this little book. To paraphrase Klyne Snodgrass, "Pound for pound, Ephesians may well be the most influential document in history" (Snodgrass, *Ephesians*, 17). What makes it so influential? Why should we study it?

Why Study Ephesians?

Ephesians deepens our understanding of the gospel. Unfortunately, we live in a day with much superficial Christianity. Much shallow teaching is going around, but when you get to Ephesians, you dive into what Paul calls "the incalculable riches of the Messiah" (3:8). It is a great place to dive in deep and discover the true meaning of the gospel.

Ephesians magnifies the importance of the church, perhaps more than any other New Testament letter. We also live in a day in which people do not really value the church. They are inclined to think, "If nothing else is going on this weekend, then I guess I will attend a corporate worship service." Yet when we look in the book of Ephesians, we read how the church is central to God's eternal purposes; the church is put in eternal perspective. Through the church God has chosen to make known His "multi-faceted wisdom" (3:10).

Lives have been forever changed by the exploration of this little book. John Mackay, former president of Princeton Seminary, recalled how, at the age of 14, he took his Bible into the hills of Scotland and studied the book of Ephesians. He wrote these words: "I saw a new world . . . everything was new . . . I had a new outlook, new experiences, new attitudes to other people. I loved God. Jesus Christ became the center of everything. . . . I had been 'quickened.' I was really alive" (in Stott, *Ephesians,* 15). May a whole new world be opened up to you also!

Ephesians may also be the "most contemporary" epistle in the New Testament. Apart from the mention of slavery, which we will address later, this letter "could have been written to a modern church" (Snodgrass, *Ephesians,* 17). This is because Ephesians is not the most situational of letters. Typically when Paul wrote letters, he wrote to correct something, but in Ephesians we encounter little of that. It is more reflective and less corrective. It was a circular letter, distributed and read by the churches in the Asia Minor region and, therefore, comes to us in a general form. Paul does not name particular false teachers, mention specific problems in the church at Ephesus, or include his travel plans as he does in other letters. As a result Ephesians resonates with contemporary Christians because it seems Paul could have written the letter to a twenty-first-century church.

Ephesians provides grace-filled encouragement. If you feel tired, discouraged, beat up, lonely, or confused, then welcome to Ephesians! Our souls need to see this description of the glorious grace of God. We need the gospel every day. Yes, Christians need the gospel every day. Remember, Paul is writing this letter to Christian churches, yet he devotes three chapters to telling them what the gospel is. Paul is writing to ordinary people just like us. Some were wealthy. Some were simple employees. Some worked at the port. Some were servants of masters. Some worked in the small villages. They were Christians living in the world. They first needed to understand who they were and then how to live in that reality, just like us.

Ephesians offers some practical answers to basic questions about the Christian life. It is a "mini theology book" every Christian would benefit from studying. Non-Christians, particularly those interested enough to learn what Christians believe, would also benefit from a study in the book of Ephesians. In this book we will address the following questions:

- Why worship? (1:3-14)
- What should we pray for? (1:15-23)
- What is so amazing about grace? (2:1-10)
- Who are we? (2:11-22)
- Why is the church a big deal? (3:1-13)
- What should we pray for? (3:14-21)
- How can we be unified? (4:1-16)
- How do "new" people live? (4:17-32)
- How can we imitate God? (5:1-14)
- What is God's plan for marriage? (5:15-33)
- How should we parent? (6:1-4)
- How should we see our vocation? (6:5-9)
- How do we fight? (6:10-24)

By way of introduction to the letter, I want to take a look at the first two verses and then look at the message of the letter. We will consider the author, the recipients, the greeting, and the message.

The Author
EPHESIANS 1:1A

The book opens with these words: "Paul, an apostle of Christ Jesus by God's will." While some argue against Pauline authorship, Paul himself says he is the author (1:1; 3:1) and also gives two strong exhortations about "speaking the truth" (4:15,25)! Further, the early church universally accepted Pauline authorship, and it was not challenged until the late eighteenth and early nineteenth centuries (O'Brien, *Ephesians*, 4; see also Thielman, *Ephesians*, 1–30 and Akin, "Invading Satan's Territory").

While Ephesians is unique in style compared to Paul's other letters, it is not different enough to cause doubt regarding his authorship. Some critics claim it is too impersonal for a man who spent three years there, but I think this is a weak argument. Paul could have simply chosen to be reflective. It is also safe to assume he did not know all the believers (especially those out in the villages and those who came to faith after he left). And as previously mentioned, the letter was probably circular and, therefore, general.

Paul follows his usual form in this prologue, providing three elements: the sender, the recipient, and a greeting.

Paul: An Apostle of Christ Jesus by the Will of God

Formerly Paul was a persecutor of the church (Acts 9:1-2), but God made him "an apostle to the Gentiles" (Rom 11:13). Paul attributes this conversion and calling to the grace of God (1 Tim 1:15). Before his conversion Paul was breathing murderous threats against Christians, yet he went on to write 13 letters in the New Testament. That is quite the transformation, isn't it? Paul's life reminds us that God can radically change anyone. Here we have a man who might formerly have been compared to a terrorist now writing the New Testament.

In Ephesians 3:7-8 Paul highlights the grace of God and his mission to the Gentiles. Paul's message of grace was something he himself experienced personally. You could say the portrait in 2:1-5 was just like Paul's experience.

He is "an apostle of Christ Jesus"; that is, his authority came from Jesus Christ. While sometimes the term *apostle* is used in a nontechnical sense, more often than not it is used in a technical way, referring to those whom the risen Christ called and commissioned (O'Brien, *Ephesians*, 84).

Paul says he was an apostle by "God's will." God's will is an important theme in the letter, emphasizing God's purposes. Paul's apostleship was not of his own choosing (Gal 1:16). God appointed him from birth.

 From where is Paul writing? Three times he mentions imprisonment (3:1; 4:1; 6:20). I believe Paul wrote this letter near the end of his two-year imprisonment in Rome, about the same time as Colossians and Philemon, approximately AD 62. He was chained to a Roman soldier during this time but free to receive visitors. Of these visitors, one probably included a secretary who took down his words. Paul then sent all three letters with Tychicus, who was with him in Rome.

According to C. L. Mitton (*Epistle*, 57), 26.5 percent of the wording in Colossians appears in Ephesians. It is a good idea to read Colossians as you study Ephesians (Thielman, *Ephesians*, 8).

Be Devoted to the Apostles' Teaching

As an apostle writing under the inspiration of the Spirit, Paul's words have the same weight for us today. Because of this we must listen with humility and attention. Paul is speaking *to us* through this letter by the Spirit. Charles Hodge says, "The epistle reveals itself as the work of the Holy Ghost as clearly as the stars declare their maker to be God" (Hodge, *Ephesians*, xv).

Later Paul says the church is "built on the foundation of the apostles and prophets, with Christ Jesus Himself as the cornerstone" (2:20). In Acts 2 the church "devoted themselves to the apostles' teaching" (Acts 2:42). We too should love the apostle Paul's instruction in this letter. It is a gift from God to us. I encourage you to memorize all or portions of it.

The Recipients
EPHESIANS 1:1B

Paul writes "to the faithful saints in Christ Jesus at Ephesus." There is a lot of discussion about whether "at Ephesus" was part of the original wording here. Although some early documents do include it, others omit it without providing any geographical name in its place, which leaves us with an awkward grammatical construction (Thielman, *Ephesians*, 13; O'Brien, *Ephesians*, 85). It could be that it was simply dropped somehow. F. F. Bruce thinks the churches of Asia Minor were supposed to insert their own name (Bruce, *Ephesians*, 240). O'Brien concludes that it "was a general epistle sent to mainly Gentile believers in Southwestern Asia Minor, and that it was linked with Ephesus at an early stage, perhaps because of its being a strategic church or because it was one of the several cities to which the letter was sent" (O'Brien, *Ephesians*, 86).

Expressing a similar position, Daniel Akin says the following, which also expresses my own view:

> It is possible (probable) that Ephesians is a circular letter addressed to various churches in Asia Minor in the general vicinity of Ephesus. The circular address of the epistle explains the omission of a city name in the address. During Paul's stay in Ephesus (the bulk of his third missionary journey recorded in Acts 18:23–21:17), the impact of his ministry was felt beyond the boundaries of the city of Ephesus. Consequently, it would be quite natural for him to write to the Christian

communities established during the Ephesian mission. (Akin, "Invading Satan's Territory")

A study of Paul's ministry in Ephesus seems valuable, though he was probably writing to the wider Ephesian region. I agree with Bryan Chapell who says, "The cultural environment of Ephesus in the first century clearly illuminates the type of Asia Minor social context Paul's audience experienced" (*Ephesians*, 10). In other words, if Ephesians was intended for several churches throughout Asia Minor, then a look at Ephesus will still help us understand the context. In fact, Acts 19 illustrates the connection between Ephesus and Asia Minor. Luke writes that as a result of Paul's ministry in Ephesus, "all the residents of Asia . . . heard the message about the Lord" (Acts 19:10; cf. Acts 20:27).

The Struggle in Ephesus

In 1 Corinthians (a previous letter to another church, written from Ephesus), Paul says, "But I will stay in Ephesus until Pentecost, because a wide door for effective ministry has opened for me—yet many oppose me" (1 Cor 16:8-9). In Acts 19 Paul mentions his long stay in Ephesus, which was about three years, the longest stay in his missionary journeys—three months in the synagogue, two years in the lecture hall, and "a while" longer (Acts 19:8,10,22).

One reason for the long duration was that he had many great opportunities for ministry. Among them was the daily public teaching in the hall of Tyrannus. Those opportunities involved great opposition, though. In Acts 20:18-19 he says he served in Asia with tears and trials. In 1 Corinthians 15:32 he says he faced wild beasts in Ephesus. This might be a figure of speech, but it is likely a reference to what happened in Acts 19 in the amphitheater.

An important application we can discern from these texts relates to trials and the will of God. Just because something is difficult does not mean you have moved out of the will of God. The will of God does not mean you are free from opposition. In fact, opportunities and opposition are often mingled together.

What made this a difficult region in which to minister? Consider first, **the size of Ephesus**. Ephesus is in modern-day western Turkey. It was a busy port city, the fourth or fifth largest city in the world at that time (Chapell, *Ephesians*, 10). Its massive amphitheater held about 25,000 people. The city hosted athletic events similar to the Olympics. It was at the junction of four major roads in Asia Minor. Several villages surrounded it. It was the gateway of Asia that became the gateway of the gospel, as Paul's ministry in the city reached out into "all . . . of Asia" (Acts 19:10).

Today much of the world is urban, and the need for churches to be planted in dense, urban areas where there is great diversity is massive. Picture a missionary today moving somewhere like Manhattan or Istanbul (another gateway city)—massive cities with great need for the gospel and local churches.

Second, consider the **spiritual warfare in Ephesus**. If the size of this city alone was not enough to overwhelm a missionary, there was also tremendous spiritual warfare in Ephesus. The city was known for different forms of paganism. Some were more sophisticated, others quite sleazy. The sophisticated types embraced the Greek notion of true enlightenment, which involved rising to high levels of mysterious knowledge. This knowledge was obtained not just by learning but by experience, through both erotic and ascetic practices (cf. 1 Tim 4:1-4). As an example of the sleaziness of Ephesus, a sign carved in stone remains today on the streets coming from the ancient dock; it used to direct sailors to brothels (Chappell, *Ephesians*, 19). The culture was steeped in materialism, sensuality, and perverted idolatrous practices.

Ephesus was also home to the Roman emperor cult. The worship of the emperor was a prominent feature of life at all levels in Asia at this time. Caesar Augustus was spoken of as the "Savior." His birth was hailed as "the beginning of good tidings to the world," and the calendar was adjusted in light of his birth (Thielman, *Ephesians*, 21). So there was a "gospel conflict." Coins, statues, temples, and other items proclaimed the gospel of Augustus, but the church was proclaiming the gospel of Jesus.

Today you can see the statue of the Roman emperor Trajan among the ruins in Ephesus. He ruled after Paul's lifetime, but you can catch the spirit of Roman rulers at his time. The statue shows Trajan's foot on top of the world, giving the idea that he was a god. Now compare this picture with 1:21-22. Only One has all things under His feet: the Lord Jesus. When Christians said, "Jesus is Lord," they were saying that Caesar is not.

• Ephesus was also the headquarters for the cult of the Roman goddess Diana (or Greek "Artemis"), whose temple was one of the Seven Wonders of the World. Once four times as large as the Parthenon, today only the scant remains of a pillar survive. It is about a mile from the ancient amphitheater, which is still standing. Paul's Ephesian ministry threatened the commerce of those who made silver models of Diana (cf. Acts 19:23-41).

Perhaps this spiritually conflicted context of the Ephesians prompted Paul to write in the particular style he uses in this letter. He uses words like "authorities," "power," and "spiritual forces," and he emphasizes Jesus' lordship over all. Ephesus seems to have been obsessed with demons, magic, and idolatry, particularly the worship of Diana.

Third, consider a glimpse of warfare in Ephesus (Acts 19:9-20). Paul had a short stay in Ephesus during which he proclaimed Christ in the synagogues (Acts 18:19-20). Then we get a flavor of the spiritual climate in Ephesus in Acts 19. We read about Paul's teaching ministry:

> But when some became hardened and would not believe, slandering the Way in front of the crowd, he withdrew from them and met separately with the disciples, conducting discussions every day in the lecture hall of Tyrannus. And this went on for two years, so that all the inhabitants of Asia, both Jews and Greeks, heard the message about the Lord. (Acts 19:9-10)

Paul began in the synagogue, speaking for three months. Then he went to the hall of Tyrannus, where he taught for two years. Paul was in a public auditorium or lecture hall where lectures were given during the midday "siesta" period. (Paul also probably took a break from his trade.)

By way of application, remember we can gather anywhere to teach the Bible. We do not need a temple or spectacular building. You might compare the hall of Tyrannus to a modern community center where classes are offered on a variety of subjects. Our church gathers in a generic facility and will probably continue to do so unless someone wants to give us a church building!

Like Paul we too should find ways to share the gospel within our daily context. Paul is using the typical siesta period to teach. This can look like doing a Bible study with colleagues before work begins, or a businessmen's luncheon, or a student starting something at school during breaks. Paul's teaching eventually spilled out from the hall into the villages!

Then we read about the demonic opposition in Ephesus:

> God was performing extraordinary miracles by Paul's hands, so that even facecloths or work aprons that had touched his skin were brought

to the sick, and the diseases left them, and the evil spirits came out of them.

Then some of the itinerant Jewish exorcists attempted to pronounce the name of the Lord Jesus over those who had evil spirits, saying, "I command you by the Jesus that Paul preaches!" Seven sons of Sceva, a Jewish chief priest, were doing this. The evil spirit answered them, "I know Jesus, and I recognize Paul—but who are you?" Then the man who had the evil spirit leaped on them, overpowered them all, and prevailed against them, so that they ran out of that house naked and wounded. This became known to everyone who lived in Ephesus, both Jews and Greeks. Then fear fell on all of them, and the name of the Lord Jesus was magnified. And many who had become believers came confessing and disclosing their practices, while many of those who had practiced magic collected their books and burned them in front of everyone. So they calculated their value and found it to be 50,000 pieces of silver. In this way the Lord's message flourished and prevailed. (Acts 19:11-20)

Paul performed miracles that confirmed his message, but we need to be careful in applying this account. Acts is a narrative, and narratives are descriptive, not prescriptive, meaning Luke is simply describing what happened; he is not prescribing we do this. We are not to go start an apron ministry! We should certainly apply the narratives, but they are different from epistles, which give us clear exhortations.

Simply consider the result of Paul's ministry here. It was marked by awe, confession and repentance, and the exaltation of Jesus. This dramatic account culminates with the burning of books, which probably contained spells, incantations, and other cultish practices. It was a spiritual awakening. Can you imagine those wrapped up in false religions, cults, and superstition burning their books and worshiping Jesus?

Not everyone was thrilled with this movement, however. Luke mentions that Paul "stayed in Asia for a while," and then he writes, "During that time there was a major disturbance about the Way" (Acts 19:22-23). These Christians were turning "the world upside down" (Acts 17:6) in Ephesus. I have been asking these questions: Is that said about our local church? Are we impacting the city? Let us pray that we can make a holy disturbance.

Notice that Christianity was referred to early on as "the Way" (Acts 9:2; 19:9; 22:4). It was a new way of life. It was entirely different from other religions. It was centered on Jesus, who said He was "the way, the truth, and the life" (John 14:6).

This holy disturbance led to some serious opposition. As you look at the next verses in Acts, you see that Paul now faces opposition from another source: the silversmiths. This highlights the materialistic, as well as superstitious, culture of Ephesus. One silversmith in particular, Demetrius, is named. He was upset because the gospel was affecting the socioeconomic system. Luke records his words:

> Men, you know that our prosperity is derived from this business. You both see and hear that not only in Ephesus, but in almost all of Asia, this man Paul has persuaded and misled a considerable number of people by saying that gods made by hand are not gods! So not only do we run a risk that our business may be discredited, but also that the temple of the great goddess Artemis may be despised and her magnificence come to the verge of ruin—the very one all of Asia and the world adore. (Acts 19:25-27)

Because many Ephesians were turning to Christ, they no longer wanted to buy silver statues. This created a massive eruption in Ephesus. As a result they dragged Paul and his companions into the amphitheater where they were all but killed (Acts 19:28-41).

Finally, if you add to the list of these trials the "plots of the Jews" (Acts 20:19), then you have an incredibly difficult place to minister! Yet, amazingly, Paul spent about three years in Ephesus (Acts 20:31), probably around AD 52–54 (Thielman, *Ephesians*, 16). He had great success there, especially among the Gentiles, but it was not without opposition.

The church in Ephesus was birthed, in large part, in the midst of opposition. If you plan on planting a church or going to a tough city, and I pray many of you will, remember this pattern. It will be a struggle. You may bleed, but take comfort in Paul's journey. Be prepared for war, but be confident in the Lord.

Though few of you will move to a massive population center, filled almost entirely with unconverted people, remember that many of us still live in a culture filled with idolatry, superstition and the occult, demonic activity, public sexual immorality, materialism, a love for education devoid of God, and the worship of political leaders. Remember, the gospel of Jesus Christ is powerful enough to break through these forces and bring people to saving faith in Jesus Christ. There is only one Lord. Proclaim Him with boldness.

The Saints in Ephesus

In the middle of this culture were "the saints." The word *saint* (1:15,18; 3:8,18; 4:12; 5:3; 6:18) has its roots in the Old Testament, which speaks of God choosing a people from among the nations to be "My kingdom of priests and My holy nation" (Exod 19:5-6). Christ has made us into a holy people (Eph 5:26). Positionally, we are holy because we are united with Christ. Now we must live in a manner that is consistent with this position. Personal holiness is about becoming in practice what we are in position.

Who were these saints? Some Jewish believers were in Ephesus before Paul's arrival (Acts 18:24-27), but later it seems that the churches were primarily Gentile. The Ephesian churches were perhaps made up of about 30 to 40 people, meeting in homes (Thielman, *Ephesians*, 27). But these churches had experienced about a seven- to eight-year absence from Paul by the time the book of Ephesians was written. They needed instruction. There may have been a lack of unity among the pre-Paul converts and those who came later, as well as division between the Jewish and Gentile groups.

Ephesians, then, provides some critically important truths about the nature of the gospel and how we are unified. Ephesians is like Romans in this regard. In Romans Paul is also trying to unite the church, Jew and Gentile, around the gospel.

Paul also calls the Ephesians "faithful." This term most likely means "believers" rather than "trustworthy." They were those who trusted Christ for salvation (1:13). While they lived physically in Ephesus, the saints were spiritually "in Christ." They lived in union with Christ.

Ephesians mentions union with Christ and being "in Christ" more than any other letter, about 36 times (Snodgrass, *Ephesians*, 39). This phrase occurs some 164 times in Paul's 13 epistles. This is the heart of Christianity: to be united to Jesus Christ. Christians are people who are in Christ. You are united in His death and His resurrection (2:5-7).

Only by being "in" Christ can one have access to "every spiritual blessing." If you are in Christ, then "Christ's riches are your riches, His resources are your resources, His righteousness is your righteousness, His power is your power. His position is our position: where He is, we are . . . what He has, we have" (MacArthur, *Ephesians*, 10). And because we are in Christ, though opposition surrounds us on every side, we are secure in Him. Your identity, therefore, is in Christ, not in your performance, your popularity, your productivity, or your prominence.

The Greeting
EPHESIANS 1:2

Paul writes, "Grace to you and peace from God our Father and the Lord Jesus Christ." This greeting is the same type of greeting Paul uses for his other letters. By saying "Grace," Paul is not saying "Hello" but is rather giving a prayer wish for grace to come to the Ephesians. Paul is the theologian of grace. Grace runs through this letter, appearing 12 times (1:6-8; 2:4-9; 4:7; 4:29). The same is true for "peace": Paul was praying for God to bring peace to his readers. We learn much about God's peace in Ephesians: "[Christ] is our peace" (2:14); "He proclaimed the good news of peace" (2:17); "keeping . . . the peace that binds us" (4:3); "the gospel of peace" (6:15).

This prayer wish introduces the letter, which would have been read aloud in corporate worship (cf. Col 4:16). This grace and peace comes from "God our Father and the Lord Jesus Christ." What a magnificent picture of the Father is in this letter (see also 1:17; 4:6). It also has a majestic picture of the Lord Jesus as the cosmic King of all. Jesus fills the mind of Paul. Notice the end of the letter in 6:23-24: Paul prays again for peace and grace from God the Father and the Lord Jesus for "all who have undying love for our Lord Jesus Christ."

The Message

The key thought in Ephesians is the phrase "in Christ." Ephesians shows us that God is forming a new humanity through Christ, by the Spirit. It describes how Jesus Christ died for sinners, was raised, is exalted above all His competitors, and is now the head of the cosmos and the church. Through our union with Christ, we share in these same events—we are raised with Christ and seated with Him (2:5-7). This great salvation is owing to the grace of God (2:8-10).

Observe also these "formerly . . . but now" expressions:

- We were dead in sin, but now we are "alive with the Messiah" (2:4).
- We were separated from Christ, but now in Christ Jesus we "have been brought near" (2:13).
- We were "foreigners," but now we are "fellow citizens" (2:19).
- We were darkened in understanding, but now we have "learned about the Messiah." We have put off the "old self" and put on the "new self" (4:20-24).
- We were "darkness," but now we are "light in the Lord" (5:8).

Paul describes the transforming power of the gospel throughout the letter.

Ephesians divides naturally into two parts: who we are in Christ (our position), and how we are to live in Christ (our practice). The first part makes up the first half of the book, and the second part makes up the second half of the book. Each part can be broken down further. Allow me to sketch out the contents briefly.

Our Position—Who We Are in Christ (1:3–3:21)

In the opening chapters we read about how God, in His glorious grace, saves sinners through Jesus Christ, granting them spiritual life. The focus is not on what we must do but rather on what God has done for us. The verb tenses are mainly passive.

We now have new life in Christ (1:3–2:10). In the first two chapters the new life we have in Christ is explained with power and beauty. Look at this new life we enjoy:

- We have been chosen and adopted by the Father (1:4-6).
- We have been redeemed by the Son (1:7-12).
- We have been sealed with the Spirit (1:13-14).
- We have been given resurrection power (1:19).
- We have been given eyes to see the lordship of Jesus (1:15-23).
- We have been brought from death to life by grace through faith in Christ (2:1-10).
- We have been raised and seated with Him in the heavens "so that in the coming ages he might show the immeasurable riches of his grace in kindness toward us in Christ Jesus" (2:5-7 ESV).
- We have been created for good works (2:10).

We find here that Christianity is not about becoming religious. It is not about conforming to a list of rules. It is not about adopting a philosophy. It is not about financial prosperity. It is not about becoming a nice person. It is about becoming a new person. It is about going from death to life. It is about going from darkness to light. The missionary's task is not to call people to religion but to call people to Jesus, who is the way, the truth, and the life.

We now have a new community in Christ (2:11–3:21). When God saves sinners, He brings them into a new community. This new community, called the church, is made up of various groups of people. Both Jew and Gentile are now one. Paul says, "He is our peace, who made both groups one and tore down the dividing wall of hostility. . . . So that He might create in Himself one new man from the two" (2:14-15). We belong to a new community, united in Jesus. We are "fellow citizens with the saints, and members of God's household" (2:19).

John Stott says,

> The church lies at the very center of the eternal purpose of God. It is not a divine afterthought. It is not an accident of history. On the contrary, the church is God's new community. For his purpose . . . is not just to save individuals and so perpetuate our loneliness, but rather to build up his church, that is, to call out of the world a people for his own glory. (*The Living Church*, 19–20)

Isn't it awesome to know we belong to something that exists to display the glory of God? Yes, it would be great to wear the jersey of your favorite team, but you belong to something much better! You belong to the church of the living God. When you become a Christian, you belong to God, and you belong to brothers and sisters in Him.

Steve Timmis says,

> It is not that I belong to God and then make a decision to join a church. My being in Christ means being in Christ with others who are in Christ. This is my identity. This is our identity. . . . If the church is the body of Christ, then we should not live as disembodied Christians. (Chester and Timmis, *Total Church*, 41)

Are we living out our corporate identity by belonging to a local, visible church? Do we have brothers and sisters with whom we love, serve, weep, rejoice, and celebrate? We were saved for community.

Our Practice—How We Are to Live in Christ (4:1–6:24)

In the second half of the letter, Paul shifts. He turns his attention to the responsibilities of the saints. Many of the verbs are imperatives.

We must now pursue unity and purity in Christ (4:1–5:14). The vision for unity that is explained in 2:11-22 is now fleshed out in these verses. He explains how we can be "diligently keeping the unity of the Spirit with the peace that binds us" (4:3). Paul describes how our distinct character (4:1-2), our doctrinal convictions (vv. 4-6), our diverse capabilities (vv. 7-14), and our dependence on Christ and one another (vv. 15-16) unite us.

Then in 4:17–5:14 Paul talks about a particular way believers are to "walk" (4:17; 5:2,8). They are to live out their new identity in purity and love.

☞ *We must now pursue submissiveness and stability in Christ (5:15–6:24).* Finally, Paul begins to talk about how we should live out Spirit-filled relationships (5:14–6:9). He emphasizes submission, love, and respect in our relationships within the church, marriage, as parents and children, and in the workplace. Christians should pursue harmony in the home, at work, and in the church.

We also have an enemy to stand against (6:10-20). The book closes with vivid imagery of our spiritual battle against the Devil. By the power of God, we are to take our stand.

So Ephesians is teaching us about a whole new way to live. New people pursue different lifestyles than the surrounding culture. That was a challenge in Ephesus, and it is a challenge today.

Don't Lose Your First Love

The final thing I would like to point out is the last phrase in Ephesians 6:23-24. Paul closes this great letter to the saints with an implicit admonition to love Jesus purely and simply: "love our Lord Jesus Christ with love incorruptible" (ESV). Reading the book of Ephesians should increase our love for Jesus.

What is interesting about the church in Ephesus is that even though it had an amazing history, the final mention in Revelation 2:1-7 about this great church is that they "abandoned the love [they] had at first." ☞

Think about it: Priscilla and Aquila, Apollos, Paul, Timothy, and later John ministered to this church. What a heritage! Yet about 40 years after the first generation of believers, they had lost their love.

Though they were commended for spotting heresy (Paul predicted wolves would enter in Acts 20, and 1–2 Timothy and 1–3 John illustrate this), they lost their love. They had a cold orthodoxy. We must ask ourselves: Is our service to Jesus mechanical? Do we love Him, or are we just using Him for our own ambitions?

Jesus told them to repent. That is what we must do if we have lost love for Christ: return to extolling Jesus for who He is and what He has done. Let's turn to the book of Ephesians now and find a view of Jesus that should lead us to such exaltation.

Reflect and Discuss

1. Which point under "Why Study Ephesians?" had the most impact on you and why?

2. How might the nature of Paul's calling on the road to Damascus (Acts 9) and his experiences in Ephesus (Acts 19) affect the way we listen to his words in this book?

3. How are grace and peace related? Why are they central in the Christian message?

4. How were the challenges faced by the Ephesian church similar to what we face today?

5. What does it mean to be "in Christ"? How might we live out this truth daily?

6. How does Paul describe the church in the book of Ephesians? How is that different from the way people describe the church today?

7. Summarize the first half of Ephesians in one or two sentences. Take a moment to read through Ephesians 1–3 slowly.

8. Summarize the second half of Ephesians in one or two sentences. Take a moment to read through Ephesians 4–6 slowly.

9. Select a passage to memorize from the book of Ephesians. Explain your choice.

10. How would you describe the temperature of your relationship with Jesus? Pray for your love for Christ to be increased through this study.

Whom Do You Worship?

EPHESIANS 1:3-14

Main Idea: Paul praises God for His sovereign grace in salvation, which believers enjoy through Christ.

I. **Made for Praise**
    A. The language of praise
    B. The reasons for praise
II. **Chosen by the Father (1:3-6)**
    A. The nature of election
    B. The goal of election
III. **Redeemed by the Son (1:7-10)**
    A. We have redemption (1:7-8).
    B. We have revelation (1:9-10).
IV. **Assured by the Spirit (1:11-14)**
    A. The sealing of the Spirit
    B. The promised Holy Spirit
    C. The guarantee of the Spirit

Paul was a theological thoroughbred, and Ephesians 1:3-14 is sort of like his Belmont Stakes. He writes like a "tremendous machine"—to quote Chic Anderson, who called Secretariat's famous Belmont Stakes race—as he exalts the triune God. He starts off in verse 3 with a general topic sentence and then widens out with phrase after phrase to touch on various redemptive themes without even stopping for a period! In Greek this is one long (202 words), complex, and glorious sentence that oozes with God-centered worship. One writer quipped that this is the "most monstrous sentence conglomeration that I have ever found in the Greek language" (E. Norden, in O'Brien, *Ephesians*, 90).

Made for Praise

This passage is so important because we were made for praise. And we must have the right object of worship. Look around and you will find expressions of praise: teenage girls screaming at boy band concerts; sports fans exalting the virtues of their team, paying big money for

19

tickets, and adjusting their schedules for the games; dads getting fired
up about going to The Home Depot to work on a new project; adulter-
ers praising their mistresses; consumers praising their favorite stores;
television viewers praising their favorite new series; and coffee drink-
ers commending their favorite coffee shop. Humanity has never had a
problem expressing praise.

In regard to functional idols, we like to take good things in creation (treasure, food, work, relationships, sex) and substitute them
for the Creator and Redeemer, turning those good things into god
things, thereby committing idolatry. This is no small matter. Paul says in
Romans 1 that this failure to worship God is at the heart of sin. Any sin
problem is fundamentally a worship problem. *Love the Lord your God with all*

Idolatry can also happen as people have the wrong view of God.
God has revealed Himself in His Word, and worship is a response to that
revelation. We are not to worship the God of our imaginations but the
God of the Bible. We are required to believe that what the Bible says is
true, not that what we want the Bible to say is true. In Ephesus the people had numerous objects of worship, from Diana to the emperor. The
question then (and today) is not, Do I worship? The question is, Whom
do I worship? Whom do we worship? We should praise the triune God.
We should praise Him for who He is and what He has done.

The Language of Praise

Unfortunately this passage has generated a lot of debate because it mentions the concepts of election and predestination. While this discussion
in itself is not a bad thing, I think we can miss the spirit of this text. The
spirit is one of worship. Let us look at the big picture of the passage for
a moment.

A note of *praise* is struck in verse 3, and the sentence ends in verse
14 with praise. Paul begins with an outburst of praise to God in a typical Old Testament, Jewish style of extended eulogy (*berakah*). Why bless
God? He says, because God "has blessed us in Christ with every spiritual blessing in the heavens" (1:3). The phrase "every spiritual blessing"
shows the wide-ranging scope of God's blessing to His people. In the
following verses Paul mentions blessing after blessing. Verse 14 rounds
out the sentence appropriately: "to the praise of His glory."

Observe also the *Trinitarian* nature of the passage. The opening
verses are Trinitarian; Paul mentions God the Father and the Lord Jesus
Christ and speaks of "every spiritual blessing" (alluding to the work

of the Spirit). Further, though the structure should not be forced too woodenly, there is an emphasis on the work of the Father in verses 3-6, the work of the Son in verses 7-12, and then the work of the Spirit in verses 13-14. Paul is calling us to praise the triune God from whom all blessings flow.

Notice also how our spiritual blessings are *in Christ.* This phrase appears 11 times in these verses. The great salvation God has provided is centered in the person and work of Jesus Christ. Only through our union with Christ do we have these spiritual blessings. He is to be exalted by believers.

Paul also points out that our salvation is ultimately for God's *glory.* Look at the phrase "to the praise of His glorious grace" in verse 6 and the phrase "to the praise of His glory" in verses 12 and 14. Why did God choose to bless us with this great salvation? That He may be glorified. God saves people for His glory.

The passage also highlights the *grace* of God in salvation. We do not deserve these blessings of salvation; we did not earn salvation. Paul speaks of "glorious grace" (v. 6) and "the riches of His grace that He lavished on us" (vv. 7-8). Those who have received these riches should praise the Giver.

Incredibly these verses highlight the *eternal* scope of salvation. This passage goes from "before the foundation of the world" (v. 4) to "the days of fulfillment—to bring everything together in the Messiah, both things in heaven and things on earth" (v. 10). It goes from eternity to eternity. We join Moses in praise: "From eternity to eternity, You are God" (Ps 90:2).

Paul speaks of being blessed *in the heavens,* a phrase only used in Ephesians. I think this gets at the "already–not yet" aspect of our salvation. Now we are linked with the heavenly realms because of our relationship with God. We have the benefits of salvation now, but we also anticipate them in the future when we will praise Him with all nations.

Finally, note *who* should share in this praise: both Jewish and Gentile. Following these words of praise, Paul stresses that these blessings already described in verses 3-10 are for both Jewish and Gentile believers (vv. 11-14). In verses 4-14 the same people are in view (O'Brien, *Ephesians,* 92). In almost every verse Paul speaks of "us" or "we" to refer to the people of God. They are for you if you are in Christ!

This passage, then—all of it written from prison—is about praising the Trinitarian God. Paul's body was in prison, but his heart was in heaven. Regardless of your circumstances, God is worthy of praise. Let us look at the reasons why.

The Reasons for Praise

Paul reminds his readers (and us) that we should bless God for the spiritual blessings we have received. He reminds us that we have been chosen by the Father, redeemed by the Son, and assured by the Spirit. Each section calls us to praise "His glorious grace" or "His glory" (vv. 6,12,14).

Chosen by the Father
EPHESIANS 1:3-6

This amazing passage highlights God's gracious election of sinners for salvation. Paul says that God "chose us" (v. 4) and that He "predestined us" (v. 5). These words concern some people, making them tense up, but they should not. These are Bible words. These words should inspire awe and worship.

The idea of God choosing a people to display His glory is not new. The Bible is a book of election. God chose to create the world for His glory. God chose Abraham to bring blessing to the nations (Gen 12:1-3). God chose the nation of Israel that they might be a light to the nations (Deut 7:6-8; 14:2; Isa 42:6-8). Further, Jesus chose His 12 disciples to bear fruit and multiply (John 15:16). Paul adds that God chose what is "insignificant and despised in the world . . . so that no one can boast in His presence" (1 Cor 1:28-29). In Ephesians, as in other NT texts (cf. Rom 9–11; Acts 13:48; Titus 1:1; 1 Pet 1:1; 2 Pet 1:10), we read that God chose individuals for salvation. These believers, both Jew and Gentile, make up the church.

Our church's statement of faith summarizes this doctrine well under "God's Purpose of Grace":

> Election is the gracious purpose of God, according to which He regenerates, justifies, sanctifies, and glorifies sinners. It is consistent with the free agency of man, and comprehends all the means in connection with the end. It is the glorious display of God's sovereign goodness, and is infinitely wise, holy, and unchangeable. It excludes boasting and promotes humility. ("Baptist Faith and Message 2000")

Some argue that election here is primarily corporate rather than individual. While I do want to emphasize the corporate purpose of our salvation, as Ephesians makes clear, I do not accept this argument. God did choose a corporate body, but that corporate body is comprised of individuals. In fact, the passage speaks about how individuals experience salvation. "Redemption," "forgiveness," "sealing," and "belief" are all individual experiences, so it is not an "either/or" but a "both-and." God chose a people for Himself, and that people is made up of believing, redeemed, forgiven members.

The Nature of Election

Let me make a few more observations about the nature of election in this text.

First, we must admit great mystery in the doctrine of election. This passage speaks about what God was doing "before the foundation of the world" (v. 4). It speaks of His eternal, secret purposes (vv. 5,10), and recognizes that He works all things according to "the decision of His will" (v. 11). We must admit mystery here. God is God and we are not. Deuteronomy reminds us, "the secret things belong to . . . God" (Deut 29:29 ESV). So we might disagree about the finer points of this mystery, but we can still fellowship and serve together. It is difficult for finite creatures with three-pound, fallen brains to comprehend how this doctrine relates to God's love for all people and His impartiality, as well as how it relates to human choices. We should be OK with mystery. Encountering mystery should be a cue to start worshiping.

Second, while we want to affirm mystery, we should also affirm the other attributes clearly affirmed in this text. In this text we see that God is perfectly loving (vv. 4-5), eternally sovereign (v. 5), gloriously gracious (vv. 6-8), and infinitely wise (v. 8). God can do whatever He pleases (Ps 115:3), and whatever He does is always consistent with who He is.

God is *loving*. Election is an expression of God's love for His children. Paul says, "in love He predestined us" (vv. 4-5).

God is *sovereign*. God's choosing is simply one expression of His eternal control over all things. Notice the language of God's sovereignty, as Paul mentions predestination (vv. 5,11), God's "favor" or "good pleasure" (vv. 5,9), God's "will" (vv. 5,9,11), God's "administration" (v. 10), and God's "purpose" (v. 11).

God is *gracious*. God's choosing is an expression of His grace to sinners (cf. Rom 11:6; 2 Tim 1:9). God did not choose us because of anything good in us.

God is *wise*. God's choosing is an expression of His infinite wisdom.

Third, the passage itself shows the necessity of personal belief in the gospel. This is true even if all of our questions about human responsibility (or will) are not answered in this passage. Look at verse 13: one must believe. Remember, this is the same sentence! Election and faith belong in the same sentence, and it is a sentence only God could write. We may not understand this, but we should fully embrace it. We embrace other truths that are mysteriously woven together like the deity and humanity of Christ and the divine-human authorship of Scripture. Someone once asked Charles Spurgeon how he reconciled God's sovereignty and man's responsibility, and he responded, "I never reconcile two friends" ("Jacob and Esau"). Someone asked another pastor about this "problem," and he replied, "That's not my problem. That's God's problem. And for God, it's not a problem." Just believe both truths and let God harmonize them.

Some get the wrong idea about election. It should not cast doubt on whether or not all are welcome to come to Jesus. All may come. That is the invitation. Russell Moore says,

> God is not some metaphysical airport security screener, waving through the secretly pre-approved and sending the rest into a holding tank for questioning. God is not treating us like puppets made of meat, forcing us along by his capricious whim. Instead the doctrine of election tells us that all of us who have come to know Christ are here on purpose. (*Adopted for Life*, 34)

Our invitation should be, "Come to Jesus! When you come, thank Him for drawing you!"

Another question that is often raised concerns the need for evangelism. Election does not lessen the need to tell people about Jesus. Election gives hope to evangelism. When Paul was discouraged in Corinth, Jesus said, "Don't be afraid, but keep on speaking and don't be silent . . . because I have many people in this city" (Acts 18:9-10). Some people will believe when you speak the gospel! The hardest of hearts can be converted because evangelism is not about the quality of our presentation but the power of God. We should fear no one because of this truth, and because God is sovereign, we should assume that God has placed us where we are for the purpose of seeing others come to Christ through our faithful evangelism.

Further, there are numerous examples of missionaries and pastors who affirmed the doctrine of election (William Carey, Andrew Fuller, John G. Paton, David Brainerd, and more). The Lord, who is the Judge of all the earth, orders us to go make disciples of all nations. Maybe the most famous example of this is the apostle Paul. Interestingly, in Romans 9–11, Paul speaks about election in detail, but the chapter in the middle (chapter 10) is about the necessity of evangelism for people to come to saving faith in Christ (see Rom 10:14-17). In that section he is burdened for lost people (Rom 9:1-3; 10:1), and love compelled him to proclaim the gospel to everyone.

Again, this passage in Ephesians is primarily focused on God's activity in salvation. Some texts we will expound will more heavily emphasize human responsibility, but we do not have the space necessary to harmonize all of these passages. And that is not Paul's purpose either. His purpose is to praise the God who saves sinners.

Fourth, our election is in Christ. We are chosen in the "Chosen One" (Luke 9:35; 23:35). F. F. Bruce says, "He is the foundation, origin, and executor: all that is involved in election and its fruits depends on him" (*Ephesians*, 254–55). O'Brien summarizes, "Election is always and only in Christ" (*Ephesians*, 100). We were not chosen for anything good in us. God accepts us because He chose to put us in union with Christ.

Finally, in light of these things, election should humble us (cf. 1 Cor 1:27-30). The proper response to God's having chosen us for salvation is awe, worship, and obedience to God. Election should not anger anyone or inflate anyone's pride. It should humble everyone. No one should be arrogant when talking about the doctrine of election.

For those who want to argue against this truth, Paul says, "But who are you, a mere man, to talk back to God?" (Rom 9:20). We should not be arrogant; we pots do not talk back to the Potter. Those who embrace this doctrine but walk in pride have not applied it properly. This doctrine should put us on our faces in worship to the sovereign, wise, loving, gracious, and mysterious God, who has chosen us in Christ.

The Goal of Election

Holiness. Paul says God chose us "to be holy and blameless in His sight" (v. 4). God's purpose is to bring us into conformity to Jesus (Rom 8:29-30).

Only in Christ are we holy positionally. We can stand before God because of Christ. In Christ our blame is removed, and His righteousness is given to us. God sees us holy as His Son is holy if we are in Him. We have that status. It is mind-boggling! Now we have the responsibility of pursuing holiness practically. Ephesians chapters 4–6 will teach us about that.

It is difficult to tell if the phrase "in love" goes with what is before it, which would mean that we are to be "holy and blameless and live in love" (O'Brien, *Ephesians*, 101), or if it goes with what is after it, referring to the motive/attitude of God in adoption. I lean toward the latter interpretation, though the former is also true. The focus seems to be on God's activity. In love God has chosen us for adoption.

Adoption. God chose ("predestined") a people to be holy, a people for sonship. His people are part of the family of God. What a privilege to know God as Father! In these few phrases Paul gives us a minitheology of adoption.

He tells us *the "what" of adoption.* What does it mean to be adopted? It means to have all the rights and privileges that belong to the Father's children. The word is a compound word meaning "to place a son." Paul uses the word for "adoption" only five times in the New Testament, each time to those familiar with the Roman context of adoption (Rom 8:15,23; 9:4; Gal 4:5; Eph 1:5). Romans were familiar with adoptions. Perhaps the most famous was Julius Caesar's adoption of Octavian, about whom we read in Luke 2:1 (Burke, *Adopted*, 62). You can imagine being adopted by a Roman ruler. Paul says, "That's nothing compared with being adopted by the glorious Father!" Now, as God's children, we can call Him "*Abba*" (Gal 4:6; Rom 8:15), which is what Jesus cried out in the garden of Gethsemane (Mark 14:36).

Adoption has a horizontal aspect, not just a vertical aspect. Not only is God our Father, but we are also now brothers and sisters with other Christians. The church is a family of adopted brothers and sisters. The greatest apologetic we have is to be a family.

He tells us *the "when" of adoption,* which is "before the foundation of the world" (v. 4). If we are God's children, then we are here on purpose. It is part of God's great plan.

He tells us *the "how" of adoption,* which is "through Jesus Christ." Only in Christ do we receive these blessings. He goes on to say that God has blessed us "in the Beloved" (6b; cf. Col 1:13; Mark 1:11; 9:7). We have been caught up in the love the Father has for the Son.

Finally, Paul tells us *the "why" of adoption*, which is "according to His favor and will" (v. 5). Why did God adopt us? We do not have all the answers. We just know that it pleased God to do so. He was delighted to adopt us. Verse 6 adds that He did it "to the praise of His glorious grace." Adoption magnifies the greatness of God the Father.

An implication of God's purpose of making us "holy" and making us His adopted children is that we have been chosen for a mission. God's children will take on the family business, carrying out God's mission. We will imitate God as beloved children (Eph 5:1). Election is a privilege, but it also contains the responsibility of making Christ known in word and deed.

Redeemed by the Son
EPHESIANS 1:7-10

Next we should praise God for the work of the Son who redeemed us. Building on what has already been said about the blessings we have in Christ, Paul now overflows with praise to God for His great redemption accomplished through Christ, the forgiveness that is ours because of His death, God's plan to sum all things up in Him, and the rich inheritance that is ours.

We Have Redemption (1:7-8)

Redemption denotes liberation from bondage or imprisonment. It harks back to Israel's release from Egypt. When they were delivered from the Red Sea, they sang the song of salvation (Exod 15), and we should as well. Our redemption is spoken of as an event that has already taken place. Paul says, "We have redemption." It is not that we hope to have redemption; we have it. Read how he describes it in Colossians, the "parallel book" to Ephesians:

> *He has rescued us from the domain of darkness and transferred us into the kingdom of the Son He loves. We have redemption, the forgiveness of sins, in Him.* (Col 1:13-14)

God has done the work of rescuing us, transferring us into the kingdom of the Beloved in whom we have redemption and forgiveness. Paul says that this redemption has come at a cost. "Through His blood" (Eph 1:7) we have this deliverance. This signifies the sacrificial death of Jesus. In Revelation 1:5 John says that Jesus "loves us and has set us free from our sins by His blood." Elsewhere, Paul says, "You were bought at a price" (1 Cor 6:20), and "Christ has redeemed us from the curse of the law by becoming a curse for us" (Gal 3:13).

We can be redeemed from the penalty of sin and from the prison house of sin, but it is not cheap. Our freedom cost Jesus His blood. He took our place. He bore our sins in His body on the tree.

Forgiveness. Paul says that this redemption is linked with the forgiveness of sins. We find forgiveness only in Christ. In Mark 2 Jesus told the paralytic who was lowered through the roof by his friends, "Son, your sins are forgiven" (Mark 2:5). The Pharisees objected, saying, "Who can forgive sins but God alone?" In that passage Jesus showed everyone that forgiveness was more important than physical healing and that He has the authority as God the Son to forgive sins.

If He has forgiven our sins, then we should pour out our hearts in adoration to Him. In Luke 7 we read of an unknown woman who poured out expensive oil to anoint Jesus in adoration. The Pharisees, who were too self-righteous to seek Jesus for forgiveness, grumbled at this. Jesus said she was lavish in her adoration because she realized how much she had been forgiven. Those who do not realize how much they have been forgiven do not praise Jesus like this. We too should love Him greatly because we have been forgiven much! The psalmist said, "LORD, if you kept a record of our sins, who, O Lord, could ever survive? But you offer forgiveness" (Ps 130:3-4 NLT).

Grace. Redemption and forgiveness are "according to the riches of His grace that He lavished on us" (vv. 7-8). Jesus has lavished grace on us. We are the recipients of Christ's extravagant goodness and kindness. We do not have words to describe God's amazing grace.

Wisdom and insight. God also expresses His grace by giving us "wisdom and understanding" (v. 8). God's lavish dispensing of grace in redemption involves forgiveness and the wisdom to know how to live in light of His saving plan (as expressed in the following verses).

We Have Revelation (1:9-10)

Verses 9-10 are the climactic note of the passage, where Paul says all things will be brought together in Christ. O'Brien says, "Syntactically and structurally . . . [this 'bringing together'] is the 'high point' of the eulogy" (*Ephesians*, 111).

History is going somewhere. By God's grace, "He made known to us the mystery of His will" (v. 9). He has revealed His eternal plan to us, and that plan centers on the Redeemer. What is this plan? It is to unite all things in Christ, things in heaven and things on earth. So there is a cosmic dimension to God's plan of salvation. Now the universe is divided and groaning for redemption (Rom 8:19-23). Now God's people groan in this fallen world. Paradise was lost in Adam, but it will be restored in Christ.

Stott summarizes this well: "In the fullness of time, God's two creations, his whole universe and his whole church, will be unified under the cosmic Christ who is the supreme head of both" (Stott, *Ephesians*, 44).

Assured by the Spirit
[EPHESIANS 1:11-14]

On top of all the other blessings already mentioned, Paul now references the believer's "inheritance" or heritage (vv. 11,14). The Holy Spirit is the guarantee of our inheritance. This too should lead us to praise. Paul says "in Christ" we have this inheritance (v. 11). Apart from Jesus our future is not hopeful. It is tragic.

The phrase "we have . . . received an inheritance" is one compound word in Greek. Paul speaks of something in the future that is sure to happen. The translation here is difficult. It could mean "we were made an inheritance (or heritage)" or "we have received an inheritance." The former is the notion that we are God's possession, an idea repeatedly mentioned in the Old Testament (e.g., Deut 4:20; Pss 33:12; 135:4). The latter use is more like 1 Peter 1:3-4, "[We have] an inheritance that is imperishable, uncorrupted, and unfading, kept in heaven for you" (see also Col 1:12).

Both are great options! We are God's possession, and through Christ we have received a glorious inheritance. My preference, based on the following phrases, which emphasize Jews and Gentiles together as God's people, is to take it as "we are God's possession" who have been redeemed "for the praise of His glory" (so Stott, O'Brien, and more).

How has this happened? How do we have such a status and such a future? From a divine perspective, it is according to God's sovereign purposes. Paul says we are "predestined according to the purpose of the One who works out everything in agreement with the decision of His will" (v. 11).

From a human perspective, we have believed. Paul mentions the responsibility of people by saying, "We who had already *put our hope in the Messiah*" (v. 12, emphasis added), and "When you heard the message of truth, the gospel of your salvation, and when *you believed in Him*" (v. 13, emphasis added). Once again we see this mystery of sovereignty and responsibility. People receive salvation when they hear the gospel and believe in Christ.

I love how Paul calls the gospel "the word of truth." Coming to Jesus for salvation is a coming to the truth. Notice also the movement from "we" (a reference to Jewish believers in vv. 11-12) to "you also" (a reference to Gentile readers in v. 13) and to "our" inheritance (a reference to both groups equally in v. 14). This anticipates the exposition of how God has reconciled us, Jew and Gentile, through the work of Christ (2:11-22).

It is correct that everything said in the previous verses is true for Jew and Gentile (O'Brien, *Ephesians*, 116), but with the pronoun shift Paul is stressing a different point here in verses 12-13. He is stressing God's sovereign plan in the ordering of salvation history. Paul is also saying that the Lord's inheritance is not limited to the Jewish believers. They obviously had a special privilege as the first to hope in Christ, but the Gentiles are also recipients of God's amazing grace.

Paul is saying there are no second-class citizens in the kingdom of God. All believers are God's possession, redeemed for His glory. Gentiles can be assured of their privileged status by the Spirit's work in their lives.

The Sealing of the Spirit

Notice, now, what Paul says about the Spirit's work. He teaches us about the sealing of the Spirit, the "promised Holy Spirit" (the same promise given to Israel), and the guarantee of the Spirit.

◉ A seal was a mark of ownership and authenticity. It was used for cattle, and even slaves were branded by their masters. Owners were guarding their property from theft by branding them (O'Brien, *Ephesians*, 120). Those seals were external of course. Our seal is internal. God puts His seal in our hearts (Stott, *Ephesians*, 49).

Paul later prays for the Ephesians to be "strengthened with power in the inner man through His Spirit" (3:16). The Spirit of God is dwelling in believers. Paul affirms this in several ways in Romans 8, saying, "If anyone does not have the Spirit of Christ, he does not belong to Him" (Rom 8:9), and "The Spirit Himself testifies together with our spirit that we are God's children" (Rom 8:16). In Ephesians 4 Paul writes,

"Don't grieve God's Holy Spirit. You were sealed by Him for the day of redemption" (Eph 4:30). God has sealed us and will keep us until the day of redemption.

The Promised Holy Spirit

Paul refers to the Holy Spirit as "promised" probably because His new covenant presence was foretold. The prophets and Jesus told of the day in which the Spirit would be sent. Ezekiel 36:27 and Joel 2:28 are examples of Old Testament predictions regarding the coming of the Spirit.

Peter mentions the promised Holy Spirit in Acts 2: "Therefore, since He has been exalted to the right hand of God and has received from the Father the promised Holy Spirit, He has poured out what you both see and hear" (Acts 2:33).

In John 14–16 Jesus also spoke of the Spirit's presence that He would send: "It is for your benefit that I go away, because if I don't go away the Counselor will not come to you. If I go, I will send Him to you" (John 16:7). He has not left us as orphans (John 14:18). How encouraging this is!

The Guarantee of the Spirit

Finally, the Holy Spirit is the guarantee of our final inheritance. The Spirit is the first installment, or the down payment, provided for the glory that is to come.

Many times people use this verse to compare the Spirit to an engagement ring. However, an engagement ring is not part of the wedding. It is a promise, but it is not a down payment. A better analogy is the down payment on a house, which is the first installment of the purchase (Stott, *Ephesians*, 49). So God is not just telling us about something in the future, He is bringing the future into the present so that we may taste what the future is like.

Once again Paul strikes the note "to the praise of His glory" (v. 14). There is nothing left to do but to join Paul in worship and declare God's praises to the nations who are not worshiping Him. God is calling the nations to praise Him for His mighty salvation.

God the Father has chosen us, God the Son has redeemed us, and God the Spirit has assured us. Let us worship the triune God. We were made for praise, and our hearts will only be satisfied when we begin praising this God.

Reflect and Discuss

1. What does this passage say about worship? How does it move you to praise God?

2. How does this passage contribute to your understanding of the Trinity?

3. How do some people describe the doctrine of election in negative terms? Why should the doctrine of election lead us to praise God?

4. Why should we reflect deeply on the doctrine of adoption? What practical benefit might a deep understanding of this doctrine have?

5. How would you explain to a non-Christian what Christ did to accomplish your redemption?

6. How is Christ central in history?

7. How does knowing that God works all things according to the counsel of His will affect you? Why do we need to reflect on this truth?

8. Explain the importance of "when you believed" in verse 13, in light of the context of verses 3-14.

9. Using concepts from this text, explain who the Holy Spirit is and summarize His role in salvation.

10. Why should this passage give us hope?

Praying to the Glorious Father

EPHESIANS 1:15-23

Main Idea: In this prayer of thanksgiving and intercession, Paul expresses gratitude to God for the Ephesian believers, and he prays for them to grow in their knowledge of God and in their awareness of all they have in Christ, who is over all.

I. **Thank God for Evidences of Grace in His People (1:15-16).**
II. **Ask God for Divine Illumination (1:17-20).**
    A. To know God better (1:17b)
    B. To know the blessings of the gospel better (1:18-20a)
        1. Hope (1:18a)
        2. Inheritance (1:18b)
        3. Power (1:19-20a)
III. **Praise God for His Exaltation of Christ (1:20-23).**
    A. Christ's resurrection (1:20a)
    B. Christ's enthronement (1:20b)
    C. Christ's supremacy (1:21-22a)
    D. Christ's headship (1:22b-23)

This text reveals some important truths about prayer, emphasizing prayer for knowledge and understanding. We need the Spirit's help to grasp the greatness of God, the supremacy of Christ, and the rich benefits of the gospel.

Verses 3-14 are a hard act to follow, but Paul does so with this magnificent prayer! Verses 3-14 are about *praise*, and verses 15-23 are about *prayer*, which is still mingled with praise. The first section is about the spiritual blessings of salvation, and the prayer is about grasping them. Praise and prayer belong together, and they are fundamental to the interior life of the Christian. As we pray with Paul, we can observe three parts to this text: thanksgiving (vv. 15-16), intercession (vv. 17-19), and praise (vv. 20-23).

Thank God for Evidences of Grace in His People
EPHESIANS 1:15-16

In light of the opening section about God's work in the believers in Ephesus, Paul expresses his gratitude to God for them. He begins with a note of encouragement, reflecting on what he has heard about the Ephesian believers. Due to the amount of time that he had been away from Ephesus, and due to the probable circular nature of the letter, he does not seem to know all the Ephesian believers who will be reading it. Yet he is still praying for them. Here we see a combination of thankful prayer to God and public commendation to the people of God. Paul prays to God, giving thanks. He lets the people know he is thankful for them.

Paul is thankful for two important characteristics of God's people: *faith* in the Lord Jesus and *love* for the saints. Paul mentions faith and love in other places also, showing us the importance of these qualities (see Col 1:4; 1 Thess 1:3; 2 Thess 1:3; Phlm 3). These are essential qualities of Christians. What is a Christian? Here is a good summary: a Christian has faith in the Lord Jesus and has love toward the saints. These are basic Christian graces, with *hope* making up the triad, as mentioned in verses 12 and 18.

God's people love one another. Jesus said, "By this all people will know that you are My disciples, if you have love for one another" (John 13:35). John mentions this as a proof as well several times in his epistles; for example, "This is how we have come to know love: He laid down His life for us. We should also lay down our lives for our brothers" (1 John 3:16).

Paul also says he is constantly praying with thanksgiving (cf. 1 Thess 1:2; 2 Tim 1:3; Rom 1:9). When Paul refers to his "prayers," he could be referring to the Jewish pattern of three prayer times per day (morning, noon, and evening). During these occasions and any other times, Paul is giving thanks to God for the Ephesians.

If Paul has this in mind, then here is another good principle for prayer: a good prayer life is both *ongoing* and *planned*. In terms of ongoing prayer, we should "pray without ceasing" (1 Thess 5:17 ESV). We can pray while we work and go about our days. We also need times to get away, like Jesus, who got up before the noise of the day began and prayed. I think it is good to have some place and time where you spend unhurried and unhindered moments in prayer.

In verses 15-16 we see a thankful, praying apostle. I love how in 1 Corinthians, though Corinth is a troubled church, Paul can say, "I always thank my God for you because of God's grace given to you in Christ Jesus" (1 Cor 1:4). Paul even thanks God for the Corinthians! How? He looked for traces of grace and found reasons for gratitude.

Let me remind you of the need to recognize grace in others. It is easy to be critical of others. It takes a mature believer to recognize grace in others. Do you wear the glasses of grace or the glasses of self-righteousness or self-centeredness? Let us thank God in our prayers for evidences of grace in God's people—namely, faith and love—and let us also encourage the saints when we see traces of grace in their lives.

② Ask God for Divine Illumination
EPHESIANS 1:17-20

Now we get into Paul's petitions. He uses three phrases that get at the idea of illumination: "spirit of wisdom" and of "revelation" (v. 17), and "having the eyes of your heart enlightened" (v. 18). He says that your heart has eyes! Paul is asking God to give them spiritual eyes to see who God is and what God has done for them.

Illumination is the simple idea that God opens our eyes to know Him and His truth. Inspiration is what we refer to as the nature of Scripture. Illumination is how we understand Scripture. It is absolutely necessary that we seek the Spirit's help in understanding His truth. God's mind is revealed in Scripture, but we need "Holy Spirit glasses" to understand it accurately and deeply. Spurgeon said that apart from the Spirit it is easier to teach a tiger vegetarianism than an unregenerate person the gospel (*An All-Around Ministry*, 322). There is that great example of Jesus opening the eyes of the disciples. Luke writes,

> Then their eyes were opened, and they recognized Him, but He disappeared from their sight. So they said to each other, "Weren't our hearts ablaze within us while He was talking with us on the road and explaining the Scriptures to us?" . . . Then He opened their minds to understand the Scriptures. (Luke 24:31-32,45)

Just as Jesus opened the eyes of the disciples to know His Word, so God opens the eyes of unbelievers' hearts at conversion, like Lydia, for example (Acts 16:14). Here in Ephesians, Paul asks God to give Christians eyes to see who they are. The psalmist prays something like this throughout Psalm 119: "Open my eyes so that I may contemplate wonderful things from Your instruction" (v. 18). "Help me understand Your instruction" (v. 34). "Show favor to Your servant, and teach me Your statutes" (v. 135).

The reason we often fail to seek the Spirit's illumination is that we have an inflated view of ourselves. We are tempted to feel self-sufficient, as if we do not need God's help. The first step to becoming a student of the Bible is having a heart of humility—a heart that says, "Please, give me understanding."

Along with this, we often have a low view of God, but Paul did not! Notice whom Paul is asking: "the glorious Father." The God of glory who appeared to Moses at Sinai is capable of opening eyes to see Him! Paul often tied "glory" and "power" together (compare 1 Cor 6:14 with Rom 6:4). By calling God the glorious Father, he is saying that God is the source of glory and power. Because of this, Paul can confidently ask God to give the Ephesians power. God is omnipotent. He is perfectly capable of giving us all the resources we need.

We are not praying to some little, weak God. We are praying to the only God, the "glorious Father." He is intimate, near, gracious to His people, like a good father; He is also glorious in His majesty, transcendence, and power. In 2 Corinthians Paul also puts glory and illumination ("the light of knowledge") together saying,

> For God who said, "Let light shine out of darkness," has shone in our hearts to give the light of the knowledge of God's glory in the face of Jesus Christ. (2 Cor 4:6)

Again, Paul is confident when he prays because he knows to whom he is praying: the glorious Father. He who spoke the universe into existence can turn the lights on in hearts to see the glory of God in the face of Jesus.

To Know God Better (1:17b)

The first reason Paul gives for our needing God to open the eyes of our hearts is so we might know God better ("revelation in the knowledge of Him"). This may seem elementary, but is anything more important? D. A. Carson says, "What is the greatest need in the church today? . . . The one thing we need in Western Christendom is a deeper knowledge of God. We need to know God better" (*Call*, 15).

Barna poll - ___ % of born agains
have a biblical world view.
(others a modern "politically correct" world view)

In Colossians 1:9-10 Paul prays for God to give them wisdom so they may continue "growing in the knowledge of God." The beginning, middle, and end of the Christian life is about knowing God. Beginning: Jesus says, "This is eternal life: that they may know You, the only true God, and the One You have sent—Jesus Christ" (John 17:3). Jesus told some who were doing ministry in His name, "I never knew you! Depart from Me" (Matt 7:22-23). Middle: Paul writes, "My goal is to know Him and the power of His resurrection" (Phil 3:10). End: John writes, "We know that when He appears, we will be like Him because we will see Him as He is" (1 John 3:2). The Christian's life is moving toward the *visio dei*, when we will see Christ. The Christian life is about knowing God and making Him known to others.

Spurgeon says it well: "I go back to my home, many a time, mourning that I cannot preach my Master even as I myself know Him, and what I know of Him is very little compared with the matchlessness of His grace. Would that I knew more of Him, and that I could tell it out better!" ("The Great Change"). J. I. Packer, in his classic book, *Knowing God*, says that those who know God have four characteristics: great energy for God, great thoughts of God, great boldness for God, and great contentment in God (*Knowing God*, 27–31). Let us pray that God will open our eyes that we may know Him better.

To Know the Blessings of the Gospel Better (1:18-20a)

Paul expands on the idea of knowing God better by praying that we may grasp certain truths about salvation. In a sense this is the same request or the other side of that request (Carson, *Call*, 175). Paul prays that they would know God, the God who has saved them and given them every spiritual blessing in Christ.

So what does Paul want his readers to understand? He mentions three particular blessings, distinguished by the word *what* in English:

- "what is the hope of His calling" (v. 18a);
- "what are the glorious riches of His inheritance among the saints" (v. 18b); and
- "what is the immeasurable greatness of His power to us who believe" (v. 19).

The third blessing just keeps going! I have made verses 20-23 a separate point, but they are really a continuation of the blessing. Let's look at these three.

Hope (1:18a). Paul asks God to open their eyes to know the hope to which He called them. In eternity past He called us. Then we believed in the present. And our hope also has a future dimension. We look forward to God summing up all things in Christ. Our salvation is marked by massive hope.

Paul prays that they may now grasp the hope of this calling. In Romans Paul describes our hope as involving sharing in the glory of God (Rom 5:2). He also speaks in other places of the hope of "salvation" (1 Thess 5:8), "righteousness" (Gal 5:5), resurrection of an incorruptible body (1 Cor 15:19,52-55), and "eternal life" (Titus 1:2; 3:7). This hope is rich, and it is varied in the New Testament. To put it simply, God has called us to a distinct way of life with a glorious future hope. When we hold out the gospel to people, we are essentially holding out hope to people (cf. Col 1:5). There is much suffering in this life; there are many dangers, toils, and snares, but glory is coming.

Inheritance (1:18b). Grammatically this could mean the inheritance God receives (i.e., we are His inheritance) or the inheritance that we receive (cf. Col 1:12). Since the text speaks of "God's inheritance," it seems best to go with the former (just as we noted in Eph 1:11). Paul wants us to appreciate the value that God places on us who are in Christ. Bruce says, "That God should set such a high value on the community of sinners rescued from perdition and still bearing too many traces of their former state, might well seem incredible were it not made clear that he sees them in Christ, as from the beginning, he chose them in Christ" (*Ephesians*, 270). In light of this, we should live for God's praise, and we should declare God's praise to the nations (cf. 1 Pet 2:9-10).

Power (1:19-20a). This third request is the climactic request in the prayer. That is made evident by how Paul expands on power in the following verses (vv. 20-23) and by the incredible labels Paul applies to God's power: "immeasurable greatness," "power" (*dynamis*), "working" (*energeia*), and "vast strength." Paul says God's almighty power is available to His saints! Only by God's power will we be able to engage in the spiritual battle described in Ephesians 6. Only by God's power will we arrive safely into His heavenly kingdom, and His power is given to "us who believe" (v. 19).

Think about where some of these Ephesians were coming from. Some were formerly caught up in magic, the Artemis cult, astrology, and emperor worship. Their lives were dark and perverted (Eph 4:17-19) until Christ saved them. The people of this culture lived in fear of hostile spiritual forces (O'Brien, *Ephesians*, 138). Paul is assuring them that God's power is supreme over all their enemies!

We need not fear when we have superior power. The power of the risen Christ is ours to do battle against worry, temptation, doubt, and demonic warfare. Why do we often fail to rely on this mighty power? Added to the exalted view of self and diminished view of God is the failure to understand the spiritual battle in which we are engaged.

✤ The evil one and his host hate us. They hate our faith. They hate the church, our marriages, and our mission. That is why we must lean into Christ and pray for His resurrection power to strengthen us and empower us to live for God's glory.

➽ To illustrate God's mighty power, Paul goes to the resurrection. In the Old Testament they measured power by creation (Isa 40) or by the exodus, but now there is another greater picture of power, the resurrection of Jesus Christ! Now, Christian, this power is ours. Paul says, "The Spirit of Him who raised Jesus from the dead lives in you" (Rom 8:11). This power is ours to witness, to overcome sin, to pursue holiness, to fight against the schemes of the Devil, and to have great faith for mission.

 Praise God for His Exaltation of Christ
EPHESIANS 1:20-23

As mentioned, these verses are a continuation of verse 19. Paul is speaking of God's great work of exalting Jesus above all. I want you to see four aspects of Christ's exaltation.

Christ's Resurrection (1:20a)

God, with His infinite wisdom and power, has done what no man can do. He raised Jesus from the dead! Death is no little bug to squash; it is a bitter enemy we will all face. Yet because of the resurrection of Jesus Christ, we do not have to fear death. Jesus has crushed it! In his famous chapter on the resurrection in 1 Corinthians 15, Paul closes by saying,

> *Therefore, my dear brothers, be steadfast, immovable, always excelling*
> *in the Lord's work, knowing that your labor in the Lord is not in vain.*
> (1 Cor 15:58)

Because of the resurrection, life has meaning. Our labor is not in vain. The resurrection of Jesus testifies to the fact that Jesus is the Messiah.

The resurrection gives believers enormous hope and sufficient power for living a life of service to God.

Paul is paving the way for Ephesians 2:4-7 where he says of believers, "Together with Christ Jesus He also raised us up and seated us in the heavens." The resurrection is a truth we need to meditate on every day.

Christ's Enthronement (1:20b)

Jesus is not only alive forevermore, but He is also *reigning* forevermore. Paul notes here the enthronement of Jesus.

In the early preaching in the book of Acts, the resurrection and Christ's enthronement were emphasized. They were the fulfillment of Messianic prophecies.

> This is the declaration of the LORD to my Lord:
> "Sit at My right hand
> until I make Your enemies Your footstool." (Ps 110:1)

When He was brought before the Sanhedrin, Jesus claimed that these verses were about Him (O'Brien, *Ephesians*, 140; see Matt 26:64; Mark 12:36; Luke 20:41-44). To be at the "right hand" was a position of privilege, honor, favor, victory, and power. This position belongs to Jesus Christ alone.

What does that mean for us? It means everything. Everything is under the reign of the seated King! The author of Hebrews says He is upholding the universe by the word of His power, and He upholds it all *sitting down* (Heb 1:3). If He is doing this, then we can trust Him with our problems—both great and small. Our hope is not in a political election but in the seated King.

Christ's Supremacy (1:21-22a)

Christ, as the risen, seated King, is now superior to every competitor. His throne is above the principalities and powers. He is above creation. He is above Satan and his system. He is above everyone and every ruler. Paul mentions His supremacy over all earthly powers. He mentions Christ's supremacy over every title or name (cf. Phil 2:6-11). And then he mentions Christ's supremacy over all His enemies with the phrase "under His feet." Paul is saying here that not only is every power inferior to Christ, they are also subject to Him (O'Brien, *Ephesians*, 145).

Christ's Headship (1:22b-23)

Finally, Paul mentions Christ's headship over the church. Here we see the amazing connection between Christ and His church. Only the church, not all creation, is said to be His body. Consequently, the church should be important to us! Jesus identifies Himself with it! He is head over it. Later in Ephesians Paul will expound on this relationship.

A lot of believers know this intellectually, but it seems that many think a pastor is the head of the church. I know of one case in which one-third of a congregation left a church when a pastor left it. The church is not about a man; it is about Christ. He is the Head.

Paul also says that the church is Christ's "fullness" (v. 23). I take this difficult phrase in the passive sense rather than active. We do not fill Christ. He fills us. Paul is saying that Jesus, as Head over the church, is "filling [the church] in a special way with his Spirit, grace, and gifts: it is his fullness" (O'Brien, *Ephesians*, 152).

As Lord over all things, He fills all things, but this filling of the church is different. Only the church is His body, and He rules it and fills it in a special way. What this means is that we as a church are entirely dependent on Christ. What makes us something significant—indeed glorious—is our relationship to Jesus. He fills the church with His presence.

What encouragement this must have given to the house churches in the region of Ephesus. What encouragement it should give to us!

Reflect and Discuss

1. Will you pause and pray like Paul—with thanksgiving, intercession, and praise?
2. Are you thankful to God for fellow believers? Have you told a fellow believer this lately?
3. What in this passage taught you the most about prayer? What is missing in your prayer life?
4. What kinds of requests are brought up at your prayer meetings? How are Paul's petitions for the believers in Ephesus different?
5. How is illumination different from inspiration? Why do we need divine illumination?
6. What practical difference would it make if we understood our hope, inheritance, and power better?
7. What do you find most difficult to believe in this passage? Why?

8. What does this passage say about the exaltation of Jesus? How might living with this awareness affect our lives?
9. How is Paul's view of the church different from the view taken by most Christians today? What would happen if we took a high view of the church?
10. Will you commit to praying through this prayer this week?

But God . . .

EPHESIANS 2:1-10

Main Idea: In His amazing grace, love, mercy, and kindness, God gave us spiritual life in Christ.

I. **Apart from Christ, We Were Spiritually Dead (2:1-3).**
  A. We were dead (2:1).
  B. We were disobedient (2:2-3a).
    1. We followed the world.
    2. We followed Satan.
    3. We followed our sinful desires.
  C. We were doomed (2:3b).
II. **With Christ, We Are Spiritually Alive (2:4-7).**
  A. God's character (2:4-7)
  B. God's work (2:5-7)
    1. God made us alive with Christ (2:5).
    2. God raised us up with Christ (2:6a).
    3. God seated us with Christ (2:6b).
    4. God will dispense grace forever to us in Christ (2:7).
III. **In Christ, We Are God's Workmanship (2:8-10).**
  A. Salvation is a gift (2:8-9).
  B. No one can boast (2:9b).
  C. Salvation results in good works (2:10).

Jeremy Bentham (1748–1832) was a philosopher (among other things) and is considered the founder of utilitarianism ("the greatest happiness principle"). He was an interesting figure in more ways than one. His name actually appears in the TV show *Lost* (as an alias of the character John Locke). In Bentham's will he apparently left a fortune to a London hospital. But there was one condition: Bentham was to be present at every board meeting. Reportedly, for more than one hundred years, the remains of Jeremy Bentham were wheeled into the boardroom every month and placed at the head of the table. His skeleton was dressed with seventeenth-century garb and a little hat, which sat on his wax head. In the minutes of every board meeting, a line read,

"Mr. Jeremy Bentham, present but not voting" (Kent Hughes, *Ephesians*, 66). This was a joke from his philosophy. Of course, he never voted because he had been dead since 1832. Today we come to a passage that shows *when we were spiritually dead, God made us alive with Christ.* We were "present but not voting" until God gave us life.

Broadly speaking, the paragraph consists of two sentences in Greek (vv. 1-7 and 8-10). The subject of the first sentence is actually "God" (v. 4), and the main verb is "made alive." By His amazing grace God has made our spiritually dead hearts beat. Further, this passage is related to the previous section, especially 1:19-20, which describes God's mighty work in raising Jesus from the dead. This same power raises us from death to life. Allow me now to highlight three truths about God's work in bringing us life.

Apart from Christ, We Were Spiritually Dead
EPHESIANS 2:1-3

Paul first begins with our pre-Christian past. The picture is not good. Verse 1 begins with "And you." To whom is he talking? The Gentiles in Ephesus. Then he says "all" and then "the others" (v. 3). Paul covers everyone with these phrases. He is not preparing to describe some degrading segment of society or some cannibalistic tribe somewhere. He's talking about everyone. This is the biblical diagnosis of our sinful nature (O'Brien, *Ephesians*, 156). Paul shows us who we were before Christ with three descriptions.

We Were Dead (2:1)

Paul says we were dead in our "trespasses and sins" (v. 1). This was our previous state of alienation from God. Paul repeats it later in the text in his amazement at what God has done "even though we were dead in trespasses" (v. 5).

"Trespasses" draws attention to acts of sin. "Sins" is a more comprehensive account of human evil (O'Brien, *Ephesians*, 157). We were dead, committing trespasses, in a sinful state. Thus we were wretched and culpable because of our trespasses and sins.

Notice what Paul says in Ephesians 4:18. We were "excluded from the life of God." That means we were dead. We were cut off from true, eternal spiritual life given and sustained by God.

Now this is the complete opposite of what the world tells us about ourselves as humans. The world tells us that we are basically good, and if we just believe in ourselves, then we can do anything. While a spiritually dead person may indeed do amazing things because she is an image bearer of God—make works of art, play sports exceptionally well, make money, do humanitarian work—she can do nothing spiritually because she is not connected to the Vine.

Ephesians 2:1-3 could not be clearer. Humans face a sad predicament. We are not morally good. We are not neutral. To quote Miracle Max in *The Princess Bride*, we were not "mostly dead." We were totally dead. And we needed a miracle that only God could perform.

If God performed this miracle in your heart, then you should celebrate His grace! In Luke 15 Jesus tells a parable about two lost sons. With regard to the first son, we find a powerful illustration of Ephesians 2. We meet the younger brother, rebelling against his father, living recklessly in sin, and eventually eating with the pigs. But when the son comes to his senses and returns home to his gracious, forgiving father, the father says, "Let's celebrate with a feast, because this son of mine was dead and is alive again; he was lost and is found!" (Luke 15:23-24).

We Were Disobedient (2:2-3a)

Paul goes on to describe how we disobeyed God like our first parents did. Instead of following God, we followed three evil forces.

We followed the world. Paul refers to sins "in which you previously walked according to the ways of this world" (2:2). The unsaved person is controlled by the world's influences, by the values of the age, which are contrary to God's values. The unsaved assume the attitudes, habits, and lifestyles of the culture, reflecting Paul's words in 2 Timothy 3:1-5. In John's words their lives are marked by "the lust of the flesh, the lust of the eyes, and the pride in one's lifestyle" (1 John 2:15-17). Consequently, we need Jesus to "rescue us from this present evil age" (Gal 1:4).

We followed Satan. Paul describes the evil one's work, "according to the ruler who exercises authority over the lower heavens, the spirit now working in the disobedient" (v. 2).

Ephesians speaks more about principalities and power than any other New Testament letter. And it draws attention to the power behind them: Satan (see 4:27; 6:11,16).

"Ruler" or "prince" in the Old Testament was a term used for a national, local, or tribal leader. In the Gospels Satan is the "ruler of the demons" (Matt 9:34; 12:24; Mark 3:22; Luke 11:15) and the "ruler of this world" (John 12:31; 14:30; 16:11). Paul also refers to him as the "god of this age" (2 Cor 4:4). "Lower heavens" in the ancient world referred to the intermediate space between heaven and earth where evil spirits dwelled. Here it refers to the place of activity of Satan. The "spirit now working in the disobedient" describes how Satan works on unbelievers. They are not completely possessed by Satan, but they do live in the world of darkness in which Satan holds sway. He lays out the bait, and sinful people take it, disobeying God. Paul mentions "the disobedient" (lit. "sons of disobedience") again in Ephesians 5:6, linking them to sins such as sexual immorality, impurity, greed, and foolish talk.

We followed our sinful desires. Paul calls these "fleshly desires" and "the inclinations of our flesh and thoughts" (v. 3). These passions are associated in Galatians 5:16-21 and elsewhere with sins like anger, sexual immorality, idolatry, sorcery, jealousy, strife, dissension, and drunkenness. In Romans Paul tells us the result of such a lifestyle: "Those who are in the flesh cannot please God" (Rom 8:8). The Old Testament prophet Jeremiah put it this way: "The heart is more deceitful than anything else, and incurable—who can understand it?" (Jer 17:9).

Did Paul get carried away here? Is our condition this bad? Yes, this is truth. While humans bear the image of God, and sin has not destroyed the image of God completely, we are radically depraved and unable to come to God apart from new birth. Our behavior is explained by all three of these influences—the world, Satan, and the flesh. They all play a part in the sinful condition of man.

Theologically, Paul is describing the doctrine of "total depravity"; that is, all aspects of our being have been infected with the deadly disease of sin. Paul is also describing our "total inability"; that is, morally we are not capable of responding to God apart from grace. The fact is we do not want to respond to God. But oh, how we need God's grace!

We Were Doomed (2:3b)

Paul follows this by saying we were "by nature children of wrath, like the rest of mankind" (v. 3 ESV). "The disobedient" in verse 2 are now children destined for wrath in verse 3, which is what we rightly deserved. Our spiritual status could not be more tragic or hopeless. We were justly under the judgment of God. He is right to condemn us in our sins (cf. Eph 5:6).

God is holy, and He will not sweep sin under the rug. Many think God in the Old Testament was a God of wrath but God in the New Testament is like Mr. Rogers. Wrong. What we have now is a period of patience. The door of mercy is open wide now, and we can come into this grace and be saved. But the coming wrath of God is worse than anything in the Old Testament. The words of Hebrews should humble us: "It is a terrifying thing to fall into the hands of the living God!" (Heb 10:31).

God will act in a righteous manner, not in unrighteous revenge or in an outburst of anger. He will punish sin and sinners justly.

The good news for the Christian is that God's wrath has been poured out not on us but on the Savior. Jesus drank the cup, a metaphor that describes the wrath of God. He drank the cup, and we drink grace. Bless His holy name.

Paul draws our attention to the depth of our depravity in order to magnify the mercy and grace of God in saving us, like a black cloth on which a beautiful diamond sits. And Paul gives us the diamond of the gospel with two of the sweetest words in the Bible: "But God." Christian, behold your biography.

With Christ, We Are Spiritually Alive
EPHESIANS 2:4-7

God's gracious initiative and sovereign action stand in wonderful contrast to verses 1-3. We were lifeless, hopeless, and under condemnation. "But God" came to our rescue. Notice how Paul describes the character of God and the work of God in these amazing verses.

God's Character (2:4-7)

What prompted God's salvation was His *mercy, love, grace,* and *kindness.* Paul can, in the same sentence, affirm the wrath of God and the love of God. In fact, you cannot understand one without the other. Notice the descriptions of God's goodness in these verses.

God is "rich in mercy" (v. 4). The Old Testament describes God as rich in faithful love (Ps 103:8), as One who delights in faithful love (Mic 7:18). The word in Hebrew, *chesed,* refers to God's loyal, merciful love. God's mercy is also sovereignly distributed. God says, "I will show mercy to whom I will show mercy" (Rom 9:15).

Next, God has shown "great love" (Eph 2:4). To the Romans Paul writes, "But God proves His own love for us in that while we were still sinners [dead, depraved, and doomed], Christ died for us!" (Rom 5:8).

Paul also highlights God's amazing "grace" in these verses (Eph 2:5,8). Being made alive when we were dead is a work of grace. Believers have experienced the undeserved favor of God. Twelve times "grace" is mentioned in Ephesians. In chapter 1 Paul said that our salvation was "to the praise of His glorious grace" (1:6).

Paul reaches for words as he also mentions "the immeasurable riches of His grace through His kindness" (2:7b). For all eternity we will be recipients of His grace, trophies of His grace. He has displayed infinite riches of grace in kindness to us.

2 God's Work (2:5-7)

Now notice what God did in His mercy, grace, love, and kindness. Paul begins by telling us that *God made us alive with Christ* (v. 5). The main verb that governs the phrase, "made us alive," is introduced. Just as Jesus raised Lazarus from the dead, He also said to us, "_____ come forth." And like Lazarus, we rise and rejoice in His grace.

We have what theologians have termed an "outer call," which goes out to everyone through the proclamation of the gospel, and "an inner call," which the Holy Spirit does in hearts. Those who are Christians have sensed this inner calling (Gal 1:6). Paul experienced this call to come to Christ (Gal 1:15).

We cannot overemphasize the importance of this doctrine of regeneration. Christianity is not about becoming a nicer person, nor is it about starting a new religious routine. It is about becoming a new person (2 Cor 5:17). One night a religious man named Nicodemus came to ask Jesus some spiritual questions. He had a lot of religious knowledge, but he had not been made alive. Jesus told him, "I assure you: Unless someone is born again, he cannot see the kingdom of God" (John 3:3).

We need to remember that no one is beyond the reach of God's regenerating grace, and no one is beyond the need for God's regenerating grace. I remember preaching at a church in the deep South. A man who was about 70 years old was handing out bulletins, as he did every week. I preached on John 3, and he came up after the service and said, "I've never heard that. Someone just asked me when I was a boy, 'Don't you think it's about time for you to join the church?' And I did. But I

good illus.

feel like God was waking me up today." Later I baptized this gentleman upon his confession of faith.

I love a particular story regarding the ministry of the eighteenth-century evangelist George Whitefield, who reportedly preached on John 3 thousands of times. He was pouring out his heart one day during a Great Awakening sermon. A man with pockets stuffed with rocks came to hear him for the purpose of physically attacking the famous evangelist once the sermon ended. But after Whitefield's emotional and powerful message, the man made his way up to the preacher, emptied his pockets, and said, "I came to hear you with my pocket full of stones to break your head, but your sermon got the better of me and broke my heart" (Dunn, *Evangelical Awakening*, 17). God gave this angry, hostile man life through the gospel. It is true that "the gospel can melt the ice or harden the clay." Praise God that He melts the hearts of the hardest men and women and gives them new life!

There is sort of a parenthesis in verse 5—"You are saved by grace!" Paul repeats this again in verse 8: "For you are saved by grace through faith." Being raised from the dead is all of grace. Both phrases are in the perfect tense emphasizing the abiding consequences of conversion. To capture what Paul is saying we could put it like this: You have been saved (past tense), you are being saved (present tense), and you will be saved (future tense).

Notice also how Paul says we have been made alive "with the Messiah" (v. 5, *synezōpoiesen*). Paul underscores our *union with Christ*. In fact, all three verbs have a prefix meaning "with" (alive *with* Christ, raised *with* Christ, seated *with* Christ).

Consider the staggering nature of God's work in uniting us with Christ. Paul says that *God raised us up with Christ* (v. 6a). This is a clear allusion to the resurrection of Jesus. Paul uses a compound word to declare that we have been raised together, *synegeiren*, which has the prefix *syn-*. We know this word from computers. We get the word *sync* from it (short for "synchronize"). We sync our phones with our computers in order to transfer the music on the computer to the phone. Well, we were synced with Christ! What God did for Christ, He did at the same time for believers (O'Brien, *Ephesians*, 170). In some astonishing way, when Jesus Christ got out of the tomb two thousand years ago, Tony Merida got up with Him. In Colossians 2:12 Paul says that this has already taken place: "You were also raised with Him." Because of it, Paul says, "Seek what is above" (Col 3:1).

Next Paul adds that *God seated us with Christ* (v. 6b, *synekathisen*). In chapter 1 Paul praised God for exalting Jesus above all powers and forces. Now he says that we are seated with Jesus. This means we have a position of "superiority and authority over the evil powers" (O'Brien, *Ephesians*, 171). It does not mean we are divine. There is only One on the throne. But we are seated with Him and have power to overcome. We do not have to succumb to the dark world and Satan's schemes. Also note here the "already–not yet" aspect of salvation. We are now raised and seated with Him, but we are awaiting the full completion of our salvation.

The final work of grace that Paul notes is future oriented. He says *God will dispense grace forever to us in Christ* (v. 7). The reason God has showed us such grace is so we might be the demonstration of His grace forever. We will be His trophies of grace. God says in effect, "Look what I can do with such a mess." Ponder the idea of grace for "ages" to come. Instead of wrath, we have everlasting grace!   *AMEN!!!*

In Christ, We Are God's Workmanship
EPHESIANS 2:8-10

Paul now elaborates on God's gracious gift of salvation by inserting "faith and works" into the discussion. Paul first emphasizes how salvation is a gift and then how true salvation results in good works.

Salvation Is a Gift (2:8-9)

Paul first highlights *God's grace*: "For you are saved by grace through faith, and this is not from yourselves; it is God's gift—not from works, so that no one can boast" (vv. 8-9). Indeed, grace captures the mind of Paul in these 10 verses. God's great rescue of us is by grace. Think of the great reversal that has taken place between verses 1-3 and 4-7.

Dead in trespasses and sins	→	Alive together with Christ
Sons of disobedience	→	Raised up with Christ
Children of wrath	→	Seated with Christ
Children of wrath	→	Recipients of generous mercy
Children of wrath	→	Recipients of great love
Children of wrath	→	Recipients of rich grace
Children of wrath	→	Recipients of God's kindness
Children of wrath	→	Trophies of God's grace

Paul says that grace comes *through faith*. This is the human response: belief (cf. Eph 1:13). How do we appropriate what has just been said? Faith. Faith is the instrument by which we lay hold of Christ. But faith is not a work. It is a gift. Notice what Paul says: "It is God's gift" (v. 8); "it" includes "faith." The grammar indicates that the whole of salvation is to be viewed as a gift. Grace is a gift. Faith is a gift. Salvation is a gift. We should never think of salvation as a transaction in which God provides grace and we provide faith (Stott, *Ephesians*, 83). No. It is all grace. We were dead and had to be awakened to believe.

By way of example, Luke writes that Apollos "helped those who had believed *through grace*" (Acts 18:27, emphasis added; cf. Acts 13:48; Phil 1:29). Because salvation is a divine gift, it cannot be earned. Your moral efforts or religious activity cannot earn salvation.   ✓

We were not saved because we were smarter than others, prettier than others, or more gifted than others. Our salvation was the work of God. God showed us astonishing grace. He put forth His Son as our substitute, and He granted us the faith to believe in the Savior.

No One Can Boast (2:9b)

There is only One who should be exalted in this salvation, and that is God. We have not worked for it, and we cannot, therefore, brag about ourselves (Rom 4:2). God in His grace sent Christ to live the life we could not live, die the death we should have died, and rise on our behalf. God raised Christ and us with Him; He has seated us in the heavens, and He will dispense grace on us forever. The glory goes only to God in salvation.

Paul says it well when he writes, "What do you have that you didn't receive? If, in fact, you did receive it, why do you boast as if you hadn't received it?" (1 Cor 4:7). And since we have received this salvation, "The one who boasts must boast in the Lord" (1 Cor 1:31).

Salvation Results in Good Works (2:10)

After saying that our works cannot save us, Paul notes the importance of works. He does not want us to think that works are unimportant. He states that works simply are not *the root* of our salvation. They are *the fruit* of salvation (cf. John 15:8; Titus 2:14). The Reformers used to say, "It is faith alone that justifies, but faith that justifies can never be alone." We are not saved by faith plus works but by a faith that does work. We have a living faith, a functioning faith!

Now that we belong to God, God is working on us and in us so that He might work through us. Paul says, "we are his workmanship" (v. 10 ESV). This word for "workmanship" (*poiema*) may be where the word *poem* comes from. The word was used to refer to any work of art, such as a statue, a song, architecture, a painting, or a poem (Hughes, *Ephesians*, 82). It is only used one other time in the New Testament. In Romans 1:20 it refers to the material creation. The heavens and earth display the glory of God's material creation. But this is a new creation, called "saved sinners." They declare the glory of God's spiritual creation (cf. 2 Cor 5:21; Gal 6:15).

Because we are God's workmanship in Christ Jesus, people should see our works and say, "That's a work of God." Jesus said, "In the same way, let your light shine before men, so that they may see your good works and give glory to your Father in heaven" (Matt 5:16).

Paul adds that we were "created in Christ Jesus for good works, which God prepared ahead of time so that we should walk in them" (v. 10). Like our conversion our spiritual growth takes place "in Christ Jesus." As we are united to Him, we have life; that life leads to good works. Chapters 4–6 spell out what these works look like (e.g., 4:12).

Luther succinctly and powerfully described the relationship between faith and works:

> Faith, however, is a divine work in us. It changes us and makes us to be born anew of God (John 1); it kills the old Adam and makes altogether different men, in heart and spirit and mind and powers, and it brings with it the Holy Ghost. Oh, it is a living, busy, active, mighty thing, this faith; and so it is impossible for it not to do good works incessantly. It does not ask whether there are good works to do, but before the question rises, it has already done them, and is always at the doing of them. (Martin Luther, *Romans*, xvii)

Indeed, the instinct of one who has new life is to do good works—at home, at work, and everywhere—to the glory of God.

Paul says these works have been "prepared ahead of time." God, in His sovereignty, had good deeds in mind when He chose us for salvation. And He planned that "we should walk in them." Notice the last line and compare it with verse 2, "in which you previously walked." This forms an *inclusio*, or bookends. We have made the full loop. We once walked in darkness, being controlled by the world, the flesh, and the

Devil. But God made us alive through faith in Christ, and now we are walking in Christ, doing good works.

Do you know this grace? If so, you can identify with John Newton, the author of "Amazing Grace," who said,

> I am not what I ought to be—ah, how imperfect and deficient! I am not what I wish to be—I abhor what is evil, and I would cleave to what is good! I am not what I hope to be—soon, soon shall I put off mortality, and with mortality all sin and imperfection. Yet, though I am not what I ought to be, nor what I wish to be, nor what I hope to be, I can truly say, I am not what I once was; a slave to sin and Satan; and I can heartily join with the apostle, and acknowledge, "By the grace of God I am what I am." (*Christian Spectator*, 186)

Reflect and Discuss

1. How does Paul describe our pre-Christian status in 2:1-3?
2. How do you think a typical unbeliever today would respond to this description of a non-Christian: "dead," a slave of Satan, dominated by appetites, and destined for wrath?
3. What was the consequence of our pre-Christian status?
4. Why are the words "But God" so sweet?
5. Why did God make us alive?
6. What does this passage teach about our union with Christ?
7. What is the believer's future? How should this impact our daily lives?
8. Why should God's salvation humble us?
9. Is faith a gift? Explain.
10. What is the relationship between grace and works (2:10)?

Our Corporate Identity

EPHESIANS 2:11-22

Main Idea: Paul makes another contrast in this passage, reminding believers of their prior alienation from God and His people, and what Christ has done to reconcile them to God and one another.

I.   **Alienation: Who We Once Were (2:11-12)**
   A.   Christless (2:12a)
   B.   Foreigners (2:12b)
   C.   Hopeless and godless (2:12c)
II.   **Reconciliation: What Christ Has Done (2:13-18)**
   A.   Christ has brought us peace (2:14a).
   B.   Christ has made us one (2:14b-16).
   C.   Christ preached peace (2:17).
   D.   Christ has given us access to God (2:18).
III. **Identification: Who We Have Now Become (2:19-22)**
   A.   Citizens of God's kingdom (2:19a)
   B.   Members of God's family (2:19b)
   C.   Stones in God's temple (2:20-22)
IV. **Application**
   A.   Let us elevate our concept of the local church.
   B.   Let us be part of a "red church."

As a kid I was not allowed to like the New York Yankees. My dad instilled in me a love for the Detroit Tigers. As a guy who walked to Tigers Stadium as a kid in the '60s, the thought of being a Yankees fan was sickening to Dad. After all, they beat Detroit a lot in his day. So his reaction when I came home from the town fair with a Yankees helmet should not have surprised me. I won a helmet by guessing my speed at the fast pitch game at the town fair. I only picked the Yankees due to a limited number of available teams. When I went home, my dad met me, his nine-year-old son, at the door, took off my helmet, and threw it in the yard. I went to get it and returned to the front door, but he insisted vehemently that I go back to town and trade it. I obeyed. I went back and got a Blue Jays helmet. Any team was acceptable as long as it was not the Yankees. (He has since mellowed, and we have family members and good friends who are Yankees fans!)

We live in a world of rivalries: Republican vs. Democrat; North vs. South; PC vs. Mac; Coke vs. Pepsi; Gandalf vs. Saruman. For Auburn fans, it is Alabama. For Michigan, it is Ohio State. For Duke, it is North Carolina. For UK, it is Louisville. Rivalries are everywhere. Then there are violent rivals who kill each other due to cultural and racial hostilities.

In Ephesians 2:11-22 Paul describes a deep, complex, hostile rivalry between Jews and Gentiles. Gentiles are non-Jews. The Greek word is *ethna* in verse 11 (non-Jewish ethnicities). This rivalry was religious: Gentiles did not know the God of Israel. It was cultural: Jews had rituals, feasts, and ceremonies that distinguished them from the nations. It was racial: the Jews could boast of having the blood of Abraham, Isaac, and Jacob flowing in their veins.

Yet through Christ these two enemies have become friends. Paul says this unity proclaims the mystery of the universe (3:10). Jesus accomplished this peacemaking work through His sacrificial death:

> But now in Christ Jesus, you who were far away have been brought
> near by the blood of the Messiah. For He is our peace, who made
> both groups one and tore down the dividing wall of hostility.
> (Eph 2:13-14)

There was a vertical *and* horizontal purpose of Christ's death. Through the cross we are not only reconciled to God, but we are also reconciled to others. Snodgrass suggests that this is "perhaps the single most significant ecclesiological text in the NT" (*Ephesians*, 123). If not the most significant, it is one of the key passages on the nature of the church. And the cross is at the center.

Verses 13-18 are sandwiched in between who the Gentiles had been and who they have now become. These middle verses describe the cross. Notice the phrases "blood of the Messiah" (v. 13), "in His flesh" (v. 14), and "through the cross" (v. 16). Through the cross we overcome our alienation from God and one another.

Paul urges the church to "remember" (v. 11) these things so they may live with a greater sense of gratitude to God and greater love for one another as members of the church. I will outline this incredible passage with three "reminders" for us (originally written for a predominantly Gentile audience).

Alienation: Who We Once Were
EPHESIANS 2:11-12

Verses 11-12 follow the pattern of verses 1-3. They paint for us the dark picture of what life apart from Christ involves. In short, we were alienated from God and from the people of God.

Paul addresses the readers by saying, "You were Gentiles in the flesh" (v. 11). He is highlighting a real physical difference between Gentile and Jew. He goes on to note how, through the work of Christ, their physical difference is of no ultimate significance (O'Brien, *Ephesians*, 186). It is not about skin; it is about the heart.

He goes on to note how the Jews looked on the Gentiles as "uncircumcised." They dismissed the rest of the world as uncircumcised not because the Jews were the only ones who practiced it but because it was a physical sign of their covenant with the Lord. To be uncircumcised was to be separated from the Lord.

Paul then says circumcision is "done in the flesh by human hands" in order to drive home the point that it belonged to the old order of Judaism with its external features. Now Paul could say, "What matters instead is a new creation" (Gal 6:15).

Paul goes on to elaborate on the pre-Christian past of the Gentiles.

Christless (2:12a)

First, he says they were Christless. They were "without the Messiah." The Gentiles were separated from the Messianic hope of Israel. Paul says of his Jewish kinsmen,

> They are Israelites, and to them belong the adoption, the glory, the covenants, the giving of the law, the temple service, and the promises. The ancestors are theirs, and from them, by physical descent, came the Messiah, who is God over all, praised forever. Amen. (Rom 9:4-5)

True, some Jews were and still are separated from Christ, but they have been told in their Scriptures of Messiah. The Gentiles were foreigners to these things.

To be separated from Christ personally, that is, separated from His salvation, is to be "excluded from the life of God" (Eph 4:18). Is there anything more terrible than this?

Foreigners (2:12b)

Second, Paul says they were foreigners. They were excluded from the citizenship of Israel and were strangers to the covenants. The Gentiles were alienated from God's people. Israel was a commonwealth or nation under God, a theocracy. Gentiles were foreigners (v. 19).

They were also not part of a covenant people. The term "covenants" implies a series of covenants: Abraham (Gen 15:7-21; 17:1-21), Isaac (Gen 26:2-5), Jacob (Gen 28:13-15), Israel (Exod 24:1-8), and David (2 Sam 7). The word "promise" probably has to do with God's promise to Abraham. To be separated from the covenants of promise meant they were missing the covenants that promised the Messiah (Rom 9:4).

Hopeless and Godless (2:12c)

Third, they were hopeless and godless. While God did plan to bless all nations through Israel, the Gentiles did not know this. Because they did not know the promises, they did not have the hope of the promises, nor did they know the God of the promises. They had opted for idols instead of God, suppressing the truth revealed to them (Rom 1:18-23). Because they did not know God, they did not know hope.

Before we trusted in Christ for salvation, we were in the same tragic position. We were separated from God and His people. We too need to "remember" this fact! You at one time were separated from Christ and gospel community. If we continue to remember where we came from, we will live with constant gratitude toward God and love toward His people.

Reconciliation: What Christ Has Done
EPHESIANS 2:13-18

As in Ephesians 2:4, there is another great "but" statement. A dramatic change has occurred. "But now in Christ Jesus, you who were far away have been brought near by the blood of the Messiah" (v. 13). By the blood of Christ we can be brought near to God. Only by His blood can we be reconciled to God.

Historically Christ died on the cross. It was public and visible. It was not on a hill far away from the sight of people. His death would be like crucifying someone today in a shopping mall.

Theologically Christ died on behalf of sinners. He bore our punishment. He took our place that we might be declared righteous. We receive the benefits of forgiveness, righteousness, and new life.

Experientially, we encounter the effect of the cross by our union with Christ. Notice it is "in Christ Jesus" that we experience the benefits of His shed blood (v. 13). There was a past event that is experienced in the present. This is what gives us peace with God and with others today.

So the cross is central. There are many who do not like all of the "blood language" in the Bible, but blood reminds us of what God has done for us in His great love. Blood also reminds us of the gravity of our sin. One hymn says, "It was my sin that held him there until it was accomplished" (Townend, "How Deep"). Consider the wretchedness of your sin and the amazing grace of your blood-soaked, but now risen and reigning, Savior!

Some think the cross is overemphasized. They think evangelicals are too "atonement centered." Stephen Finlan says, "It is a mistake to identify the atonement as the Central doctrine, although it is central in Pauline tradition, to First Peter, Hebrews, First John, and Revelation. But these books in their entirety compose only 39 percent of the NT" (*Problems*, 120). I do not agree with his assessment, but even so, if it is central in 39 percent of the New Testament, then you cannot pretend it is not important!

Others think the cross is too violent. One writer says, "The church's inability to shake off the great distortion of God contained in the theory of penal substitution, with its inbuilt belief in retribution and redemptive power of violence, has cost us dearly" (Chalke, in Packer and Dever, *In My Place*, 105). They are embarrassed by such a claim of substitution.

In *Recovering the Scandal of the Cross*, Joel Green and Mark Baker think the cross is irrelevant. They say, "We believe that the popular fascination with and commitment to penal substitutionary atonement has had ill effects in the life of the church and in the United States and has little to offer the global church and mission by way of understanding or embodying the message of Jesus Christ" (*Recovering*, 220–21). It has little to offer? I think it has everything to offer! According to Paul, the cross is the main thing we have to offer (1 Cor 2:2; 15:3-5)!

C. J. Mahaney gets at the importance of the cross in his great little book *Living the Cross-Centered Life*. He writes, "This is what I hold out to my young son as the hope of his life: that Jesus, God's perfect, righteous Son, died in his place for his sins. Jesus took all the punishment;

Jesus received all the wrath as he hung on the cross, so people like Chad and his sinful daddy could be completely forgiven" (*Cross-Centered Life*, 29–30).

After saying Christ's death has brought us near, Paul goes on to add more results of Christ's sacrifice. Notice the verbs in this section; they emphasize what Christ has done in order to reverse our condition: "made one," "tore down," "made of no effect," "create," "reconcile," and "proclaimed." What a Savior!

Paul also shifts from "you" to "we" and "our" in this section. Both Jew and Gentile have the same hope: Christ's atoning death. Consider three things the Savior has done for "us" through His reconciling work on the cross.

Christ Has Brought Us Peace (2:14a)

Jesus has brought us peace with God and others. Jesus is the peace-maker. "For He is our peace," Paul says. Peace is found in a person, Jesus. This was described in the Old Testament (e.g., Isa 9:6; Mic 5:5), affirmed in the Gospels (e.g., Luke 1:79; 2:14; 19:42; John 14:27), and explained in the Epistles (Rom 5:1; Col 1:20; 3:15).

Christ Has Made Us One (2:14b-16)

Paul says that He "tore down the dividing wall" (v. 14b). Christ's blood has obliterated the old, long-standing division between Jew and Gentile.

While Paul was writing this letter, there was a literal wall standing in the temple that excluded the Gentiles. Josephus tells us that attached to this barrier at intervals were messages in Greek and Latin, warning that the Gentiles must not proceed further lest they die. The temple was destroyed physically in AD 70, but it was destroyed spiritually around AD 33 or so, when Jesus Christ died on the cross for sinners. "In His flesh" Jesus tore down the wall that separated these groups.

While Paul could be referencing a literal wall in the temple, it seems more likely that he is referring to the barrier of "the law consisting of commands and expressed in regulations," the ceremonial law (v. 15). The parallel passage in Colossians 2:11 and 16-21 alludes to circumcision, questions about food and drink, and regulations about festivals, new moon, and the Sabbath. These commandments as regulations put up a huge wall between Jew and Gentile. Jesus set all of this aside by dying on the cross. At the cross Jesus fulfilled all the shadows and types of the ceremonial system.

Paul might also be saying that Jesus abolished the law as a means of salvation through His death on the cross. As Paul says to the Colossians, Jesus has "erased the certificate of debt, with its obligations, that was against us and opposed to us, and has taken it out of the way by nailing it to the cross" (Col 2:14). A person is only accepted by God through the work of Christ, not through his own work. Stott summarizes: "Jesus abolished both the regulations of the ceremonial law and the condemnation of the moral law. Both were divisive. Both were put aside by the cross" (*Ephesians*, 101).

As a result, Christ created "in Himself one new man from the two, resulting in peace" (v. 15). Jesus' abolishing of something old has led to something new: *one new humanity.* Christ has created one new man. In Christ and in Christ alone this new man exists. In Christ a new corporate entity exists, which is the church. It is not as though Gentiles have been transformed into Jews or vice versa, but rather God has created one new man.

They did not merely become one (though that is true); they have become *better.* Chrysostom said, "It is as though one took a statue of silver and a statue of lead, put them into a forge and they came out a statue of gold" (in Chapell, *Ephesians*, 110). This is part of God's plan of summing up all things in Christ (Eph 1:9-10).

We like to build fences today. People do it in all types of ways, but the cross of Jesus Christ brings unity. Racism among believers cannot be justified, and it must be resisted. Paul says elsewhere,

> There is no Jew or Greek, slave or free, male or female; for you are all one in Christ Jesus. (Gal 3:28)

> In Christ there is not Greek and Jew, circumcision and uncircumcision, barbarian, Scythian, slave and free; but Christ is all and in all. (Col 3:11)

Diversity in the church is a glorious demonstration of the work of Christ. It is to be celebrated as it pictures heaven. It demonstrates the one new man.

Paul elaborates: "He did this so that He might reconcile both to God in one body through the cross and put the hostility to death by it" (v. 16). Paul speaks of the double reconciliation that has taken place, stating that the hostility has been put to death. As Stott says, "God turned away his own wrath, and we, seeing his great love, turned away ours also" (*Ephesians*, 102). Jesus' death has ended the hostility.

Consequently, Christians are to be a people who forgive one another because of the forgiveness of Christ (Eph 4:32). Jesus taught us to pray, "Forgive us our debts, as we also have forgiven our debtors" (Matt 6:12). The best antidote to disunity and hostility between believers is a fresh comprehension of the cross of Christ.

Christ Preached Peace (2:17)

The cross of Christ is how our peace was *achieved*, but now it is to be *announced*. Commentators debate if this refers to Jesus' earthly ministry of preaching, the crucifixion itself (as a symbol of proclaiming peace), His postresurrection proclamation of peace (John 20:19-21), or the ongoing proclamation through the apostles and now through the church. I am not sure it has to be limited to any one of these. Jesus certainly proclaimed the gospel of peace before the cross, on the cross, and after the resurrection. And now the followers of Jesus must be ready to preach the gospel of peace (Eph 6:15). We are to tell the world how people can have peace with God. Paul could have also adopted this phrase "preached peace" from Isaiah: "How beautiful on the mountains are the feet of the herald, who proclaims peace, who brings news of good things" (Isa 52:7; cf. 57:19; Rom 10:15).

The application is simple enough. Christ proclaims peace through His followers today. By the Holy Spirit, Christ proclaims His peace through ordinary believers like us. The world wants "peace," and only when we preach Christ can people find out how to have it.

Paul adds that this good news was preached to those "far away" and those "who were near"—that is, to Gentiles and Jews (cf. Isa 57:19). The whole world needs this gospel. Let us be faithful in sharing it.

Christ Has Given Us Access to God (2:18)

Those who respond to Jesus' work and message now have access to God. Notice the Trinitarian language: Paul says it is "through Him [Christ] we both have access by one Spirit to the Father."

This is what prayer is about. Prayer is conversation with the Father, through the Son, by the Spirit. The ongoing benefit of Christ's reconciliation is that we today have access to God. We can now come to God with boldness (Eph 3:12) because of what Christ has done. Marvel at the privilege of prayer and the stunning grace of the Savior.

However, Paul is not just emphasizing this personal privilege. He is emphasizing that Jew and Gentile together approach God through

Christ by the Spirit. We live out our new position in Christ and in our new community by the Spirit of God.

Before we move to the final point, consider the personal testimony of a faithful saint, Charles Simeon. He had no mother to nurture him. His father was an unbeliever. His boarding school was a godless and corrupt place. And he knew of no Christian at Cambridge for almost three years after his conversion! His acceptance of Christ was a miracle of grace. He was 19 years old, sitting in his dormitory room as Passion Week began at the end of March 1779. He wrote,

> But in Passion Week, as I was reading Bishop Wilson on the Lord's Supper, I met with an expression to this effect—"That the Jews knew what they did, when they transferred their sin to the head of their offering." The thought came into my mind, What, may I transfer all my guilt to another? Has God provided an Offering for me, that I may lay my sins on His head? Then, God willing, I will not bear them on my own soul one moment longer. Accordingly I sought to lay my sins upon the sacred head of Jesus; and on the Wednesday began to have a hope of mercy; on the Thursday that hope increased; on the Friday and Saturday it became more strong; and on the Sunday morning, Easter-day, April 4, I awoke early with those words upon my heart and lips, "Jesus Christ is risen to-day! Hallelujah! Hallelujah!" From that hour peace flowed in rich abundance into my soul; and at the Lord's Table in our Chapel I had the sweetest access to God through my blessed Saviour. (Moule, *Charles Simeon*, 13–15)

Yes, we have sweet access to God through the Savior and peace that flows in abundance because of the Substitute! If you are not a believer, then transfer your guilt to Another! Look to Christ and believe.

Identification: Who We Have Now Become
EPHESIANS 2:19-22

Paul summarizes Christ's reconciling work by reminding the Gentiles of who they now are. He says that they, joined together with Jewish believers, now belong to a new community.

In Ephesians 2:5-6 I noted the three "with" (*syn*) words that show how we have been synced with Christ. In 2:19-22 there are three more "with" or "together" words: *sympolitai* ("fellow citizens"), *synarmologeo* ("put together"), and *synoikodomeo* ("built together") (Snodgrass, *Ephesians*, 136). These words emphasize that we have been synced not only to Christ but also to other Christians. This is our identity. To illustrate this identity, Paul uses three word pictures: citizens, family, and stones in a temple.

Citizens of God's Kingdom (2:19a)

First, Paul says that they are no longer refugees; now they have a citizenship. This citizenship is kingdom citizenship. The Gentile believers are not second-class citizens in someone else's territory. They are full members of the kingdom. While in reality God rules over everything, here the kingdom of God refers to where God has special rule over His people, that is, where His privileges are enjoyed and the responsibilities are carried out. We are waiting for the King to return and set up the full realization of this kingdom.

Paul is writing during a time in which Roman citizenship was prized. Roman citizens had wonderful privileges. Citizenship in a great country is a blessing, but there is nothing like being a citizen of the kingdom of God (cf. Phil 3:20).

Foreigners in another city or country feel vulnerable. They have to keep their papers with them at all times. But Paul says we do not have to feel this way. We belong. We are part of the kingdom that has no end, the only kingdom that has no end.

Members of God's Family (2:19b)

Paul's metaphor of God's new community changes to something more personal: a family. One might imagine Jew and Gentile together in one kingdom, but to think of them as one family is stunning. Elsewhere Paul says we are "God's household" (1 Tim 3:15).

How are we one family? We have the same Father. Paul just made that point in 2:18. We have access to "the Father." We are adopted children, as Paul asserted in 1:5. The church is made up of adopted brothers and sisters. We have responsibilities in the family. We are one family, each fulfilling his role, bringing glory to our Father (Eph 5:1). In 1 Timothy 5:1-2 Paul says we should treat one another like family.

We have five adopted children in our family. If you visit our home on a Saturday at the right time, you will find all of them doing chores—sweeping, mowing, dusting, collecting garbage, and vacuuming. My wife even has a chore chart for each kid! Everyone is serving, loving, and sharing responsibilities.

The church is not a building we go to or an event we attend. The church is family, living life together on mission. Be careful not to treat the church as a hotel—visiting a place occasionally, giving a tip if you are served well. Rather, see the church as part of your Christian identity, and understand that we all have a role in God's household.

Stones in God's Temple (2:20-22)

Paul's third metaphor would have been vivid for his audience. For nearly one thousand years, the temple had been a focal point of Israel—from Solomon to Zerubbabel to Herod. Now there was a new temple, made up of people. In verse 20 Paul says the foundation of the temple is God's Word. The apostles and prophets were teachers, and here Paul emphasizes their teaching. (Paul is probably referring to NT prophets, but even with the range from the OT prophets to the apostles and NT prophets, there was continuity in their teaching.)

This emphasis should not surprise us. The church stands or falls based on its faithfulness to God's Word. Luke says the early church "devoted themselves to the apostles' teaching" (Acts 2:42). That is foundational.

Next we see the cornerstone mentioned. There is only one cornerstone: Jesus. He makes the whole building possible. The whole community is built on Him. He gives security to the building, and He gives it alignment (cf. Isa 28:16; Rom 9:32; 10:11; 1 Pet 2:4-8). While the apostles' teaching is being emphasized, Jesus' person and work are also emphasized. Jesus is also how the church grows and is held together. There is no unity or growth if Christ is not the cornerstone.

Paul likens the people to stones. He says that in the Lord "you also are being built together for God's dwelling." Peter says something like this as well, calling us "living stones" (1 Pet 2:5). We are carefully shaped building blocks fitted to build this temple. Each new member is added to it. In 1 Corinthians 6:19 Paul refers to individuals being a temple of the Spirit, but here (and in other places like 1 Cor 3:16-17; 2 Cor 6:16) the people make up the temple.

By saying, "You also," Paul is referring to the Gentiles being added to this building. Previously the Gentiles were not allowed to enter the temple, but now they are a part of it! Even though the Israelites knew God did not dwell in temples made by hands, they recognized that God promised to dwell in the temple's inner sanctuary. Now His special presence is not limited to a place or a building or an ethnicity. God's presence is spread worldwide, wherever people believe in Christ. Notice it is "in the Lord" that we are a dwelling place for God by the Spirit. Through Christ, by the Spirit of God, God dwells in us personally and as a community. Ultimately, this reality will be fully realized and enjoyed in the new heavens and new earth when God makes His dwelling place with man.

A great temple stood in Ephesus (the temple of Artemis). In Jerusalem they had a great temple. But Paul says, through Christ, by the Spirit, there is a better temple; it is made up of people from every tribe and tongue. We are joined together and built together. Each one is related to the other in a special way, and we are all growing together in Christ.

Practically, that means every person counts. We need one another's time, talent, treasure, love, resources, encouragement, and rebuke. We are to live the Christian life together as a multiethnic temple, centered in Christ, rooted in the teaching of Scripture.

Application

Let me make a few applications from this important passage. This passage confronts the typical Western mind-set in two major ways, including the way people in the Western church think.

Let Us Elevate Our Concept of the Local Church

An obvious implication from these three pictures is that Christ wants to create a people, not merely isolated individuals who believe in Him. This passage confronts Western individualism. To be separate from the church is to say, "I want to be a stone apart from a building" or "a son or daughter separated from my family" or "a refugee away from my country." Many people treat the church as something that is unnecessary, unimportant, or even a hindrance to doing great things for God. I used to believe this. I did not want to pastor. I felt I was superior to others, not needing the church. I felt I could do more apart from the church. I hopped around visiting different churches, but did not have community. That is not God's design for the Christian.

Some think the church is fine for others, but they do not feel the need to take membership seriously. The New Testament positions it as our fundamental identity. Belonging to a local church should be more important than where you go to school, where you work, or to what club you belong. Sometimes people ask whether college students should join a church. I think students should consider the church they may belong to *before* they go off to school. If we are apart from community, we are not following the New Testament pattern, and we are not helping ourselves. It is not good to be apart from the oversight of shepherds or apart from the accountability and support of brothers and sisters.

The New Testament assumes every Christian is part of a local church. It knows nothing of lone-ranger Christianity or the position that claims, "I'm a member of the universal church; I don't need to join a local, visible church." We show we are part of the universal church by identifying with a tangible people locally. Is this not what we do in our union with Christ? We live out spiritual union with Christ visibly. In the same way, we should live out our union with other believers visibly. Identify yourself with a people. Avoid being a "ninja Christian," just slipping into a worship service and leaving without a trace. Be a family member instead.

Church discipline assumes local church members are *identifiable* (Matt 18:15-17). When Paul directs the Corinthians to expel the immoral brother, he assumes there are people who are in and people who are out (1 Cor 5:9-13). In 2 Corinthians 2:6 the "majority" of members voted to remove a man from its membership. The New Testament also mentions lists, which illustrates that people were identifiable (e.g., 1 Tim 5:9). The book of Acts counts people (e.g., Acts 2:41). People knew who was part of the church. The writer of Hebrews says overseers will give an account for their people (Heb 13:17). If there are no identifiable members, then there is no one for whom to give an account. Electing leaders (Acts 6; 13), submitting to them, regulating membership, keeping lists, and voting only make sense if there is an identifiable group of members. The metaphors for the church—stones in a temple, members of a family, citizens of a kingdom, members of a body—all assume individuals are part of an actual church.

There is certainly flexibility as to how one works out the membership process in a local church, but the New Testament emphasis on the importance of belonging to a local church is abundantly clear. We cannot read this passage honestly without seeing the importance of the church.

This is how God intends for us to live out our faith and love one another: in community. It is an incredible gift of God's grace to have a family of faith. It is a gift of grace to gather corporately and stir up one another to faith and good works (Heb 10:24-25). It is a gift of grace to love one another as Christ has loved us (John 13:34-35). It is a gift of grace to carry one another's burdens (Gal 6:2). It is a gift of grace to encourage one another and to be encouraged by one another (1 Thess 5:11). It is a gift of grace to be taught and admonished by one another (Col 3:16). It is a gift of grace to be allowed the privilege to give financially to further the gospel (2 Cor 8–9). It is a gift of grace to come to the table for communion (1 Cor 11:26).

All of these privileges have come to us via the cross-work of Jesus Christ. He has brought us near and made us one.

Let Us Be Part of a "Red Church"

This passage confronts not only Western individualism, but it also confronts the racist impulse in many believers. Manmade distinctions of a "black church" or a "white church" are not acceptable to gospel-centered people. Let us be part of a red church—a group of people, from every tribe and tongue, that has been redeemed by the torn-apart Christ, who spilled His red blood that we may be reconciled to God and to one another!

The main way we can work to cultivate diversity is by proclaiming the gospel. When a person understands the gospel, and that the entire human race is fallen and in need of grace, unity comes naturally.

With that said, I do think it is good for us to think about how we might display our love for the gospel by intentionally cultivating diversity. Could anything be more powerful before a lost world than to see people from all ethnicities united in Christ? Ponder the corporate implications of the cross. See what has happened corporately because of the cross. Race is a cross issue. Piper states,

> But let us also dwell on this: that God ordained the death of his Son to reconcile alien people groups to each other in one body in Christ. This too was the design of the death of Christ. Think on this: Christ died to take enmity and anger and disgust and jealousy and self-pity and fear and envy and hatred and malice and indifference away from your heart toward all other persons who are in Christ by faith—whatever the race. ("Race and Cross")

Truly value people of other ethnicities. An attitude that says, "They are not my kind," destroys the body of Christ and reveals a deep sin problem. Welcome new people, regardless of their skin color, every week, in corporate worship and in small groups. Intentionally invest in Christians of other ethnicities. Demonstrate that other groups matter to you. Do not just make this a theory. Practice it. Invite them over for dinner in your home. Invite people of diverse backgrounds to corporate worship. Passionately seek justice and display mercy for other ethnic groups. Love the poor. Seek justice for those sold into slavery. Care for orphans of every skin tone. Gladly work together with those of other nationalities for the advancement of the gospel. Pray for wisdom and diversity in your local church, and be glad when you see new elements in worship. This is hard work, but it is worth it. These intentional acts glorify the crucified Savior, who died to bring us to God and to one another.

Reflect and Discuss

1. How does it affect you to "remember" your situation before you knew Christ (2:11-12)? How are you encouraged by meditating on your new status (vv. 13,19-22)?

2. How does this passage speak of a non-Christian (vv. 12,17,19)? What are your reactions to this description?

3. How does this passage emphasize the corporate nature of Christianity?

4. Explain the work of Christ in this passage.

5. Why do you think people object to the idea of substitutionary atonement? How would you defend this doctrine to a skeptic?

6. How does verse 18 relate to prayer? How should it affect our view of prayer?

7. Which of the three illustrations of the church in 2:19-22—citizens, family, or stones—made the biggest impact on you? Explain why.

8. How should this passage change the way we think about the church?

9. What is a "red church," and do you long to be part of such a church? What can the church do to promote racial diversity, if anything?

10. Why is a unified church a great witness to the unbelieving world?

A Christ-Centered Missionary

EPHESIANS 3:1-13

Main Idea: Paul explains how God appointed him to proclaim God's marvelous plan of uniting both Jews and Gentiles together in Christ.

Six Marks of a Christ-Centered Missionary

I. A Christ-Centered Missionary Follows the Will of Christ (3:1,13).
   A. A prisoner of the King (3:1)
   B. A shepherd of people (3:13)
II. A Christ-Centered Missionary Understands the Message of Christ (3:2-6).
III. A Christ-Centered Missionary Is Overwhelmed by the Grace of Christ (3:7-8a).
IV. A Christ-Centered Missionary Proclaims the Incalculable Riches of Christ (3:8b-9).
   A. Proclaiming Christ (3:8b)
   B. Shedding light (3:9)
V. A Christ-Centered Missionary Has a High View of the Church of Christ (3:10-11).
VI. A Christ-Centered Missionary Draws Near to God Through Christ (3:12).

Have you ever been interrupted in prayer? Many things can cause this—babies crying, microwaves dinging, phones buzzing, doorbells ringing, or sirens sounding. Sometimes my wandering mind just goes elsewhere. I can begin to pray, and then all of a sudden I remember something I need to do or I get lost thinking about a ball game or some problem in the church. Before I know it, I have chased a rabbit for several minutes. Staying focused in prayer is a challenge at times. I have found that prayer walks and Scripture meditation and memorization are helpful for me in persevering in prayer.

Paul appears to begin an intercessory prayer for the church in Ephesians 3:1, but then he goes on a holy rabbit trail and does not pick up the actual prayer until 3:14. Perhaps his digression is prompted as he reflects on his position as "the prisoner of Christ Jesus on behalf of you Gentiles" (3:1).

Realize though that Ephesians 3:1-13 is more than a digression. The passage is part of God's inspired Word and contains central themes in the book of Ephesians. Paul speaks of his sufferings, the incorporation of the Gentiles into the people of God, the cosmic nature of the church, the proclamation of the riches of Christ, believers' access to God, and more.

In addition to these key themes, we also find powerful personal application for our own lives. Paul's life serves as an example to believers. Like the Ephesian church, we are also called to love the church and fulfill her mission of making Christ known to everyone. We should acknowledge and appreciate Paul's unique role in redemptive history, but we should not distance ourselves from his mission. God gave Paul the ministry of proclaiming Christ and explaining the unfolding plan of God to people; we as believers have that same purpose.

If we accept that this passage has such application for our lives, then it is appropriate to see this passage as a "missions text." Like the parallel text in Colossians 1:24-29, this passage contains missional language. We read of the *Gentiles* or "nations" (Eph 3:1,6,8; see Col 1:27-28), *suffering* for the sake of the mission (Eph 3:1; see Col 1:24), the *administration* of grace given (Eph 3:2; see Col 1:25), the revelation of *the mystery* or the plan of God (Eph 3:4-6; see Col 1:26-27), and the *proclamation of Christ* who is at the center of the plan (Eph 3:8; Col 1:28). This passage is saturated with Paul's passion for the nations to worship the reigning Christ.

Spurgeon said in a sermon, "Every Christian here is either a missionary or an impostor. . . . You either try to spread abroad the kingdom of Christ, or else you do not love him at all. It cannot be that there is a high appreciation of Jesus and a totally silent tongue about him" ("A Sermon and a Reminiscence"). Indeed. While not everyone will serve the nations in the same way, every Christian should assume the posture of a missionary and testify to the grace of Jesus. Believing this to be true, and with this missionary passage in view, let us consider **six marks of a Christ-centered missionary** from the holy digression of the apostle Paul, the greatest of all missionaries.

A Christ-Centered Missionary Follows the Will of Christ
EPHESIANS 3:1,13

Paul opens and closes this passage by speaking of his present condition and the associated sufferings. He says he is a "prisoner" (v. 1) suffering "afflictions" (v. 13).

Paul's imprisonment illustrates the nature of a Christian missionary. Jesus called Paul to a special ministry; that ministry involved suffering. Christ told Paul this from the beginning (Acts 9:15-16). And Paul was willing to suffer on behalf of Christ, for the sake of the mission (Col 1:24).

While we do not go looking for suffering, we should not be surprised by it (cf. 2 Tim 3:12; 1 Pet 5:8-10; 1 John 3:13). It comes with the territory. Baseball players should not be surprised if a baseball hits them, and soldiers should not be surprised if the enemy fires on them. We go looking simply to obey the will of Jesus; yet, we understand that following the Savior's plan might involve suffering—just as He told us (John 15:20).

A Prisoner of the King (3:1)

Strikingly, in verse 1 Paul does not refer to himself as a prisoner of Caesar, but "of Christ Jesus." The will of Christ took Paul to prison. But Paul did not see this imprisonment as thwarting the mission of Christ. They could chain Paul but not the message (Eph 6:20; 2 Tim 2:9).

The most important thing to Paul was not safety, security, and a retirement plan but the mission of the King. He knew he was not imprisoned because of some moral lapse or because he had displeased God in some way; instead, because of his sacrificial commitment to the will of Jesus, he was chained to a Roman soldier, writing this letter from prison. Most important to Paul was the glory of the real King.

Paul was Christ's prisoner. Are you? Do you belong to Jesus Christ? Do you say to the King, "Send me anywhere, only go with me! I'm Yours. Use me!"? While we must always be wise as we take the gospel to hostile places, we must not shrink back in fear, for the sovereign King is over all, and we go in His presence and power.

Elsewhere Paul says, "Imitate me, as I also imitate Christ" (1 Cor 11:1). Let us follow Paul down the Calvary Road, knowing that the King and His mission are worth sacrifice.

A Shepherd of People (3:13)

Verse 13 speaks of the loving, pastoral heart of Paul. He is the one in prison, yet he appears to want to set the people's minds at ease. He tells his readers/hearers that they should not be overly discouraged by his situation. He reminds them of the big picture. His suffering "hastens the second coming of Christ, which will lead to their glorification" (Arnold, *Ephesians*, 199). Paul does not want the church to be downhearted, and he wants them to see that his suffering is part of God's grand plan for the end of the age (cf. Col 1:24).

In this we see Paul's amazing care for people and his pastoral skill pointing people to the glory that will be revealed. Suffering will give way to glory, and because of this, believers endure with hope. Keep this in mind, believer. And remind others that the best is yet to come. The King in all His splendor will arrive soon, and then this "momentary light affliction" will seem as nothing in light of the "eternal weight of glory" (2 Cor 4:17).

A Christ-Centered Missionary Understands the Message of Christ
EPHESIANS 3:2-6

Paul speaks now of the administration, or responsibility, he has to communicate the message of Christ, and he expresses his desire for the church to understand this message.

It should go without saying that missionaries are called not only to go, but they are to go with the right message. Many false religions have missionaries. What makes Christian missions distinct is the message about the crucified, risen, reigning, and returning King. We must make sure, as missionaries, that we are not exporting a deficient gospel.

As I travel to the nations, I am always angered and grieved by the prosperity gospel that has taken root in different parts of the world, especially in impoverished countries. All of this is done in the name of "gospel" and "Christ" and "Christianity." But it is not the gospel. Therefore, it is absolutely essential that we understand the real gospel and help others understand it properly. We need to saturate the nations with sound doctrine.

Paul has a unique role in redemptive history. He is given "insight about the mystery of the Messiah" (v. 4). As God's steward (cf. 1 Cor 4:1; 9:17; Col 1:25), Paul's responsibility involves explaining God's intent to create a special people, or a "household" of both Jews and Gentiles, through Christ (Eph 2:19; 3:5-6). Paul's role is to explain this "mystery," and the church's role is to "understand" (v. 4) and then communicate it. This "mystery" was not like Ephesian mystery cults. It was not a mystery of esoteric knowledge, reserved for a secret few. This mystery, this message about Christ, is for all nations. Paul urges the Ephesians to forsake any other pseudo-mysteries and focus their attention on Christ alone (Arnold, *Ephesians*, 188).

This mystery was "hidden" or "not made known to people in other generations" (v. 5); but now, at this point in history, it can be understood. While the plan of God was present in the Old Testament, parts were unclear or "hidden" in a sense (v. 9). But when Christ appeared, the lights came on, clarifying the nature of the Messiah's death, the fact that Gentiles do not have to become Jews, that Gentiles and Jews have equal access to God, and the degree of nearness one has with God in the new covenant (Arnold, *Ephesians*, 190). Now these things have been made known. And people should know them and celebrate them!

While we will not "reveal" (v. 5) the message as Paul did, we can "re-reveal," meaning that we teach apostolic doctrine to others. But that implies study on our part. Sometimes the church is too quick to appoint missionaries to the nations. Not every missionary has to be a tremendous theologian, but every missionary does need to have a firm grasp on the gospel. If you are a new Christian, keep exploring the glories of Christ. Study the great doctrines of the faith—creation, fall, redemption, and new creation. Meditate on the atoning death of Jesus and the centrality of the church. A Christ-centered missionary understands (and delights!) in the message of Christ.

We also must make the main thing the plain thing in Christian missions. Our goal in going overseas is not to make people conform to our culture. Our goal is to proclaim the centrality of Christ. Therefore, focus your studies on that which everyone, everywhere needs.

As we meditate on Paul's words today, we are reminded of the faithfulness of Christians who have understood, preserved, and passed on the Christian gospel for generations (2 Tim 2:2). Paul was writing from prison, chained to a Roman guard, and about two thousand years later we can know and worship Christ around the world. Always appreciate the value of understanding the gospel message and making it known to the world.

God message not bound

A Christ-Centered Missionary Is Overwhelmed by the Grace of Christ
EPHESIANS 3:7-8A

The theme of grace permeates Paul's writings. Paul experienced God's saving grace at conversion. The former blasphemer refers to himself as the worst of sinners who experienced an overflow of redeeming grace and mercy from the Savior (1 Tim 1:14-15). But he also experienced God's empowering grace for ministry. He tells the Corinthians,

> For I am the least of the apostles, unworthy to be called an apostle, because I persecuted the church of God. But by God's grace I am what I am, and His grace toward me was not ineffective. However, I worked more than any of them, yet not I, but God's grace that was with me.
> (1 Cor 15:9-10; cf. Gal 1:15-16)

God's grace had a humbling effect on Paul, and it also had an empowering effect. The same is true here in Ephesians.

Faithful missionaries love grace. Paul's love for grace teaches us at least two lessons about grace. First, *God's grace should humble us*. Because Paul understood grace, he lived with a profound sense of humble gratitude to God. He knew that apart from grace he would not be doing what he was doing. So he says, "Grace was given to me" twice (vv. 7,8). He deflects attention away from himself, toward the proper place of praise: the God of all grace.

Paul refers to himself as "the least of all the saints" (v. 8). This does not seem to be false humility but something Paul firmly believes. His position and place in redemptive history does not puff him up; it leaves him to boast only in Christ. He feels privileged to serve the King. Do you? We do not *have* to serve Jesus; we *get* to serve Jesus. Notice how Paul refers to himself as a humble "servant of this gospel" (v. 7; cf. 1 Cor 3:5; 2 Cor 11:23; Phil 1:1). Even though he is an inspired apostle, Paul knows he is following our foot-washing Suffering Servant. Do not forget this.

When you view yourself as the "least of all the saints," you will gladly serve "the least of these" (Matt 25:40). Grace humbles you and causes you to identify with everyone, including the poor and the weak. No one is beneath you. The "least of all the saints" give love, time, and energy to everyone created in God's image. Oh, how we need the grace of God to be worked down deeply into our hearts, as it is here in Paul's heart! Such identity formation comes through long and rich meditation on the grace of God, the sinfulness of humanity, and the glory of the cross, and through regular repentance.

Second, we should realize that *we need God's grace to empower us.* Paul ties "grace" and "power" together in verse 7. The Lord powerfully called Paul on the Damascus Road, and the Lord's power continued to sustain Paul for ministry (Rom 1:5; 12:3; 15:5; 1 Cor 3:10; 2 Cor 12:9; Col 1:29). Arnold points out, "By the time Paul writes this letter, he has had an abundant experience of God's empowering hand upon his life and ministry, in spite of the most difficult circumstances, including sickness" (*Ephesians*, 193). Indeed, the mighty power of God (Eph 1:19-20) provides sufficient strength for weak, fragile, ordinary people as they make the glories of Christ known.

Bryan Chapell speaks of Christ's servants being "enraptured with grace":

> Being enraptured with grace is the nature of Christian calling. Such awe of grace certifies our calling as genuine and energizes it in the face of sacrifice. The truly called are so enraptured by the grace of God toward them that the attacks of others, the difficulties of circumstances, their lack of worldly comfort, and their lack of recognition in the world do not dissuade them from the joy of proclaiming Christ. (*Ephesians*, 143)

May we never lose the awe of grace or the joy of proclaiming Christ, who is "full of grace and truth" (John 1:14).

A Christ-Centered Missionary Proclaims the Incalculable Riches of Christ
EPHESIANS 3:8B-9

Paul provides the purposes of God's enabling grace. He uses three purpose clauses in verses 8-10; the first two are linked together in verses 8b-9 by the use of "and" as well as their similarity in form and subject (Arnold, *Ephesians*, 196).

Proclaiming Christ (3:8b)

God empowered Paul to proclaim the "incalculable," or unsearchable, or incomprehensible, riches of Christ. This particular word appears nowhere outside of biblical Greek. When Paul thought about the glory of Christ, he made up a word! Arnold says this word is built on the word for "footprint." That word was used literally in Greek literature for a tracker, someone who pursues another by following footprints (*Ephesians*, 194). It has the sense of "tracing out" or "searching." Other biblical writers convey the incalculable nature of God's attributes as well. Job speaks of the "unsearchable" ways of God (Job 5:9; 9:10). Paul elsewhere describes the "unsearchable" wisdom of God and His "untraceable" ways (Rom 11:33).

Consider how Paul, this former persecutor of Christ, is now consumed with proclaiming the crucified Messiah (cf. 1 Cor 2:1-5). Jesus transformed Paul's life, and Christ and His redemption became Paul's resounding theme. To the Colossians Paul says, "We proclaim Him" (Col 1:28). Paul's all-consuming subject of proclamation was a person: Christ. Is Christ the all-consuming subject of your teaching and preaching?

Some may object that proclaiming Christ every week will get old. Based on Ephesians 3:8, we should not agree. If our preaching is boring, it is not because Christ is boring. His glories are incalculable. As long as we are proclaiming Christ, we should never run out of material, we should never be left without something to talk about, and we should never talk about Him without passion. Proclaim the riches of Christ to your own soul daily, and out of the overflow of your communion with Him, declare His glory to others.

The goal of our proclamation—either in informal evangelism or in public preaching—is not to attract personal praise but rather praise for the Savior. We should desire for people to say, "What a great Savior!" not "What a good sermon."

Let us once again recognize what must always remain central in Christian missions—the Christ of Christian missions. Make the hero of the Bible, of "the mystery," the hero of your preaching, teaching, and evangelism. Jesus changes lives; keep the Life-changer at the heart of your messages.

Shedding Light (3:9)

Paul also had received grace in order to explain the global nature of God's plan of salvation. He was sent to "shed light for all about the administration of the mystery hidden for ages in God who created all things." Paul has the responsibility of helping those who receive the message of salvation to understand God's truth. Earlier he prayed for illumination (1:18), and now he uses the same word to describe his role in illuminating God's plan to converts (Arnold, *Ephesians*, 195). What is this plan? It goes back to Ephesians 3:2-6—how the Jew and Gentile are one in Christ. Paul is commissioned to explain this glorious reality (cf. 2:11-22). Paul emphasizes the sovereignty of God in all of this, referring to Him as "God who created all things." This plan was not an afterthought, but part of the Sovereign Lord's eternal purposes.

As we look back over these verses, we are struck by the centrality of Christ and the global nature of Christianity. Both are revealed in Scripture. If someone asks you, "Where did you get your passion for missions?" a proper response is "from the Bible." From cover to cover, there is a missions thrust in the Bible because there is a messianic thrust in the Bible.

We have a global God, and we proclaim the only King of the nations. Let us remember that every tribe and tongue needs to hear of the incalculable riches of Christ. If you are preaching in New York or in a leper colony in Nigeria, remember that everyone needs Jesus. Proclaim Him to everyone; then shed additional light concerning the wonderful plan of God revealed in the Bible for everyone.

A Christ-Centered Missionary Has a High View of the Church of Christ
EPHESIANS 3:10-11

If you have a high view of Christ, you should have a high view of the church. Ephesians contains a lofty view of the church, which we have already observed in 2:11-22. In the next passage Paul prays for God to be glorified "in the church" (3:21). In 4:1-6 he discusses the unity of the church. He goes on to explain how God has gifted His people with spiritual leaders to equip them for ministry (4:11-12). In chapter 5 he says that Christ "loved the church and gave Himself for her" (5:25).

Here in Ephesians 3:10-11, Paul adds another amazing point to our theology of the church with this third purpose clause. The apostle tells us that the church has implications that reach throughout heaven and the entire spiritual realm. The church—made up of Jews and Gentiles—is making known the manifold wisdom of God to "the rulers and authorities in the heavens." I agree with O'Brien, who says that these "rulers and authorities" are probably both bad and good heavenly beings, "although the apostle's particular concern is obviously with hostile forces" (*Ephesians*, 246–47). It seems to me that the angels look on at grace and marvel while demonic forces look on in fear and tremble. The evil forces have already been defeated at the cross, and they await their final subjugation. The existence of the church is announcing that their rule is coming to an end once and for all.

While we have limited knowledge of all of these beings, it appears that they are not omniscient (Stott, *Ephesians*, 124). Peter seems to allude to this idea when he says, "Angels desire to look into these things" (1 Pet 1:12). Further, we can infer that God intends to make His plan known to them through the church. Stott says, "They watch fascinated as they see Gentiles and Jews being incorporated into the new society as equals" (*Ephesians*, 124).

There is more going on with the church than meets the eye. If you are part of the church, then you are part of a cosmic sermon that is being preached to spiritual rulers and authorities. Kent Hughes says, "The inescapable conclusion is that the angels watch us because we are part of the mystery! . . . We have a far bigger and more observant viewing audience than any of us realize!" (*Ephesians*, 109).

To be clear, the emphasis here is not on us preaching to unseen powers and principalities. The point is that God is revealing His plan to the powers through the existence of the church (Arnold, *Ephesians*, 196–97).

According to verse 11, Jesus came and "accomplished," or fulfilled, or achieved, God's plan. Christ is the central character in this plan, and all things will be summed up in Him (Eph 1:10). The crucified and risen Christ is at the Father's right hand, and He will soon come to put all of the hostile principalities and powers under His feet.

So consider how the church is a witness of the glory of Christ. We make known the "multi-faceted" wisdom of God (a related word is used for Joseph's multicolored coat in Gen 37:3,23). This wisdom is so great that God uses it to proclaim to heavenly beings. His grace and glory are displayed in a diverse people—a many-colored fellowship, a multicultural and multiethnic fellowship—who have been called, redeemed, forgiven, made alive, and united in Christ. The angelic host look on at the reconciling work of Christ, "which is the model for the reconciling of the universe when everything in Heaven and earth will be brought together in Him (cf. 1:9-10; Col 1:17-22)" (Hughes, *Ephesians*, 109).

How such a vision must have encouraged the churches in Ephesus! Can you imagine the people gathering from normal backgrounds, leaning in to listen to the reading of this letter—farmers, bankers, metal workers, carpenters, shop keepers, servants, masters, moms, dads, and children? As the readers get to chapter 3, they are told that they are testifying to the heavenly beings! Stunning! Do not underestimate the glory of God in the church.

Christ-centered missionaries have a high view of the church. They see the church as being central to human history. They see that Christ loves His bride. They understand that God's redeemed people—from every tribe—proclaim the incalculable riches of Christ to the nations. And they marvel at how God's people make known to "the rulers and authorities in the heavens His manifold wisdom."

A Christ-Centered Missionary Draws Near to God Through Christ

EPHESIANS 3:12

Part of the mystery is that believers can experience a nearness to God that far exceeds that of the old covenant. Christians can boldly approach God because of Christ. In the previous passage Paul said, "For through Him we both have access by one Spirit to the Father" (2:18). We do not come to God with a type of arrogant boldness but rather acknowledging that we have "freedom of access" (Arnold, *Ephesians*, 198). We can come freely, openly, and without constraint (ibid.).

Christ-centered missionaries take advantage of the marvelous privilege of prayer. They live by prayer. They love by prayer. They make the gospel known by prayer.

If you are a Christian, you can pray anytime, anywhere. We can draw near to the throne of grace and find help in our time of need (Heb 4:14-16). We seek God in prayer, through Christ, by the Spirit. We can know that He hears us. He is for us. He is with us. A Christ-centered missionary is never alone.

When Paul returns to what was presumably his initial thought—namely, intercessory prayer—in Ephesians 3:14-21, he asks God to empower the church. That is what we as Christ's ambassadors need. We need God's power to sustain us for the mission.

Let us go on to read what Paul says in the following prayer, but let us pause and give thanks to God for this inspired rabbit trail. The apostle has painted for us a compelling vision of a Christ-centered missionary.

May the Spirit of God deepen in us a greater love for the Messiah, for the grace of God, for the church, and for this global and cosmic mission!

Reflect and Discuss

1. If you were imprisoned for your faith like Paul, do you think it would make you stronger or discourage you? What steps can you take to strengthen your faith to face all kinds of challenges?
2. How does Paul's pastoral heart challenge and/or encourage you?
3. Why should missionaries have a solid grasp on the essentials of the faith? How might you grow in your understanding of sound doctrine?
4. How would you explain the "mystery" Paul describes?
5. Are you overwhelmed by Christ's grace? Why or why not? What can you learn from Paul regarding gratitude for God's grace?
6. Why is it right to say the riches of Christ are "incalculable" or unsearchable?
7. Do you think a local pastor should preach Christ in every sermon? Why or why not?
8. In light of this passage, why should one have a high view of the church?
9. Why is this passage an encouragement to pray?
10. Which of the six points of a Christ-centered missionary impacted you the most? Why?

Praying for Power

EPHESIANS 3:14-21

Main Idea: In his second intercessory prayer, Paul prays for God to empower the Ephesian believers and grant them a greater knowledge of His extraordinary love for them.

I. **Pray with Humility (3:14-16a).**
   A. Humble gratitude
   B. Humble desperation
   C. Humble confidence
II. **Pray for the Fullness of God's Power and Love (3:16-19).**
   A. We need to be strengthened by the Spirit's power (3:16-17a).
   B. We need power to grasp Christ's love (3:17b-19).
      1. Know that you are secured in God's love (3:17b).
      2. Know the limitless dimensions of God's love (3:18).
      3. Know that this love surpasses knowledge (3:19a).
      4. Know God's love that you may be mature (3:19b).
III. **Pray with Great Expectations (3:20-21).**
   A. What (3:20a)?
   B. How (3:20b)?
   C. Why (3:21)?

In the film *Gravity*, astronauts Ryan Stone (Sandra Bullock) and Matt Kowalski (George Clooney) undertake a routine space mission. However, debris created by a Russian missile disrupts their mission. The rest of the movie is about them trying to survive and return to earth. Eventually, Ryan, a medical engineer and mission specialist on her first trip to space, finds herself in a desperate situation, stranded alone. Having given up all hope of living, she tries to prepare herself to die. She says, "I'm going to die. . . . Everyone dies, but I'm going to die today. . . . No one will mourn for me. No one will pray for my soul. . . . I've never prayed. . . . Nobody ever taught me how."

Tears ran down my 3-D glasses as I thought about how common her experience is. People do not want to die. And people do not know how to pray. The answer to both problems is the same: Jesus. Jesus Christ has given us access to God (2:18), and the crucified and risen Savior has defeated death (1:20).

Ephesians contains many important truths related to prayer. We have already learned that prayer is conversation with the Father, through the Son, by the Spirit (2:18). We have already prayed for divine illumination (1:17-23). Now we learn some more petitions that should fill our prayers.

In 3:14-21 we see Paul showing us what it is like to pray in view of God's greatness and our human need. This section is a transitional section of the book. The first three chapters are about who we are in Christ. The next three chapters are about how we are to live. Understanding both is essential for Christians, but you need more than knowledge of these things. Sandwiched in between these two sections is this prayer for *power*.

This is a good reminder for us. We must have God's power to do God's will. Let me make three points regarding our need to pray with a high view of God.

Pray with Humility
EPHESIANS 3:14-16A

The first thing to notice here is Paul's posture. Kneeling was not common for the Jews. The typical position was one of standing, as we see today at the Wailing Wall. Whenever someone is kneeling in prayer in the Bible, he is indicating deep humility and deep emotion before God. I do not want to suggest that this is the only correct posture for prayer, for we have people praying in all kinds of postures in the Bible (my favorite way to pray is by walking), but I do want to emphasize the heart of the idea of kneeling.

As we consider this posture, I think we can draw application about three things: gratitude, desperation, and confidence.

Humble Gratitude

The context shows us that Paul is praying with humble gratitude to God. I draw this from "For this reason" (v. 14). What prompted this prayer? What was the "reason"? Paul began this prayer in verse 1 it seems, but he took a holy rabbit trail to talk about his calling in 3:2-13. So, what preceded 3:1?

Two chapters of God's amazing grace preceded chapter 3. Gratitude for the grace of God in chapters 1–2 prompted this prayer in chapter 3. Paul was stunned at God's grace in saving sinners individually and at His grace in uniting them corporately. When we reflect on God's amazing grace, it should lead us to get on our faces before God, who called us, adopted us, redeemed us, and forgave us. Christ died on our behalf. The Spirit has sealed us. God has brought us from death to life, has raised us with Christ, and has seated us with Christ. God has made us part of His church. In light of these realities, Paul says, "For this reason I kneel before the Father." And so should we.

Prayer is not striking a piñata or asking God for goodies. It begins and ends in *worship*. That is what Paul is doing here. He is worshiping. Paul knew God had taken the initiative to call sinners to Himself in order to form a people, and that made him fall to his knees. Paul loved God because God had called sinners to Himself, dressed them in the robes of Christ, and said there are no second-class citizens in the kingdom. Did He do this because they were good? No. God did it because God is good.

When was the last time we bowed in humble gratitude to God like this? The psalmist captures this spirit:

> *Come, let us worship and bow down;*
> *let us kneel before the LORD our Maker.*
> *For He is our God,*
> *and we are the people of His pasture,*
> *the sheep under His care.* (Ps 95:6-7)

Let us kneel before the Lord God our Maker, or as Paul says here, "Before the Father from whom every family in heaven and on earth is named" (vv. 14b-15). Let us kneel before the sovereign Father over all and worship Him for His grace and glory.

Humble Desperation

Kneeling is also a sign of desperation. When we realize that we are approaching the only One who can act on our behalf, it gives us a proper sense of helplessness.

From this text we see that Paul is not a cold theologian, busy writing sophisticated arguments for philosophers to consider. He is a deeply passionate leader. We see him with Ephesian elders in Acts 20 shedding "tears" as he left them (Acts 20:19,31,37). In that context we also see him kneeling in prayer (Acts 20:36). He sets a good example for us. Earlier in Acts, Stephen falls to the ground in desperation and prays for his persecutors (Acts 7:60).

Why is Paul so passionate and desperate in Ephesians 3:14? I think because he knows what the Ephesians need is something that can only come from God: power. Notice how Paul prays that God would "grant" them to be strengthened (v. 16). He knew God's power was a gift, so he was desperate for God to answer.

Are you coming to God desperately? Do you realize you are helpless and powerless without God? A vivid illustration of this is found in a story titled "Palm Monday":

> The donkey awakened, his mind still savoring the afterglow of the most exciting day of his life. Never before had he felt such a rush of pleasure and pride.
>
> He walked into town and found a group of people by the well. "I'll show myself to them," he thought.
>
> But they didn't notice him. They went on drawing their water and paid him no mind.
>
> "Throw your garments down," he said crossly. "Don't you know who I am?"
>
> They just looked at him in amazement. Someone slapped him across the tail and ordered him to move.
>
> "Miserable heathens!" he muttered to himself. "I'll just go to the market where the good people are. They will remember me."
>
> But the same thing happened. No one paid any attention to the donkey as he strutted down the main street in front of the market place.
>
> "The palm branches! Where are the palm branches?" he shouted. "Yesterday, you threw palm branches!"
>
> Hurt and confused, the donkey returned home to his mother.
>
> "Foolish child," she said gently. "Don't you realize that without him, you are just an ordinary donkey?" (Rice, *More Hot Illustrations*, Kindle)

Apart from Christ we can do nothing (John 15:5). This should humble us and make us desperate, but it should also encourage us. You can do ministry with His help.

Humble Confidence

Finally, Paul's introduction here shows us that we should also come before God with confidence. We should not come with arrogance, thinking God owes us His blessings, but with humble confidence. Why? We can pray with confidence because of our position in Christ. Paul said in Ephesians 2:18 that because of the reconciling work of Jesus and our union with Him, we have access to God. Then in chapter 3 he says, "We have boldness and confident access through faith in Him" (3:12). We can also pray with confidence because we are approaching our Father who loves us (John 16:26-27).

Our Father is the sovereign Father. Paul calls Him "the glorious Father" (1:17) and the "Father of all" (4:6). Here Paul says that "every family in heaven and on earth is named" from God. This is an expression of the Father's authority and rule over all.

Our Father is rich and powerful! Paul prays for God to answer "according to the riches of His glory" (cf. Phil 4:19). God's resources never run out. Therefore, bring your petitions to Him confidently.

Our Father is gracious. Paul asks for God to "grant" the church strength. God loves to give good gifts to His children, particularly those things pertaining to the Spirit, not just material blessings but the Spirit's guidance and work (cf. Luke 11:11-13).

Pray for the Fullness of God's Power and Love
EPHESIANS 3:16-19

As we move to Paul's petitions, two main requests emerge: power and love (Carson, *Ephesians*, 182; see also O'Brien, *Ephesians*, 253). Verse 19b is considered "the third and climactic request, or the summarizing request in which the contents of the two preceding petitions are realized" (O'Brien, *Ephesians*, 253). Stott points out that they are like a "staircase" (*Ephesians*, 134). We begin with the lead request "to be strengthened with power" (v. 16); then we move through the next requests (notice the use of "that") until we reach the climax: "so you may be filled with all the fullness of God" (v. 19b).

Notice all the phrases about *power* and *love* in verses 16-19, and then peek into verse 20:

- "strengthened with power" (v. 16)
- "rooted and firmly established in love" (v. 17)

- "able to comprehend [God's love]" (v. 18)
- "to know the Messiah's love" (v. 19)
- "filled with all the fullness of God" (v. 19)
- "according to the power that works in us" (v. 20)

Paul is essentially praying for the readers to experience what he has just talked about in the previous chapters: Christ's supreme power and God's great love toward sinners. We should remember that prayer and teaching always go together (Stott, *Ephesians*, 132). It is one thing to teach it or hear it; it is another to experience it. Let us look closer at what Paul believed the Ephesians desperately needed, which is what we desperately need also.

We Need to Be Strengthened by the Spirit's Power (3:16-17a)

Paul asks God to strengthen the believers with power in the "inner man." This is where we need strength and power—on the inside. This is how we fight sin, proclaim the gospel with courage, and love people the way Christ has loved us. In 2 Corinthians 4:16 Paul says that the outer man is perishing but the inner man is being renewed. Our bodies may be wearing out, but while our bodies are weakening, our inner man may be renewed by the Spirit.

Our culture places primary importance on the outer person, but the inner person is far more important (cf. 1 Sam 16:7; Prov 31:30). Make sure you give attention to your inner being.

Why do we need to be strengthened by the Spirit in the inner man? Paul says, "That the Messiah may dwell in your hearts through faith." These two petitions in verses 16-17 clearly belong together. Paul uses the language of the inner man (v. 16) and the heart (v. 17). He uses the language of the strength of the Spirit (v. 16) and of the indwelling Messiah (v. 17). Paul does not intend to separate the Second and Third Person of the Trinity. To speak of the indwelling Christ and the indwelling Spirit is to speak of the same thing (Stott, *Ephesians*, 135). Christ dwells in our hearts by the Spirit.

It is indeed part of the "mystery" that Christ dwells in believers, not in a tabernacle or temple. Some might say, "I thought Christ was already in my heart as a Christian." Yes, He is (John 14:15-17). But Paul is speaking about something more than just Christ *dwelling* in our hearts. Paul is talking about Christ *ruling* in the heart. Paul's choice of words for "dwell" is important. He uses a strong word. He could use the word that means "to inhabit," but instead he uses the word that means "to settle down." It carries the idea of a permanent resident, not a short-lived resident.

D. A. Carson points out Paul's word choice and then illustrates the difference between a short-lived resident and a long-term resident. Carson says, when Christ takes up residence in a believer, it is like a couple who purchases a home that needs a lot of work. Over time they clean it up, repair it, and eventually say, "This house has been shaped to our needs and taste and I really feel comfortable." Then Carson says,

> When Christ by his Spirit takes up residence within us, he
> finds a moral equivalent to trash, black and silver wall paper,
> and a leaking roof. He sets about turning this residence
> into a place appropriate for him, a home for which he is
> comfortable. . . . When a person takes up long-term residence
> somewhere, their presence eventually characterizes that
> dwelling. . . . When Christ first moves into our lives, he finds
> us in bad repair. It takes a great deal of power to change us;
> and that is why Paul prays for power. . . . [He is] transforming
> us into a house that pervasively reflects his own character.
> (*Spiritual Reformation*, 186–87)

Christ enters the heart of a Christian that He may live, abide, and reign there. He enters our hearts that we may reflect His character. In Colossians Paul says that we are to let the peace of Christ rule in our hearts and let the word of Christ dwell in our hearts (Col 3:15-16). Let us pray the same as Paul!

We Need Power to Grasp Christ's Love (3:17b-19)

Paul moves from talking about strength to love, but strength is still in view since we need God's power to understand the limitless dimensions of His love. Sure, the Ephesians knew of God's love. But Paul is asking for them to know it better.

Understand that this petition does not focus on the Ephesians' love for Christ (though that is a good thing for which to pray), but rather it is a prayer that the Ephesians may know Christ's love for them! Paul apparently thinks they do not appreciate Christ's love as they should.

I think the same could be said of us. When we begin to grasp Christ's love for us, we live a crucified life. Consider how Paul ties an understanding of Christ's love to a Christian's radical obedience:

> *I have been crucified with Christ and I no longer live, but Christ lives in me. The life I now live in the body, I live by faith in the Son of God, who* loved me and gave Himself for me. (Gal 2:19-20, emphasis added)

> *And walk in love, as the Messiah also* loved us and gave Himself for us. (Eph 5:2, emphasis added)

It is not a mere intellectual appreciation of the love of Christ that Paul is after. Carson says,

> Paul is not asking that his readers might become more able to articulate the greatness of God's love in Christ Jesus or to grasp with the intellect alone how significant God's love is in the plan of redemption. He is asking God that they might have the *power to grasp the dimensions of that love in their experience.* (*Spiritual Reformation*, 191, emphasis added)

God's love is rooted in history, most magnificently at the cross, but that love is to be tasted. It is to be experienced. Numerous verses refer to the idea of experience (e.g., Ps 143:8). Peter says, "And though not seeing Him now, you believe in Him and rejoice with inexpressible and glorious joy" (1 Pet 1:8). That is not mere head knowledge. Paul goes on to say that this love "surpasses knowledge." It is a love that is knowable and explainable to a degree; yet, it must be experienced.

Let me point out two ditches to avoid regarding experience. First, watch out for *experiential abuse.* Some base too much on experience. They do not filter experience through God's Word. This can lead to mysticism. This is dangerous, as it can lead to heresy and all kinds of problems. God's revelation must be primary. We must understand our experience through the lens of Scripture, which alone is perfect. Second, watch out for *experiential avoidance.* Some are so afraid of the abuses of experience and the work of the Spirit that they have their own problem, that is, an avoidance of the Spirit and experience. They have a cold, dead orthodoxy as a result.

Paul shows us what we need. He has spent three chapters on God's truth. Now he says he wants us to know it, to experience it. God's salvation, God's power and love, are to be known and experienced. Many people have known right doctrine but committed grave sins because they were not walking in the fullness of God's presence and love personally.

They were straight as a gun barrel but just as empty. Notice four aspects of love that we need to know in our minds and in our experiences:

Know that you are secured in God's love (3:17b). Paul describes Christians as "being rooted and firmly established in love." Stott says, "Love is to be the soil in which their life is rooted; love is to be the foundation on which their life is built" (*Ephesians*, 136). Paul says a similar thing in Colossians 2:6-7: "rooted and built up in Him" (Col 2:7).

We are to build our lives on the love of Christ. We must let our roots go down into the love of Christ and draw strength from there, living moment by moment knowing we are loved by God. This love has come to us before the foundation of the world (Eph 1:3-6). In love God has called us and brought us to life (2:4-5).

Know the limitless dimensions of God's love (3:18). Next Paul goes on to express his desire for the Ephesians to grasp something of the greatness of God's love. He uses the expressions: "length and width, height and depth" (cf. Rom 8:31-39). It is difficult to understand precisely what Paul is getting at, but God's love is certainly extensive! Scripture speaks of the breadth of God's love in that He has included all ethnic groups as part of His family; Jew and Gentile are one. Scripture speaks of His love being as long as eternity. Jeremiah says He has "loved you with an everlasting love" (Jer 31:3). Scripture speaks of God's love being higher than the heavens (Ps 103:11-12). Scripture speaks of His love in terms of depth in that God casts our sins into the bottom of the sea (Mic 7:19).

Notice that we should try to "comprehend" it. But it takes God's "power" to do so! This love has been expounded beautifully in chapters 1–2.

Notice also that we should try to grasp it "with all the saints." All the saints—rich and poor, black and white, young and old—should think on the love of Christ together. Discuss His love; share stories of His love; study the Bible together. This is another reference to the importance of the church. God intends to shape us through community as we reflect on His gospel. We are not intended to live the Christian life in isolation.

Know that this love surpasses knowledge (3:19a). Paul urges us to grasp and experience God's love as much as possible. We cannot get to the bottom of God's love since it "surpasses knowledge." How do we experience God's love? Vertically, we need to stop and marvel at God's love (2:1-2) and rest in God's forgiveness (4:32).

I meet many people who often say, "I know God has forgiven me, but I can't forgive myself." That is idolatry. If God has forgiven us, we need to move on. He is the ultimate authority, not us. When we think we need something more than God Almighty's forgiveness, it is clear that we are not finding our identity in Jesus Christ and the gospel. We are living in a works-based system that does nothing but enslave.

Horizontally, we need to experience God's love by showing love to the world. And we need to show this love in the church, to everyone, regardless of socioeconomic background (2:11-22). We need to forgive others because Christ has forgiven us (4:32). We must show God's love by putting up with difficult people and offering patient, forbearing love (4:2-3): the same type of patient love that God has for us.

Know God's love that you may be mature (3:19b). Paul concludes his prayer with this great phrase: "filled with all the fullness of God." Paul wants them to know the love of God in Christ to the end that they might "be all that God wants them to be" or "be spiritually mature" (Carson, *Spiritual Reformation*, 195).

Paul uses a similar expression in 4:13 to talk about spiritual maturity: "until we all reach unity in the faith and in the knowledge of God's Son, growing into a mature man with a stature measured by Christ's fullness."

As individuals, we are to go on being filled with the Spirit of God (5:18). And as a church, although we are already filled with His fullness (1:23), we are to grow up into Him until we reach fullness (4:13-16). God is growing us up into maturity in Christ, which means He is growing us up into the fullness of Christ. In Colossians Paul says that God's fullness dwells in Christ, and we have come to fullness (Col 1:19; 2:9-10).

Jesus got at this idea when He prayed, "So the love You have loved Me with may be in them and I may be in them" (John 17:26). We cannot be mature unless we know and experience the power and love of God in Christ. We need the fullness of God's love and power in order to be like Christ. Each of us should seek the fullness of God's power and love that we may love our neighbors, our churches, our families, and this broken world. This leads us to the following doxology.

Pray With Great Expectations
EPHESIANS 3:20-21

Finally, Paul moves to praise. He shows us the greatness of God. Consider the "what," "how," and "why" of this doxology.

What? (3:20a)

Paul says God is "able" (20a)! Able to do what? Notice how he heaps up phrases to describe God's sovereign might:

- to do above [But that's not all!]
- to do above and beyond [But that's not all!]
- to do above and beyond all that we ask [But that's not all!]
- to do above and beyond all that we ask or think

God can do more in response to one prayer than we can do in one hundred years of planning and plodding. Do we believe God alone is the only Sovereign? He is the One who raised Jesus from the dead and placed Him as head over the church, and He has put all things under His feet! If so, then pour out your heart to Him, believing He is able.

We need a vision of God that increases our faith in God's greatness. The best way to do this is to fill our minds with the Word of God.

How? (3:20b)

How does God work beyond our imaginations? Paul says it is "according to the power that works *in us*" (20b, emphasis added). Think about the examples of this in the Bible. Think of His work in the lives of Abraham, Moses, Gideon, David, Elijah (a man like us according to Jas 5:17-18), Isaiah, Nehemiah, the disciples, and the church. God is able to do extraordinary things through ordinary people by His power at work within them.

Why? (3:21)

Why does God do these things? Paul says it in verse 21. This should be the ultimate goal for our prayers for power and love: "To Him be glory in the church and in Christ Jesus to all generations, forever and ever. Amen." God blesses His people for His own glory.

But notice Paul says that God desires His glory *in the church* and *in Christ Jesus*. Stott says, "God desires glory in the bride and in the bridegroom; in the community of peace, and in the Peacemaker" (*Ephesians*, 141).

For how long? *Forever.* Forever, God will be glorified for His power and love. Forever, God will be glorified by His people. Forever, God will be glorified in Christ Jesus, the Lamb who was slain. Forever, God will be glorified in the Christ, who fell to *His knees* before the Father in the garden of Gethsemane, who took the cup of wrath that we could receive the cup of grace, who has reconciled us to the Father and one another, and who now dwells in our hearts, through faith by the Spirit. To God be the glory forever!

Fictional astronaut Ryan Stone was correct: we are all going to die. But you can live forever through Jesus Christ, who also gives us access to the Father in prayer right now.

Reflect and Discuss

1. What prompts Paul to pray with such humility and gratitude?
2. What keeps you from feeling humble desperation in your praying?
3. What does this passage teach us about the resources of God?
4. For what does Paul pray? Pause and pray through these petitions.
5. Why is it important to meditate on the love of God?
6. Why do we need the power of God?
7. How is the love of God conveyed throughout the book of Ephesians?
8. Why do verses 20-21 encourage us to pray with great expectations?
9. Why should we pray for God to do amazing things, according to verse 21?
10. Will you consider memorizing this prayer? If so, begin now.

A Healthy Body

EPHESIANS 4:1-16

Main Idea: Paul exhorts the Ephesian church to maintain unity, to use their gifts, and to grow in spiritual maturity.

I. **A Healthy Church Is Marked by Spiritual Unity (4:1-6).**
   A. United by divine calling (4:1)
   B. United by Christlike conduct (4:2-3)
   C. United by gospel confession (4:4-6)
II. **A Healthy Church Is Marked by Spiritual Diversity (4:7-12).**
   A. We have diverse gifts (4:7-10).
   B. We have diverse responsibilities (4:11-12).
III. **A Healthy Church Is Marked by Spiritual Maturity (4:13-16).**
   A. Maturity involves Christlikeness (4:13).
   B. Maturity involves doctrinal stability (4:13-14).
   C. Maturity involves truth joined with love (4:15-16).
   D. Maturity involves contribution (4:16).

If your church is like ours, you have a lot of health-conscious individuals in the community. We have nurses, pharmacists, and fitness center coaches, just to name a few. Some have disciplined eating habits. Many of them exercise daily (even running marathons!). I am also interested in health and enjoy exercising (I used to teach health class in high school). Recently my wife was told to drink "parsley water" to help an ailment. I decided to have a few glasses myself. There is nothing like a mouthful of grass water at 9:00 p.m.! (Well, not really.)

In Ephesians 4 Paul describes another body, the body of Christ. We should be even more interested in its health. We should listen closely to Paul, for we are *part* of this body as Christians. And we should pay attention because, unlike a lot of changing health opinions, this is eternal truth. I am not sure about the benefit of parsley water, but I am sure about the apostle's instruction. This plan will do a body good.

So, what is the nature of a healthy body of Christ, and how should it function? This essential passage helps us answer this question. Snodgrass says, "No passage is more descriptive of the church in action" than this passage (*Ephesians*, 194). We can trace Paul's teaching by noting **three marks of a healthy church**.

A Healthy Church Is Marked by Spiritual Unity
EPHESIANS 4:1-6

United by Divine Calling (4:1)

Paul says, "Therefore I, the prisoner for the Lord, urge you to walk worthy of the calling you have received." The word *walk* is important. You will see it appear a lot in the following sections. It essentially means "to conduct one's life." After Paul has expounded the gospel in the first three chapters, he now wants his readers to know how they are to conduct their lives in a way that is in keeping with the gospel.

Realize that there is no sharp divide between the sacred and the secular. Our whole lives are to be lived in light of the gospel. Jesus Christ is Lord of all, and as believers we are to walk in step with Him, under His lordship.

This idea of "calling" goes back to the beginning of the book. God has called us to Himself by His grace. He has blessed us with every spiritual blessing in the heavens (1:3). Now we are to live worthy of that privileged calling. Paul says this calling is for every Christian, not just professional clergy or the elite. Christians are "little Christs." There is nothing more noble and great than this. Remember who you are as you live this life.

Paul illustrates what a worthy walk looks like in his own situation. He is a "prisoner for the Lord" (4:1; cf. 3:1). He does not consider himself a prisoner of Rome but rather of Christ. He has surrendered his life to the lordship of Christ, and it has taken him to prison. While you may not be sent to prison for obeying Jesus, you, as a redeemed believer, are called to sacrificial obedience.

This common calling unites us. Recognize its divine nature. God called us. We share a common experience of His grace.

United by Christlike Conduct (4:2-3)

Paul now explains what it looks like to "walk worthy." In short, it looks like Jesus! Paul mentions the following character qualities we must pursue as Christians: "With all humility and gentleness, with patience, accepting one another in love, diligently keeping the unity of the Spirit with the peace that binds us."

No one exemplified these virtues better than Jesus, who was the supreme example of humility (Phil 2:5-11). As for gentleness, Jesus said, "Come to Me . . . because I am gentle" (Matt 11:28-29). His patience is unparalleled (1 Tim 1:16). As for love, Christ demonstrated it in manifold ways and most vividly at the cross (Rom 5:8). As for being eager to maintain peace, He was the Peacemaker (Eph 2:14). Therefore, the more we look like Jesus individually, and the more we live like Christ relationally, the more united we will become.

Humility. Paul holds up humility throughout his letters as an essential characteristic of believers. He also speaks of humility in relation to unity (Rom 12:3-8; Phil 2:1-11; Col 3:12-15). For unity to exist, humble, selfless people must be living for the good of others. Interestingly, the term *humility* was uncommon in first-century Greek literature; when it did appear, it was used with a negative connotation (Thielman, *Ephesians*, 253). Pride was more highly valued. Christians were ridiculed for humility (ibid.). However, this virtue is valued throughout the Old Testament Scriptures (Prov 3:34; 11:2; Isa 66:2).

We live in a similar day. The opposite of humility is "self-exaltation." Our culture says, "Exalt yourself," "Pamper yourself," "Think about yourself first." That is the problem! You only think of yourself! Pride means being filled with self. Conversely, humility is being filled with God (Eph 3:19). Paul describes humility in Philippians 2:3 within the context of considering others more important than ourselves and not being conceited or having rivalry. Keller puts it this way: "The essence of God gospel-humility is not thinking more of myself or thinking less of myself, it is thinking of myself less" (*Freedom*, Kindle, 32).

Gentleness. This does not mean timidity. It involves being "mild spirited" or "self-controlled." Moses was described as the meekest man on the face of the earth (Num 12:3). Yet he was a dynamic leader who challenged the power of the throne of Egypt. His strength stood under God's control (albeit imperfectly). Pastors, who are to exemplify Christlikeness, are required to be "not a bully but gentle" (1 Tim 3:3). Gentleness is a fruit of the Spirit, and it is the way we are to care for one another (Gal 5:23; 6:1).

Patience. How are you doing with this virtue? For some of us the microwave is too slow! "O Lord, give me patience, and hurry!" is our prayer. Lack of patience displays a lack of humility and a lack of love.

Paul says, "Love is patient" (1 Cor 13:4). To have patient love, we must endure annoyances and challenges over a period of time. How do you cultivate patience? By relying on the Spirit! And by meditating on the patience that Christ has shown you (cf. 1 Tim 1:15ff; 2 Pet 3:9). It is easy to learn facts; it is difficult to be patient with people.

Accepting one another in love. This means "to put up with each other in love." Peter says, "Love covers a multitude of sins" (1 Pet 4:8). This is the only way a marriage works. If I had to put up with me, one of us would have to die. But my wife puts up with me. This is the way relationships in the body of Christ work, as well.

Diligently keeping unity. Unity is active, not passive. We should be zealous to maintain unity. Notice we do not work to *create* unity but to *keep* unity! God unites us, and we are to seek to maintain unity by the Spirit's help.

In order to pursue these qualities, we must be willing to renounce the opposite of each (Snodgrass, *Ephesians*, 218). We must renounce self-centeredness in order to walk in humility. We must renounce harshness in order to walk with gentleness. We must renounce the tyranny of our own agendas in order to walk with patience. We must renounce idealistic expectations in order to walk in forbearing love. We must renounce indifference and passivity in order to be eager to maintain the unity of the Spirit in the bond of peace. The church is unified and God is glorified when we live with such Christlike conduct.

United by Gospel Confession (4:4-6)

Paul cites what was probably an early Christian creed. Paul points out seven "one" statements to emphasize the oneness we share in the gospel. It is important to note that Ephesians 4 is not teaching unity at any cost. It is a unity in Christ.

One body. We share a common existence in Christ's church. We are diverse in background and gifting, but we are united as one.

One Spirit. We share a common origin in the Holy Spirit's work. The Spirit is the One who creates unity and empowers us to maintain it.

One hope. We share a common hope in Christ. Formerly, we were "without hope" (2:12) until we were called to Christ. Now we have hope, and we must live in a manner worthy of our calling.

One Lord. Believers confess and proclaim, "Jesus Christ as Lord" (2 Cor 4:5). When the early Christians said, "Jesus is Lord," they were saying, "Caesar is not lord." When Jewish Christians said this, they were boldly identifying Jesus with the God of the Hebrew Scriptures (cf. Deut 6:4). So this was not merely an empty creedal affirmation for early believers. This confession could cause you to lose your head.

One faith. The creed reminds us that we embrace the essential truths together, for "faith" here seems to refer to the body of truth we believe.

One baptism. We share a common experience of being spiritually baptized into Christ. We are united with Him. The act of baptism into water pictures this reality. This ordinance may be in view here.

One God and Father. As His adopted children, we share the same Father (cf. Eph 1:5). He is the God over all and the Father of all His children—regardless of their ethnicities. We are one big, adopted family.

Notice also the Trinity here in this creed. The triune God not only creates the unity we have as believers but also serves as the ultimate picture of unity. Jesus prayed for unity, reflecting on His relationship with the Father: "May they all be one, as You, Father, are in Me and I am in You. May they also be one in Us, so that the world may believe that You sent Me" (John 17:21). A healthy church is characterized by such unity, and it is a marvelous testimony to the watching world.

(2) A Healthy Church Is Marked by Spiritual Diversity
EPHESIANS 4:7-12   *unity ≠ uniformity*

Unity does not mean sameness. Our diverse roles and abilities enrich and bless the church. In the following verses Paul shows us how the church, with all of its glorious diversity, functions in a healthy way.

We Have Diverse Gifts (4:7-10)

Here Paul provides one of the key passages on spiritual gifts in the New Testament (cf. Rom 12:4-8; 1 Cor 12–14). He says every believer has received a gift, or "grace" (v. 7). This is not "saving grace" but "ministry grace." It is grace to serve and build up the body. In 3:8 Paul said, "Grace was given" that he might preach to the Gentiles. Here grace is given to every believer to do ministry.

Perhaps what is most distinctive about this text, compared to the other texts on gifts, is its exalted, Christ-centered focus. Paul highlights Christ's generosity and authority. Christ Jesus died, rose, and ascended into heaven as the victorious King with all authority and gave gifts to His people, displaying extravagant generosity (v. 8).

Here is another example of how Jesus is portrayed as a *giver*! In turn, we are to be givers. We are to be generous with the gifts and resources we have received.

These gifts are ways in which we extend the ministry of Jesus on this earth. When you see gifts at work, you should adore Jesus who gave them. When someone's gifts bless you, you should see that as Jesus blessing you.

In verse 8 Paul cites Psalm 68 and relates it to Christ's triumph and authority. Instead of directly quoting Psalm 68:18, Paul apparently gave a general summary of the entire psalm.

Psalm 68 is a victory hymn. Historically it was typical to bring back the spoils of war after a king won a significant military victory (Num 31:7-9; 2 Sam 12:29-31; see also Exod 3:19-22). Here, having triumphed over sin, death, hell, and the grave, our Savior gave His congregation spiritually gifted people that they might minister to His church.

In verses 9-10, which function like a parenthesis, Paul speaks of Christ's descent and ascent. Paul sees the incarnation (descent) and ascension of Christ as evidence that Christ is Savior and King. Therefore, Christ is our ascended Lord. He came all the way down (Phil 2:5-8) and has now gone all the way up (Phil 2:9-11). Christ is above all. Christ fills all. Christ gives gifts to all. Marvel at His generosity and authority!

We Have Diverse Responsibilities (4:11-12)

Christ gave us gifts so that we would use them (cf. 1 Pet 4:10-11). These responsibilities are different for different believers. Here Paul notes the leaders and the members. Each of them has the same value to God, but they share different roles. In baseball pitchers are not known for hitting, and hitters are not known for pitching. In football you usually do not want the nose guard playing quarterback! In basketball you do not want five seven-footers on the floor at one time! Likewise, the church needs people playing different positions to be a unified and effective team. Some have gifts of encouragement, some have gifts of administration, some have gifts of hospitality, and so on.

The leaders equip the saints (4:11). Paul mentions those in unique positions of leadership in the church: apostles, prophets, evangelists, pastors, and teachers. He focuses on those gifted in articulating the gospel, teaching the Word, and shepherding God's people.

The titles *apostle* and *prophet* have a broad range of meaning. In one sense the apostles and prophets were foundational to the church (2:20;

3:5). *Apostle*, in a technical sense, refers to the Twelve (defined in this way, we do not have apostles anymore). In a general sense it can refer to a "sent one." *Prophets* were forth-tellers even more than future-tellers. We see prophets throughout the Old Testament and also mentioned in the early church in the New Testament (Acts 11:27-28; 13:1; 15:32; 21:9; 1 Cor 14:32). Used in a technical sense, as with apostles, we do not have biblical prophets any longer. In a general sense prophets are those who apply God's Word to God's people.

Evangelists are those gifted in proclaiming the gospel (Acts 21:8; 2 Tim 4:5). Everyone is called to evangelize, but some are uniquely gifted in this area.

The term *pastor* is used here to refer to a ministry in the church, though the related verb *shepherd* appears elsewhere (e.g., 1 Pet 5:2; Acts 20:28; John 21:16). *Pastor* is to be understood alongside the terms *elder* and *overseer*. I take them as the same office and use the terms interchangeably at our local church (cf. Acts 14:23; 20:17,28; 1 Tim 4:14; 5:17,19; Titus 1:5,7; 1 Pet 5:1-4). The noun *flock* refers to the church (Acts 20:28-29; 1 Pet 5:2-3). In addition to the important role of teaching, pastors are to oversee the flock (1 Thess 5:12; Heb 13:17). They nurture, defend, protect, know, and sacrifice for the flock. In turn the New Testament says they should be honored and respected (1 Tim 5:17; 1 Thess 5:12-13).

The imagery of the shepherd applied to God in the Old Testament; He is the ultimate Shepherd who cared for and protected His people (Gen 49:24; Pss 23:1; 80:1; Isa 40:11). Leaders in the Old Testament were also referred to at times as "shepherds" (e.g., 2 Sam 5:2; Ps 78:71-72; Jer 23:2; Ezek 34:10). In the New Testament Jesus is the good shepherd (John 10:11-18), the great Shepherd (Heb 13:20), and the chief Shepherd (1 Pet 5:4). He is "the ultimate Senior Pastor," and pastors today are undershepherds.

Some take *teacher* as the same office as pastors, translating them "pastor-teacher." O'Brien provides a helpful conclusion:

> The *pastors* and *teachers* are linked here by a single definite article in the Greek, which suggests a close association of functions between two kinds of ministers who operate within the one congregation (cf. 2:20). Although it has often been held that the two groups are identical (i.e., "pastors who teach"), it is more likely that the terms describe overlapping functions (cf. 1 Cor 12:28-29 and Gal 6:6, where "teachers"

are a distinct group). All pastors teach (since teaching is an essential part of pastoral ministry), but not all teachers are also pastors. The latter exercise their leadership role by feeding God's flock with his word. (*Ephesians*, 300)

While we wrestle with these distinctive positions and gifts, one thing is abundantly clear: God has blessed His people throughout redemptive history with gifted proclaimers of His Word. The author of Hebrews tells us, "Remember your leaders who have spoken God's word to you. As you carefully observe the outcome of their lives, imitate their faith" (Heb 13:7). Such leaders are instruments in the Redeemer's hands, used for our sanctification. Their teaching strengthens us and, as Paul says next, equips us for ministry.

The saints do the work of ministry (4:12). Church leaders prepare, complete, train, and equip God's people for ministry. We all have a work of ministry because we all have spiritual gifts given by Christ (1 Cor 12:7,11; 1 Pet 4:10).

This is not the first time Paul has mentioned "work." Earlier, he said that God saved us for good works (Eph 2:10). Later he will tell us to imitate God (5:1). God works, and we imitate God by working. The pastor works and the people work. The church is to have an "every-member ministry."

What are you doing with what God has given you? The church will be enriched in worship and mission when everyone is serving. When members give, work in child care, visit those in need, make meals for new parents, and minister to one another in groups, the body is edified, blessed, and built up (4:12).

Every member should grow up and use a towel, not wear a bib. They should not be immature consumers but eager servants. This is how Paul Tripp puts it:

> Your life is much bigger than a good job, an understanding spouse, and non-delinquent kids. It is bigger than beautiful gardens, nice vacations, and fashionable clothes. In reality, you are part of something immense, something that began before you were born and will continue after you die. God is rescuing fallen humanity, transporting them into his kingdom, and progressively changing them into his likeness—and he wants you to be part of it. (*Instruments*, 20)

There is nothing greater to do with your life than to spend it for the glory of our Redeemer-King and the advancement of His kingdom.

A Healthy Church Is Marked by Spiritual Maturity
EPHESIANS 4:13-16

The result of the church's unity and diversity is the church's maturity. Notice how this body metaphor in verse 13, "a mature man," is contrasted with "children" in verse 14. Paul wants the people to grow up. Notice also that while one is doing the work of ministry (v. 12), one grows into maturity. We tend to think that one must be totally mature to serve in the church, and while we must be careful not to appoint leaders too quickly, we need to recognize that spiritual growth is not merely cerebral. Service is a means of growth in maturity.

Paul mentions four traits of a spiritually mature person.

Maturity Involves Christlikeness (4:13)

The ultimate picture of maturity is Christ: "a stature measured by Christ's fullness." "Christ's fullness" is an expression of completion or perfection. This makes obvious sense. The goal for us is to be like Jesus. We should long for the character qualities Paul mentions in verses 2-3 to be present in our lives. We should long for maturity individually and corporately.

Maturity Involves Doctrinal Stability (4:13-14)

Paul mentions the need to grow in our "knowledge" of truth. In verse 13 he mentions growth in "unity in the faith" (the body of doctrine) and "the knowledge of God's Son" (which involves both the intellect and the heart, cf. Phil 3:10). In verse 14 he says we should no longer be "little children" thrown around by every wind of doctrine.

Children are gullible and easily deceived. False teachers can creep in and toss them around. They prey on the gullible, saying things like:

- All religions are the same.
- If you are a good person, you'll go to heaven.
- The Bible is just one among many other religious books.
- Believe in the idea of resurrection, not a bodily resurrection.

Children must be taught as they grow up. I would not say to my youngest daughter, "Hey Victoria, drive your brothers and sisters to corporate worship!" She is only nine years old! She has to be taught. And so do believers. We enter the Christian life as babies, but we are to grow through the Word and become disciple-making teachers (1 Pet 2:1-3; Heb 5:11-14).

Maturity Involves Truth Joined with Love (4:15-16)

God means for Christians to present the truth to others, and it should always be presented in love. We must hold the truth high (1 Tim 3:15). And Christians must remember the centrality of love (1 Cor 13). The wording in Greek in verse 15 is "truthing in love" (Stott, *Ephesians*, 172). Of course, "truthing" is not a word in English, but the idea is clear. Maturity involves a truth-telling, truth-maintaining, truth-doing love.

I pray that folks would say this about my church: "They teach the Bible faithfully." I hope they also say, "They love each other like family and their neighbors as themselves." If people do not agree with our doctrine, I pray they will see that we love them. Are you known for truth and love personally, and is your church known for truth and love corporately?

Maturity Involves Contribution (4:16)

Paul returns to the body metaphor, where every member is a "limb" in Christ's body. Because you are a body part, you are important! We need one another. Every member is to contribute, using what he or she has.

Our ultimate need is Christ. We grow up into Him (v. 15). We are *dependent on Christ*, who is the head and source of the church. But we are also members of the body, and we are *dependent on one another*. "[E]ach part . . . working properly, makes the body grow so that it builds itself up in love" (4:16 ESV). As we grow into Christ and as we use our gifts in love, the body becomes healthy. What an unspeakable privilege it is to be united to Christ and to one another!

It is wise and good to be health conscious—taking care of our physical bodies. But let us be more concerned about the health of the body of Christ. May our local church bodies be marked by spiritual unity, spiritual diversity, and an ever-increasing maturity. Paul's teaching serves as a "spiritual checkup" in these vital areas. Let us make the necessary changes with the Spirit's help.

Reflect and Discuss

1. Why is unity important in a local church? Describe a typical church that models unity and one that demonstrates division.
2. What do all believers share in common? What should all believers pursue?
3. How can you grow in Christlike character?
4. How are believers different? Is this good or bad?
5. Explain the relationship between the ascension of Jesus and the distribution of gifts to the church.
6. Explain the relationship between leaders in a local church and members of a local church.
7. What responsibilities do you have as a member of a local church?
8. Which of the marks of spiritual maturity (vv. 13-16) impacted you the most?
9. Explain the importance of doctrine for growing in spiritual maturity.
10. How would you describe the health of your local church? Stop and pray for it.

A New Set of Clothes

EPHESIANS 4:17-32

Main Idea: Believers are called to live out their new identity in Christ with a lifestyle that is different from the world and different from their pre-Christian past.

I. **Our New Identity (4:17-24)**
   A. Do not live like a pagan (4:17-19).
   B. Live as a new creation (4:20-24).
II. **How to Live Out Your New Identity (4:25-32)**
   A. Replace lying with truth-telling (4:25).
   B. Replace unrighteous anger with righteous anger (4:26-27).
   C. Replace stealing with working and giving (4:28).
   D. Replace corrupt talk with edifying talk (4:29-30).
   E. Replace bitterness and rage with kindness and forgiveness (4:31-32).

We have heard the saying, "Clothes make the man." Of course that is not true physically, but it is true spiritually. When you become a Christian, you get a new set of clothes. You are clothed in Christ, and these clothes make the man (or woman).

When soldiers, firemen, policemen, or astronauts first put on their distinct uniforms, they are taking on new responsibilities corresponding to their new identity. So it is with the Christian. When we put on Christ, we receive a new spiritual identity and new corresponding responsibilities. Having put off the corrupt garment of the old self (4:22) and put on the new garment (v. 24), we must live in light of our new identity.

The Old Testament uses this metaphor of putting on particular virtues, especially God being clothed in majesty (Job 29:14; 40:10; Pss 93:1; 104:1; 132:9). Paul uses this picture of putting off and putting on in several places. He tells the Colossians, "You have put off the old self with its practices and have put on the new self" (Col 3:9b-10). To the Romans: "Let us discard the deeds of darkness and put on the armor of light. . . . But put on the Lord Jesus Christ" (Rom 13:12,14). To the Galatians: "For as many of you as have been baptized into Christ have put on Christ like a garment" (Gal 3:27). Some early traditions even gave the baptized person a different garment after baptism.

So Ephesians 4:17-32 is all about our new identity in Christ and what it looks like to live in light of it. The first paragraph is the doctrinal section, explaining **who we are** (vv. 17-24). The second paragraph is practical, illustrating **how we must now live**, especially in our relationships with one another (vv. 25-32).

Our New Identity
EPHESIANS 4:17-24

In these verses Paul provides another "formerly . . . but now" contrast (see 2:1-10). He tells believers what used to mark their lives (vv. 17-19). Then he reminds them of their new status (vv. 20-24).

Do Not Live Like a Pagan (4:17-19)

Paul begins with a strong, urgent exhortation: "Therefore, I say this and testify in the Lord: You should no longer walk as the Gentiles walk, in the futility of their thoughts" (v. 17). Some translations read "insist" instead of "testify." Paul stresses the importance of his exhortation. He intensifies it by saying, "in the Lord." Paul is pointing to his source of authority: the Lord Jesus. What is this intense exhortation? It is simple: Do not live ("walk") like non-Christians ("Gentiles"). *Gentiles* could be used in an ethnic sense (2:11), but Paul also used it in a moral sense, similar to how we might use the word *pagan*. Paul calls Christians to live no longer like the surrounding pagan culture.

This calls to mind Johnny Cash's hit song "I Walk the Line." It was his first number one song. Evidently he wrote it backstage just after being married, as a pledge of devotion to his wife. He wrote, "Since you've been mine I walk the line. . . . Oh, I admit I'm a fool for you, since you've been mine, I walk the line." Something similar is going on here in Ephesians. Since Ephesian believers entered a new relationship with Christ, they are to "walk the line." They are to walk worthy of the calling with which they have been called (4:1), to devote their lives to their Savior.

In verses 17-19 Paul reminds the Ephesian Christians (and us) that before we came to Christ, our minds, feelings, and actions were bleak. He says that we lived in the "futility" of our minds (v. 17). One writer said, "With one single word Paul describes the majority of the inhabitants of the Greco-Roman empire . . . as aiming with silly methods at a meaningless goal" (Barth, *Ephesians 4–6*, 499). What a description of meaninglessness: a foolish method aiming at a foolish goal. We were also "darkened" in "understanding" (v. 18). We had no light; we were blacked out. Sin produces a malfunction of the mind (Snodgrass, *Ephesians*, 230).

Regarding the heart, Paul builds on what he has already said in this letter concerning the unregenerate heart (e.g., 2:1): the unbelievers are "excluded from the life of God, because of the ignorance that is in them and because of the hardness of their hearts" (v. 18). They are cut off from spiritual life, and their hearts are hard. In addition, he says that they became "callous" (v. 19). They have had opportunities to respond to the good news, but they refused repeatedly.

As a result of this dead, hardened, and callous heart, Paul says their lives are marked by "promiscuity" and "every kind of impurity with a desire for more and more" (v. 19). They lack moral restraint, which leads to sexual obsession and a total perversion of the way God made us.

Compare this passage with Romans 1:18-32; Galatians 5:16-21; and Ephesians 5:3-12. In these texts Paul also speaks of the corrupt nature of the flesh and how idolatry leads to immorality. Left to ourselves, we are vile. And even though some may seem less vile, all are still in desperate need of Christ.

The good news in this passage is that God can transform anyone by His grace! Many in the Ephesian church matched this dark description, but they became new creations.

The point is clear: As new creations in Christ, we are to think differently, respond to the truth differently, and act differently from the pagan culture. God enables us to live holy lives by His Holy Spirit (cf. 4:29; 5:18). To be clear, it is not that you should never be around unbelievers. You should! But as Jesus demonstrated, our goal is to be separate from sin, even though we must not be isolated from unbelievers.

Live as a New Creation (4:20-24)

Paul now explains why we must not live as pagans. In these four remarkable verses, he first describes coming to Christ with three images: a school (vv. 20-21), changing clothes (vv. 22-24), and a new creation (v. 24b).

Remember your Christ-centered education (4:20-21). Paul says, "But that is not how you learned about the Messiah, assuming you heard about Him and were taught by Him, because the truth is in Jesus." This education is not formal education but transformational education.

The first thing to note about this education is that Christ is the *subject* of the teaching. Paul says, "You learned Christ" (v. 20 ESV). This is an unusual and awe-inspiring phrase. Christianity is about knowing a living person, Jesus Christ. O'Brien says, "The phrase 'to learn a person' appears nowhere else in the Bible and to date, has not been traced anywhere else in pre-biblical Greek documents" (*Ephesians*, 324). Paul is using "relational" language (Thielman, *Ephesians*, 300). When you become a Christian, you do not merely learn about the teaching of Jesus; you develop a relationship with Him.

Paul says, "Assuming you heard about Him" (v. 21). It had been a long time since Paul was in Ephesus. He knew false teaching abounded. So here, in passing, he notes the necessity of hearing about the real Jesus. He wants to make sure they have heard of Christ and have come to know Him.

So, have you? Have you come to know Jesus Christ? If not, then you cannot live this new life. It begins with conversion to Christ. Christianity is not about moral rule keeping, religious attendance, having "warm feelings" at a religious event, merely believing in a god, doing good things, or knowing facts about Christ. It is about knowing Christ. Jesus said, "This is eternal life: that they may know You, the only true God, and the One You have sent—Jesus Christ" (John 17:3).

I heard of a little girl who was getting a swine flu shot, and the nurse asked, "Which arm do you want it in, Sweetie?" The little girl said, "In Momma's arm." Well, Momma cannot take your shot, and she cannot believe for you. Do you know Christ personally?

We should also note that Christ Himself is the *Teacher*. Paul says you "heard about Him" (v. 21). But there is no preposition "about." It is literally, "You heard Him." Thielman says, "As with that expression, the implication is that Christ is alive and that when one hears the gospel preached, as Paul assumes his readers have, one is put in touch with a living person" (*Ephesians*, 300). Have you heard His voice?

But there is more: Christ is the *context* of the teaching. Paul says you "were taught in him" (v. 21 ESV). Paul is probably referring to the ongoing instruction that happens after you become a Christian. However, it is more than just ethical instruction, for we were taught "in Him." That is, the teaching has taken place in the sphere of the living Christ. Christ is the school, if you like. All ethical instructions are to be understood in light of our union with Christ.

Finally, we see that Christ is the truth. The result of teaching that is centered on Christ, that comes from Christ, and that is in the context of our union with Christ is that you can be assured you are walking in the truth because "the truth is in Jesus" (v. 21). Coming to Christ and learning Him is coming to the truth. Earlier Paul called the gospel "the word of truth" (1:13 ESV). But that is another way of saying coming to Jesus. For the truth is not just a set of propositions. The truth has fingernails and scarred hands. Jesus said He is the truth (John 14:6).

While Paul often refers to "Jesus Christ" or "Christ Jesus" or "Lord Jesus" or "the Messiah, Jesus," in 4:21 we find the only mention of just the name "Jesus" in Ephesians. It seems deliberate. Paul is talking about the historical person, Jesus. He lived, died, and rose from the dead in human history. Find Him and you find truth. Find Him and you find life.

Take off and put on (4:22-24). Next the apostle uses three infinitives: "to put off," "to be renewed," and "to put on" (ESV). There is a discussion about how we should take these infinitives. Should we take them as imperatives or as a description of what has already happened at conversion?

The parallel text in Colossians 3:8-10 helps us:

> But now you must also put away all the following: anger, wrath, malice, slander, and filthy language from your mouth. Do not lie to one another, since you have put off the old self with its practices and have put on the new self. You are being renewed in knowledge according to the image of your Creator.

The command to put away particular sins (Col 3:8-9) is based in the fact that the old self *has already been removed* and the new self *has already been put on* (Col 9-10). In Colossians "the verbs are aorist participles indicating what the Colossians did at the time of their conversion" (Stott, *Ephesians*, 180). In other words, since we have taken off the old and have put on the new, we must put away sin practically, daily, continually. We must live differently since we are new people. Stott summarizes my view:

> It is because we have already put off our old nature, in that decisive act of repentance called conversion, that we can

logically be commanded to put away all these practices which belong to that old, rejected life. (*Ephesians*, 180)

In verse 22 the old self refers to all that we once were, described in verses 17-19. We were "corrupted by deceitful desires" (v. 22). Remember that you do not wear this garment any longer! In verse 24 the "new self" refers to our new identity in Christ. Paul says, "You put on the new self, the one created according to God's likeness in righteousness and purity of the truth" (v. 24). The language echoes Genesis 1:26: "Then God said, 'Let Us make man in Our image, according to Our likeness.'" God made humanity in His image, but sin entered the world at the fall. Now, through Christ, we are re-created into His image. When we put on Christ, we put on a new person.

After spending about 35 days in Ukraine in an effort to adopt our four children, my wife and I finally had permission to go home with them. All of the legal work was done. We were eager to show them love in many ways, including cleaning them up and giving them some new clothes. They had been wearing the same smelly clothes and the same worn-out shoes every day since we arrived. Once we had permission to leave, we brought them some brand-new outfits. Kimberly took the older two children, and I took the younger two. I told the girls (via a translator), "Girls, we're going home." Little Victoria asked, "Forever?" I said, "Yes. Forever." Their faces lit up as I then gave them their denim dresses, socks, shirts, and more. They went to the bathroom and changed every garment. In their orphanage, upon leaving, the children had to leave behind every piece of clothing they had been wearing. What a picture of the gospel! They put off their old orphanage garments and put on the clothes from their adoptive parents. New clothes. New identity. New home. New security. And a new way to live.

Remember you're a new creation (4:23-24). Paul also says the new self is a life of renewal: "You are being renewed in the spirit of your minds." In Colossians Paul says you "have put on the new self. You are being renewed in knowledge according to the image of your Creator" (Col 3:10). "Being renewed" is in the present tense, like "being corrupted" (Eph 4:22). The present tense indicates that this renewal is an ongoing process God performs in us. We need a continual renewal of our minds. We need to be reminded constantly of our new identity. God created us but sin separated us from Him. Through Jesus we can be new creations, reflecting the glory of God by living holy righteous lives as His redeemed image bearers.

Practically speaking, the primary means of ongoing transformation in our lives is the Word and the Spirit. God does this work in us, but we also have the responsibility of setting our minds on what is above (Col 3:1-3). Paul tells the Romans, "Be transformed by the renewing of your mind" (Rom 12:2). We must give attention to our minds for growth in godliness (cf. 2 Cor 3:18; 4:16; Phil 2:5; 4:8; Titus 3:5). We must renew them, wash them, clean them with the Word of God, and meditate on that which is good, right, and true in order to live the new life.

We have come to know Christ. We are new creations. We have minds that are being renewed. Because of this change, we are empowered to live out this identity in everyday life. Verses 17-24 are absolutely essential because they tell us from where the power for change comes! It comes from God. We need new hearts. We need new desires. We need new minds and new power. That is what you have when you come to Jesus.

How to Live Out Your New Identity
EPHESIANS 4:25-32

This new lifestyle involves replacing sinful habits with righteous and holy habits. I could write a book on each of these verses, but I do not think that would capture the spirit of the text. While Paul seems to have had contextual reasons for highlighting these particular actions, we still should not take this as an exhaustive list of examples on how to live out our new identity. These are behaviors we should all be careful to pursue, but these are not the only behaviors that should mark our lives.

Before we look at these behaviors, consider a few important, over-arching observations. First, these practical exhortations are *relational*. Our new union with Christ should change the way we live in community. Our sin affects others negatively, just as our righteousness will bless others positively.

Second, notice how there is a *negative* action stated first and then a *positive* action. That is important. Get this: Holiness is not just about saying no to sin; it is also about saying yes to God. We must not only throw our dirty clothes in the hamper; we must put on the new suit as well!

Third, notice that there is a *theological reason* given for why we should throw off these sinful vices and put on these Christian actions. For example, Paul does not simply say, "Put away lying"; he relates it to the doctrine of the church: "Because we are members of one another" (v. 25). He does not stop with the exhortation, "Be angry and do not sin" (v. 26); he relates it to a belief in the "Devil" (v. 27). He commands the church to no longer "steal" and follows it by speaking of honest work, stewardship, and care for the poor (v. 28). When talking about unhealthy speech, he relates it to grieving the Holy Spirit (vv. 29-30). Regarding forgiveness, he takes us to the cross and God's amazing forgiveness (vv. 31-32). Do you see this? Our practice and our theology are tied together. Christians should not only live differently from unbelievers, but they also should live differently *for different reasons*. We believe in God, sin, the Devil, the Spirit, the church, and Christ's death on the cross. These truths should affect the way we live. Now let us consider each of these exhortations specifically.

Replace Lying with Truth-Telling (4:25)

This imperative is a quote from Zechariah: "Speak truth to one another" (Zech 8:16). Paul not only brings the weight of the Old Testament prophet here, but he also adds, "Because we are members of one another" (Eph 4:25). Your words greatly affect the whole body. If my eye says to my hand, "The iron is *not* hot," and my hand touches it, I'll get burned! Since we are united together, false words hurt the whole body. Falsehood stifles unity; truth strengthens unity.

Paul has already emphasized truth in this chapter (vv. 15,21,24). God's people are to be truth-tellers. Just like God desired for Jerusalem to be a city of truth, He longs for the church to be the same.

The word translated "lying" is actually "the lie" (singular), which is understood in the sense of lying (Snodgrass, *Ephesians*, 249). It may also carry the idea of idolatry—exchanging the truth of God for a lie (Rom 1:25; cf. Jer 10:14; 13:25). We learn from Scripture that God hates lying (Prov 6:16-17; 12:22; 12:19; 20:17; 21:6) and that Satan is a liar (John 8:44). When you tell the truth, you are imitating God. When you lie, you are imitating Satan.

Replace Unrighteous Anger with Righteous Anger (4:26-27)

This text is an echo of Psalm 4:4. The Scriptures permit a particular type of anger, what you might call *righteous indignation*. What does this righteous anger look like? Someone said, "It's when you get mad but you don't cuss." Not exactly. Righteous indignation is a holy anger against sin. We need to feel anger as Christians. If we are indifferent to injustice, then evil will prevail. Do not encourage the spread of evil through indifference. We should hate sin like God hates sin! David wrote, "Hot

indignation seizes me because of the wicked, who forsake your law"
(Ps 119:53 ESV). In Mark 1 Jesus expressed righteous indignation
when He turned over the tables in the temple. Later, in response to
the religious leader's question about healing on the Sabbath, Mark says
that Jesus "looked around at them with anger, grieved at their hardness of heart" (Mark 3:5 ESV). He displayed an anger that was mingled
with grief (Piper, "Satan Seeks a Gap"). We too should be grieved and
angered over sin.

Verse 31 mentions unrighteous anger. This anger is self-defensive
and out of control. It leads to murder, jealousy, envy, and a host of
other sins.

To make sure we keep our anger holy, Paul gives us three reminders.
The first qualification is "do not sin" (v. 26). Paul is therefore not giving
us permission to throw a fit, seek revenge, and dishonor the name of
God in public. Next Paul says, "Don't let sun go down on your anger."
This does not mean Eskimos at the North Pole may be angry and hold a
grudge for six months while the sun is up (Piper, "Satan Seeks a Gap").
Paul is saying, Do not let it fester. Resolve it quickly. Even "good anger"
can lead to problems like bitterness, so the time to be angry is short!
The final qualification is, "And don't give the Devil an opportunity."
Someone said, "Don't go to bed with unresolved conflict or else you will
sleep with the Devil." Seek forgiveness and reconciliation quickly. Satan
would love to use your anger as an opportunity to make you violent and
divisive.

Replace Stealing with Working and Giving (4:28)

Historians tell us that stealing was typical in the first century in Asia
Minor. Paul tells the church to break free from these societal norms.
Further, stealing violates the eighth commandment!

Paul possibly has in mind day laborers and skilled tradesman,
whose work was seasonal. When out of work and without assistance,
such workers would have been tempted to steal in order to survive.
While this sin may have been part of their lives before becoming
Christians, Paul reminds them that it has no place now: "The thief must
no longer steal."

Paul then says, "Instead, he must do honest work with his own
hands, so that he has something to share with anyone in need." Notice
a few applications from this statement.

Paul reminds the believers of the need for honest work. We are created to work. Work is a gift from God. Jesus put in an honest day's work for years as a carpenter/stone mason. Paul worked throughout his ministry so that he would not be a burden on the church (Acts 18:3; 1 Cor 9:15,18; 1 Thess 2:9). Work was highly valued in the Old Testament (Exod 20:9).

Additionally, Paul says we should not only see the goodness of work, but we should also remember the need for work. He insists, "If anyone isn't willing to work, he should not eat" (2 Thess 3:10-12). The writer of Proverbs says, "The one who works his land will have plenty of food, but whoever chases fantasies will have his fill of poverty" (Prov 28:19). If you want food, then work. (Christians should help one another find honest work when a brother is in need.)

But the apostle also tells us that we should work "to share with anyone in need" (v. 28). Paul tells the Romans, "Share with the saints in their needs" (Rom 12:13).

I like the way John Wesley put it: "Work as hard as you can, make as much as you can, then give as much as you can." Piper tells us there are really three options regarding work: you can steal to get, you can work to get for yourself, or you can work to get in order to give. Paul is obviously commending the third option ("The Purpose of Prosperity").

Who in the New Testament met Jesus and became a radical giver? Zacchaeus. What a remarkable story of grace in his life! He was a taker his whole life but was made into a giver because he met Jesus (Luke 19:1-10).

Replace Corrupt Talk with Edifying Talk (4:29-30)

Paul tells the Christians to bid farewell to "rotten, putrid, filthy" talk (Hughes, *Ephesians*, 152). He says, "No foul language is to come from your mouth, but only what is good for building up someone in need, so that it gives grace to those who hear." The word for "foul" or "corrupting" (ESV) is used in the New Testament to refer to rotten fruit (Matt 7:17-18) and rotten fish (Matt 13:48-49) (O'Brien, *Ephesians*, 344). Both are appropriate pictures of sinful speech. Corrupt talk does not nourish you; it makes you sick. And corrupt talk comes from a corrupt heart. Examples include, but are not limited to, lying, abusive language, vulgar references (5:4), vicious and unkind words, gossip, and slander (4:31).

Jesus said we will give an account on the final day for every careless word spoken (Matt 12:36). Augustine hung a sign on his dining room wall: "Whoever speaks evil of an absent man or woman is not welcome at this table" (Hughes, *Ephesians*, 153).

In place of corrupt talk, Paul says we need well-chosen talk (cf. Prov 25:11). Speak constructive words that are helpful and build up others. Speak encouraging words that give grace to the hearers.

The Christian life involves the constant encouragement of others. If your disposition is cynical and critical and there is no warmth and encouragement, you will not be a good leader—in your job, in your family, or in a church (small group or large). Sam Crabtree says, "We can sin in two ways: by idolatrous commendation (the praise of men), or by failing to commend the commendable." He goes on to say, "Generally, it is easier to practice affirmation early in a relationship and it can get harder later" (*Practicing Affirmation*, 13). This is probably true in a marriage or in a church.

Paul adds, "And don't grieve God's Holy Spirit" (v. 30). This warning is tied to verse 29, though all of the sins mentioned in this section grieve the Holy Spirit. The Spirit can be lied to, offended, dishonored, and disobeyed. Anything inconsistent with the Spirit's nature grieves Him. Sins of the tongue lead to the withdrawal of the influences of the Spirit.

Instead, Christians must be sensitive to the One who sealed us "for the day of redemption" (v. 30). Ask this question: Will what I'm about to say or do please the Spirit or grieve the Spirit?

Verse 30 reminds us that more is going on than meets the eye in relationships in the local church. Relationships involve spiritual warfare. Let us learn to walk by the Spirit and yield to Him in our conversation and attitudes, eagerly maintaining the unity of the Spirit. One of the ways we must learn to do this is by practicing the next two verses.

Replace Bitterness and Rage with Kindness and Forgiveness (4:31-32)

Paul says we must put off resentful attitudes (bitterness), festering anger, indignant outbursts (wrath), public shouting, abusive language (slander), and hostility (malice). In their place put on kindness and forgiveness. Wear these virtues like you wear clothes—every day.

Oh, if only the church would practice this! We should be a people known for kindness and forgiveness based on the depth of God's kindness and forgiveness that has been shown to us. God's kindness brought us to repentance (Rom 2:4). Paul tells us, "But when the kindness of God our Savior and His love for mankind appeared, He saved us" (Titus 3:4-5). The psalmist says, "The LORD is gracious and compassionate, slow to anger and great in faithful love" (Ps 145:8). And, "Yahweh, if You considered sins, Lord, who could stand? But with You there is forgiveness, so that You may be revered" (Ps 130:3-4). God is kind and forgiving, and we are to imitate Him. We see this throughout the Scriptures.

In Ephesians Paul gives us what is one of the most powerful verses on forgiveness: "God also forgave you in Christ" (4:32). The implication is obvious. If Jesus can forgive us, then there is nothing for which we should not forgive another person. Should there be consequences for actions? Sure. But we must be forgiving people. Jesus taught us to dwell on how He forgave our infinite debt and then to be quick to forgive others when they sin against us (Matt 6:12,14-15; 18:21-35; Luke 6:36). Not to forgive is to not rightly understand or appreciate Jesus' forgiveness. Think on His kindness, His love, and His forgiveness daily. It will change you. It will make you like Him.

So, what do you wear? Have you come to know Christ? Are you dressed in His righteousness? If so, live out your new identity as a new creation in Christ for the good of others and the glory of God.

Reflect and Discuss

1. Which of the cross-references on the "new set of clothes" metaphor (Job 29:14; 40:10; Pss 93:1; 104:1; 132:9; Rom 13:12b,14a; Gal 3:27; Col 3:9b-10) provides you with the most encouragement or motivation?
2. How does Paul explain the process of personal change? Does it happen by "trying harder" or by becoming a new creation?
3. How does this passage show the importance of relationships in the Christian life?
4. Explain the theological reasons that undergird each of these ethical exhortations (4:25-32).
5. How are these ethical exhortations (4:25-32) reflected in the life of Jesus?
6. Distinguish between righteous anger and unrighteous anger.
7. What is your philosophy of work? How does working for money fit into the meaning of life? How does this passage inform your opinion?

8. What characters in movies or television reflect the good and bad speaking habits of verses 29,31, and 32?
9. How does one "grieve the Holy Spirit"?
10. What does 4:32 say about forgiveness? Do you need to forgive anyone?

Imitate God

EPHESIANS 5:1-17

Main Idea: Believers are called to imitate God by walking in love, light, and wisdom.

I. **Walk in Love (5:1-2).**
   A. Love like the Father (5:1).
   B. Love like the Son (5:2).
      1. The power for love
      2. The pattern of love
      3. The perfume of love
II. **Walk in Light (5:3-14).**
   A. Exalt God, not idols (5:3-6).
      1. Sexual immorality and impurity (5:3a)
      2. Greed (5:3b)
      3. Corrupt speech (5:4)
      4. Warning (5:5-6)
   B. Exhibit the fruit of light (5:7-10).
      1. Display light by not joining those in darkness (5:7).
      2. Display light by living out your identity (5:8).
      3. Display light by doing all that is good, right, and true (5:9).
      4. Display light by pleasing the Lord (5:10).
   C. Expose the darkness (5:11-14).
      1. Light exposes the sin of unbelievers (5:11-13).
      2. Light transforms unbelievers into the realm of light (5:14).
III. **Walk in Wisdom (5:15-17).**
   A. "Not as unwise people but as wise" (5:15)
   B. "Making the most of the time" (5:16)
   C. "Understand what the Lord's will is" (5:17).

You have probably heard the expression, "Like father like son." Many sons take on characteristics of their dads and want to grow up to be like them. When I was a boy, I had a toy shaving kit so I could shave

like my dad. I had shirts that matched my dad's shirts. On Fridays my
dad and I would go to the bowling alley and stop at McDonalds, where I
would order exactly what he ordered: a Big Mac.

Sadly, many children are fatherless or have a father who is absent
or abusive. This generation has been called the "fatherless generation."
But thankfully, every believer gets to call God "Father." In 5:1 Paul urges
us to imitate our heavenly Father.

Paul paints a glorious picture of the Father in Ephesians (1:3,17;
3:14-15; 4:6). Now he adds that we must take on the Father's character.

In other places Paul holds himself up as an example saying, "Imitate
me, as I also imitate Christ" (1 Cor 11:1; cf. 1 Cor 4:16; Phil 3:17;
1 Thess 1:6; 2 Thess 3:7,9). Paul also tells congregations to imitate other
congregations (1 Thess 2:14). Only here in Ephesians are we told to
"imitate God."

Of course, we cannot imitate God in everything. For example, we
cannot create the world out of nothing, and we cannot know all things.
But we can reflect God's character in some ways as His image bearers
who have been changed by the gospel. Paul described this already in
Ephesians 4:24: "You put on the new self, the one created *according to
God's likeness* in righteousness and purity of the truth" (emphasis added).
In 5:1-17 we find many of the same themes found in 4:17-32. Paul contin-
ues describing how we may live holy and compassionately like our God.

This passage is heavy, like the previous one. Paul does not hold back.
Though it may feel like a right-left combination, we need this passage.
Paul answers how we should imitate God with three "walks." He urges
us to walk in love (5:2), walk in light (5:8), and walk in wisdom (5:15).

Walk in Love
EPHESIANS 5:1-2

In verses 1-2 Paul highlights the love of the Father and the love of the
Son. Of course it is the Spirit who enables believers to love in such a way
(Gal 5:22). Paul tells the Romans, "God's love has been poured out in
our hearts through the Holy Spirit who was given to us" (Rom 5:5). The
Spirit empowers us to love like the Father and the Son.

Love like the Father (5:1)

We are told to imitate God "as dearly loved children." How did we
become His children? Paul answered this already: "He predestined us

to be adopted through Jesus Christ for Himself, according to His favor and will" (1:5).

God adopted us. He made us His sons and daughters. He sent the Spirit of His Son into our hearts, enabling us to cry out "*Abba*, Father" (Gal 4:6). God has given us a family called the church, filled with brothers and sisters. He has given us family chores to do as members of the family. Consider these amazing privileges and this sacred responsibility.

Therefore, an appropriate application of *Ephesians 1:5*, is *Ephesians 5:1*. These two verses belong together. Amazingly, the Father has loved us in the Beloved (1:6). We share in the love the Father has for the Son. Believers now show God's fatherly love by great acts of compassion and mercy. Jesus said, "Be merciful, just as your Father also is merciful" (Luke 6:36).

God's people should be known for practical acts of mercy, like caring for orphans and widows (Jas 1:27), practicing hospitality (Rom 12:13), and caring for the poor (Eph 4:28). They should also give particular attention to meeting the needs of those within their own fellowships (Gal 6:10), as well as showing kindness and forgiveness to one another (Eph 4:32).

Love like the Son (5:2)

Paul moves to the cross of Christ in verse 2 to talk about love. He just stated that Christ's forgiveness of us is the motive for our forgiveness of others (4:32). Now he goes back to the cross again to talk about love. To understand the Father's love more clearly, we need to look at Christ, who is the ultimate imitator of the Father (John 14:9). Consider the power for love, the pattern of love, and the perfume of love.

The power for love. "Love others like Jesus" sounds good, but everyone fails at it. Non-Christians generally can't grasp the concept of sacrificial love, and they certainly have no interest in submitting to God by loving Him with their whole being. But even Christians have not loved God and neighbor perfectly. Paul shows us that we need not only Jesus' example; we also need His redeeming grace. We need a Savior who forgives us, and we need the Holy Spirit in us to empower us to love the world, demonstrating the fruit of salvation.

We still fail—frequently! We would be crushed today under the weight of guilt were it not for the cross. We would give up in frustration. But Jesus loved the Father and others perfectly, and He died in the place of lawbreakers like us. What a Savior!

A Christian brother was ministering at a local university and began speaking to a Jewish student about the gospel. He began, "Now, I'm sure you've been told that one of the main beliefs of Christians is that Christ died for us, right?" His Jewish friend, who grew up in the heart of the U.S. Bible Belt, looked stunned and said, "No. I didn't know that." After a good conversation, the Jewish student started attending this Christian's Bible study. One of the guys made a passing comment during the study, "I just wish Jesus would come back." The Jewish friend said, "What? Jesus is coming back? OK, put that aside; I've got to figure out the first coming first."

I assume you know this, but if not—Christ Jesus came to earth and lived a perfect, sinless life. He kept the law perfectly, and then He died the death we deserved, as a substitute for sinners like us (cf. 2 Cor 5:21; Gal 3:13). He rose on our behalf. If you have faith in Him, He will receive you. He will save you. Once people come to know Jesus, the Spirit of God then indwells them and empowers them to love sacrificially.

The pattern of love. How did Jesus love? This verse provides a marvelous description of genuine love. Love involves giving ourselves away for the good of another. Paul says Christ "loved us and gave Himself for us." He repeats this idea when he talks about marriage: "Husbands, love your wives, just as Christ loved the church and gave Himself for her" (5:25). Christ gave us the ultimate pattern of love.

Love is not just sentimentalism. It is not merely feeling sorry for someone. It involves sacrifice and action. John writes, "Little children, we must not love with word or speech, but with truth and action" (1 John 3:18). Jesus demonstrated His love with flesh-and-blood action (Rom 5:8). Some of these actions include loving one another (John 13:34-35), forgiving others (Eph 4:32), giving financially (2 Cor 8:9), spreading the gospel (2 Cor 5:14-21), being patient with others (1 Cor 13:4; Eph 4:2), loving those who annoy you (Eph 4:26), repenting of racism and displaying love to different people groups (Eph 2:11-22), and aiding those in need (Eph 4:29).

How can we grow in our love for others? We must think on Christ's love for *us*. Paul says Christ "loved us and gave Himself for us" (v. 2). He says a similar thing in Galatians as he describes his sacrificial life:

I have been crucified with Christ and I no longer live, but Christ lives in me. The life I now live in the body, I live by faith in the Son of God, who loved me and gave Himself for me. (Gal 2:19b-20, emphasis added)

In light of Christ's love for him, Paul lived a life to the glory of God and for the good of others. Meditate much on the love of Christ, and may it compel you to love like the Savior.

The perfume of love. Christ's death was a "sacrificial and fragrant offering to God." In the Old Testament, sacrifices were placed on an altar. A "pleasing aroma" was an Old Testament description of God's acceptance of a sacrifice given from a sincere and wholehearted worshiper (Gen 8:21). Here in Ephesians, Christ's offering of Himself was the ultimate acceptable sacrifice. It gave the perfume of grace and glory, the most pleasing aroma of sacrifice ever.

Notice Christ gave Himself up *for us,* but it was an offering *to God.* This is the pattern of love for us. While we cannot love like Christ in an atoning sense, we can love in this "horizontal-vertical sense." Let there be a holy fragrance of love in your life as you care for others practically, sincerely, and generously *for the glory of God.* An example of this horizontal-vertical love is in Philippians. There the church gave an offering to Paul, and Paul said their offering *to him* was a "fragrant offering" *to God* (Phil 4:18). They gave to Paul, but God received it as worship.

Amy Carmichael exemplified this type of love. She was a great missionary to India who spent much of her ministry caring for ill-treated children, and she saved many from forced prostitution (which took place in the temples). She founded the Dohnavur Fellowship, which became a refuge for more than a thousand children. She died in India in 1951 at the age of 83. Before dying, she asked that no stone be put over her grave. But the children she cared deeply for decided to put a birdbath over her grave, with the single inscription "Amma," which means "mother." Carmichael lived out her saying: "One can give without loving, but one cannot love without giving." Sherwood Eddy said of her, "Her life was the most fragrant, the most joyfully sacrificial, that I ever knew" (*Pathfinders*, 125). May God make us a people that love others like Christ loves us, and may our love be a pleasing aroma to God.

Walk in Light
EPHESIANS 5:3-14

In this section Paul describes the themes of light and darkness by contrasting the works of darkness and the fruit of light. Notice in verse 8 Paul states, "For you were once darkness." He does not say that you "were walking in darkness." Rather, "you *were* once darkness." But through the gospel, he says, "You *are* light in the Lord." So your identity has changed. Because you are light, Paul says, "Walk as children of light." Once again Paul calls believers to become what they are! You are light! (cf. 1 Pet 2:9; 1 John 1:1-5).

Now, the question for the believer is, How do we walk in the light? We can answer this by observing three exhortations: exalt God and not idols, exhibit the fruit of light, and expose the darkness.

Exalt God, Not Idols (5:3-6)

Paul mentions several sins here to describe a dark life: sexual immorality, impurity, greed, and filthy speech. These sins grow out of a heart that has replaced God with functional saviors. Paul says that these sins should "not even be heard of among you" (v. 3) and that they are "not suitable" for a believer (v. 4).

Sexual immorality and impurity (5:3a). One might think we are advanced in the twenty-first century. But when you read this, you see that we have the same sin issues faced by the first-century church.

Impurity is a broad word that refers to any type of filth. It is sometimes combined with sexual immorality, but when Paul says "any," it should not be limited to sexual sin (cf. 4:19). It basically means we should live lives of pervasive holiness, following the command, "Be holy, because I am holy" (1 Pet 1:16).

Sexual immorality is at the top of Paul's sin lists elsewhere. In the parallel text in Colossians, he states, "Therefore, put to death what belongs to your worldly nature: sexual immorality, impurity, lust, evil desire, and greed, which is idolatry" (Col 3:5; cf. Gal 5:19; 1 Cor 6:9-11). The word used here for sexual immorality is *pornei*, which Snodgrass defines as a "broad word covering any sexual sin" (*Ephesians*, 268). Scripture condemns particular types of sexual sin (homosexuality, fornication, adultery, bestiality) and also lustful thoughts (Matt 5:27-30).

People will try to work around this teaching of Scripture, but remember what Paul says: there should not be even a hint of sexual immorality in a believer's life. Paul's words are clear. You were darkness. Now you are light. Become what you are!

We must resist the temptation to *rename* sin. Popular illustrations of this abound: "It's for mature audiences" or "The Gentlemen's Club." We must not *redefine* sin. We often hear, "If it feels good, it must be good." We must not merely try to *manage* sin. I saw an in-flight magazine promoting a particular club this way: "It's just the right amount of wrong."

God's people must seek to *kill* sin (Col 3:5) and *flee* from sin (1 Cor 6:18; 1 Thess 4:3).

Ultimately, *pornei* is idolatry. Much of the ancient world had sexual practices wrapped up in their idolatry (as in Ephesus). Paul does not specifically call *pornei* "idolatry" as he does with the sin of greed, but sexual sin is the result of not honoring God. Paul shows us this progression in Romans 1:18-32. Your life is an overflow of your heart. Your sexual sin problem is fundamentally a worship problem. To be clear, the Bible is not antisex. Rather, it is pro-intimacy within the covenant of marriage. But if you do not get the worship problem solved, you will never enjoy the beautiful gift of sex the way God intended.

Though this is not a new sin, the fact is, pornography is more accessible today than ever. Some have told me that it is regularly played on the TVs where they work. It is viewed in the dorms at universities. Pornography is viewed on the smart phones of middle-school boys as they sit in the cafeteria before class begins. It is everywhere. Paul's words are timely and timeless.

We should add that churches should be known for restoring those who have fallen into deep sexual sin. However, people cannot have healing apart from repentance. Repentance involves acknowledging the sin, believing that you need to change, experiencing the grace of Jesus, and then changing your life. Let us humbly repent and call others to repentance.

Greed (5:3b). Greed (or covetousness) is the insatiable desire for more. Paul identifies it as idolatry in verse 5 and in Colossians 3:5. The tenth commandment addresses coveting (Exod 20:7). Breaking this commandment means you are not keeping the first commandment, "Do not have other gods besides Me" (Exod 20:3).

So greed is about the heart. It is about desiring something more than God. Jesus told His followers to "watch out and be on guard against all greed" and not to become a rich fool (Luke 12:15-21). Perhaps Jesus had to tell us to "watch out" because none of us thinks we are greedy. Greed is sneaky.

I once heard Tim Keller describing a sermon series that he decided to present on the seven deadly sins. His wife predicted, "Your lowest attendance will be for the message on greed." Keller said she was correct. And of those who did show up for the greed sermon, no one was observably moved or upset. Why? It is because few think the topic applies to them. Keller went on to say that no one has ever confessed, "Pastor,

greedy" or "I think I love money too much." Why? Is it
is guilty or because we are not "watching out" for this
blind spot. I think we know the answer. In materialistic cultures greed is
the air breathed. We must seek to put this idol to death.

Jesus' command is to delight in God and store up treasure in heaven
(Luke 12:32-34). Echoing these words, Paul states, "But godliness with
contentment is a great gain" (1 Tim 6:6). The apostle says greed kills
(1 Tim 6:9-10) and the rich should not "set their hope on the uncer-
tainty of wealth, but on God, who richly provides us with all things to
enjoy" (1 Tim 6:17).

Ultimately, the god of money will not satisfy. It is empty. The call
is for believers to find their satisfaction in God alone. Christians are to
make money, thank God for money, and use money for the right purposes while worshiping God alone.

Corrupt speech (5:4). Christians must also avoid "coarse and foolish
talking or crude joking." Those walking in the light will not use language
that is shameful or disgraceful (cf. Col 3:8). Some suggest that "foolish
talking" may be associated with sexual sin and drunkenness (Thielman,
Ephesians, 330). And while there is nothing wrong with humor and
laughter, humor can be abused in malicious and vulgar ways. Therefore,
Paul forbids "crude joking."

Paul says that in place of corrupt speech, the Christian should be
known for "giving thanks" (cf. 1 Thess 5:18). Let us cultivate a heart of
gratitude and adopt a vocabulary of thanksgiving. Here again the issue
is worship. Thanksgiving, not sinful speech, will come out of your mouth
when gratitude fills your heart. Snodgrass says it well: "Thanksgiving is
an antidote for sin, for it is difficult [impossible] to both give thanks and
sin at the same time" (*Ephesians*, 276).

Sexual sin, greed, and corrupt talk are about self-centered ways of
thinking. We sin in these ways when we seek to gratify our sinful desires.
But thanksgiving is the attitude that says, "Thank You for Your generosity, Father. You have given me everything I need. I don't need to go looking to substitute gods for pleasure and joy."

Paul reiterates this note of thanksgiving in 5:18-21. He says thanksgiving is a result of the Spirit's work in the believer. Here is where we
find the power for replacing idols with true worship: the filling of the
Holy Spirit.

Warning (5:5-6). Paul says those who persist in this dark lifestyle
will not inherit the kingdom of heaven (cf. 1 Cor 6:9-10; Gal 5:19-21).

Hughes is instructive here: "Do Christians fall into these sins? Of course! But true Christians will not persist in them, for persistence in sensuality is a graceless state" (*Ephesians*, 159). Paul told the Corinthians, "And some of you used to be like this. But you were washed, you were sanctified, you were justified in the name of the Lord Jesus Christ and by the Spirit of our God" (1 Cor 6:11).

This warning emphasizes how foolish worldly pursuits are from a kingdom perspective. Consider Jesus' words: "For what does it benefit a man to gain the whole world and lose his life?" (Mark 8:36). Indeed, this warning is instructive to the believer as it calls him or her to pursue the kingdom and its righteousness over fleeting pleasures.

Paul strengthens his argument by speaking of the fate of the unrepentant: "Let no one deceive you with empty arguments, for God's wrath is coming on the disobedient because of these things" (Eph 5:6; cf. Col 3:6). Paul says God's wrath is coming on the unrepentant and people had better not listen to the scoffer who mocks God's judgment.

Believers have a God more satisfying than sexual sin and greed, a God worthy of endless thanksgiving, a God who has given them a kingdom. Worship the triune God alone, not cheap substitutes.

Exhibit the Fruit of Light (5:7-10)

Paul reminds us of our new identity and gives us four instructions on how we can exhibit the fruit of light amid darkness.

Display light by not joining those in darkness. He says, "Therefore, do not become their partners" (v. 7). To the Corinthians he says, "Do not be mismatched with unbelievers. For what partnership is there between righteousness and lawlessness? Or what fellowship does light have with darkness?" (2 Cor 6:14).

Paul calls Christians to be salt in society, to love and befriend those outside the faith. However, our mission does not involve participating in the sins of unbelievers. We must flee from, and not share in, the world's greed, sexual immorality, and corrupt speech.

Display light by living out your identity. He says, "For you were once darkness, but now you are light in the Lord. Walk as children of light" (v. 8). Snodgrass highlights the force of this statement: "No text is as strong in its explanation of conversion" (*Ephesians*, 271).

Paul makes an important distinction here: Christians are not light in themselves; they are light *in the Lord.* Because He is light and we are in Him, we are light. And because the Christian is light (a fact), we are now called to "walk as children of light" (an imperative). We are to pursue total holiness before the eyes of God, who has made us new people.

Display light by doing all that is good, right, and true. Paul says, "For the fruit of the light results in all goodness, righteousness, and truth" (v. 9). The phrase "fruit of the light" describes the result of dwelling in God's light. God is *good* and *right* and *true.* As His imitators, Christians are to do that which is good and right and true. Here this trio of virtues seems to be a summary of the ethical content previously covered in Ephesians and resembles the fruit of the Spirit. Those who walk in light do "good works" (2:10), they live righteously (4:24), and they speak truthfully (4:15).

Display light by pleasing the Lord. Paul says, "Discerning what is pleasing to the Lord" (v. 10). As a believer, you may not please everyone. You may be mocked for following Jesus. Some may think you are living in the Stone Age because you believe the Bible. But we must keep coming back to this fundamental question: What will please the Lord? Walking in the light pleases the Lord.

Expose the Darkness (5:11-14)

Paul goes on to say that believers must not only avoid participation in darkness but they must also actively expose the darkness. The latter is the positive counterpart to the former negative exhortation. Believers are to let their light shine as Jesus said and did (Matt 5:16). Notice two effects of shining the light.

Light exposes the sin of unbelievers. The word *expose* carries the idea of correcting or convincing someone. Walking in the light does not mean avoiding contact with people. It means living a holy life, and it means confronting darkness.

Though the text does not tell us how to do this specifically, it surely means with words and deeds. We need wisdom, discernment, gentleness, and courage to know how to confront and expose the works of darkness. Paul says the light illuminates darkness (these secretive and shameful deeds), as evil is seen for what it is. Here the life and actions of the believer expose the works of darkness in the world.

Verse 12 notes these works done in secret are too "shameful" to mention. Do not participate in that which is shameful. Expose that which is shameful, and live a life that is honorable.

Light transforms unbelievers into the realm of light. Paul says, "For what makes everything clear is light" (v. 14). This verse seems to speak of the transforming power of the light of truth and purity. O'Brien summarizes it well:

> The disclosure of people's sins effected through believers' lives enables men and women to see the sinful nature of their deeds. Some abandon darkness of sin and respond to the light so that they become light themselves. This understanding is confirmed by verse 8, which speaks of the transformation that had taken place in the readers' experience, and by the confession of 14b. (*Ephesians*, 372–73)

J. B. Philips's paraphrase is helpful: "It is even possible (after all, it happened to you!) for the light to turn the thing it shines upon into light also."

The believer is called to expose the darkness in the corrupt places of our world—like where young children are trafficked, enslaved, and forced to work against their will, and where power is abused in other ways. We must bring the light of justice, exposing shameful, secretive sins, and bring the transforming light of the gospel to everyone—including the guilty enslavers themselves.

The last part of verse 14 is about the transforming light of Christ. It seems to combine passages on the resurrection and light such as Isaiah 26:19; 60:1; and Jonah 1:6. These words are probably a hymn or an early confession that was used at baptism. Those baptized would be reminded to "rise and shine." Paul says, "Get up, sleeper, and rise up from the dead, and the Messiah will shine on you" (v. 14).

To summarize 5:7-14, when awakened Christians, who were once darkness but are now light, shine the light of truth and righteousness in a dark world with their words and deeds, they make visible the shameful and secretive deeds of darkness; they may also be used to help those in darkness come to the light themselves.

Walk in Wisdom
EPHESIANS 5:15-17

In the same spirit of verses 7-14, believers must wake up and live wisely. Paul exhorts us to walk carefully, to make the most of our time, and to understand the Lord's will.

The verses that follow explain what it means to pay attention to how you walk. Those who walk carefully do not walk foolishly, like an unwise person. In the Colossians parallel Paul says, "Act wisely toward outsiders, making the most of the time" (Col 4:5), with speech that is "gracious, seasoned with salt" (Col 4:6). The believer is to "walk" in front of outsiders in hopes that they may see the life-changing power of the gospel.

"Not as Unwise People but as Wise" (5:15)

With regards to walking in wisdom, Proverbs is instructive (Prov 1:7; 9:10; 10:1; 12:15; 13:16,20; 14:16; 28:26). The fool lives recklessly. He flaunts folly, hangs with fools, and despises wisdom. The wise man, in contrast, values wisdom and pursues it diligently (Prov 2:1-5).

How does the believer gain wisdom? The writer of Proverbs tells us to walk with the wise in order to become wise (Prov 13:20). James says God gives wisdom if you ask for it (Jas 1:5; cf. Prov 2:6). Further, Paul states that in Jesus all the treasures of wisdom are found (Col 2:3). Jesus says fools build their lives on sand, but the wise build on the rock of His Word (Matt 7:24-27). Let us follow these instructions.

"Making the Most of the Time" (5:16)

Paul reminds the Ephesians that they, like us, are living in the last days. Therefore, how we live matters. This text calls us to identify the things that fritter our time away and to prioritize everything relentlessly.

Christians should make the most of their time because they do not want to waste their lives. The phrase "The days are evil" refers to the idea of "this present evil age" (Gal 1:4) in which all are living. We must passionately shine our light in this dark world while we have breath. When we see the King, we will not regret having spent our lives wisely.

"Understand What the Lord's Will Is" (5:17)

Usually when Christians talk about God's will, they are referring to God's will regarding major decisions about things like their careers. But I do not think that is what Paul has in mind here. He is referring to God's already revealed will, and for us today that means understanding the Bible.

Believers need to understand what God has called every believer to pursue and what He has called every believer to avoid. In short, understanding the Lord's will means to pattern our lives after Jesus (cf. Rom 8:29).

We should remember today that Christians are new creations because Jesus submitted to God's will. He cried out, "It is finished," after doing God's will obediently. He rescued those who did not love others perfectly, those who committed these dark, shameful deeds, and those who were living a life of folly. Now the Spirit indwells His people, enabling them to imitate God by walking in love, by walking in light, by walking in the Spirit. Let there be thanksgiving to God for His Son, Jesus.

Reflect and Discuss

1. Explain the relationship between Ephesians 1:5 and 5:1.
2. Paul commands us to love others as Jesus loved us (5:2). Does that seem like an unreachable ideal, or does Jesus' example give you hope?
3. How did Jesus model both horizontal and vertical love (v. 2)?
4. To walk in light we are called to exalt God, exhibit fruit, and expose darkness. What about these points resonates with you?
5. How would you explain to a youth Sunday School class that immorality, greed, and corrupt speech each amount to idolatry?
6. Explain the relationship between sin, God's wrath, and salvation in this passage. How can one escape the wrath of God?
7. What virtues and practices from this passage should we pursue as people of light?
8. What does it mean to expose the works of darkness (v. 11)? How might we do this today? How does the Holy Spirit provide wisdom and boldness for this task?
9. What does it mean to walk in wisdom (v. 15)? What are your sources for this kind of wisdom?
10. What does it mean to make the most of the time (v. 16)? Are you doing this?

A Spirit-Filled Marriage

EPHESIANS 5:18-33

Main Idea: Christian marriages flourish when husbands and wives are filled by the Spirit and reflect the picture of Christ's relationship to the church.

I. **Spirit-Filled Relationships (5:18-21)**
    A. Be filled by the Spirit (5:18).
    B. The effects of the Spirit (5:19-21)
        1. Singing (5:19)
        2. Giving thanks (5:20)
        3. Submitting (5:21)

II. **Spirit-Filled Wives and Husbands (5:22-33)**
    A. Spirit-filled wives (5:22-24) .
        1. The instruction (5:22-24,33)
        2. The illustration (5:23-24)
            a. This illustration gives us the ultimate picture of marriage.
            b. This illustration gives us the ultimate purpose of marriage.
            c. This illustration provides amazing hope for marriage.
    B. Spirit-filled husbands (5:25-33)
        1. Sacrificial love (5:25)
        2. Sanctifying love (5:26-27)
        3. Satisfying love (5:28-31)

We learn about our new life in Christ in Ephesians. One of the most important results of our new life is that we have new relationships. Sin separates us from God and people. But through Christ everything changes. Our relationships with one another are now different (2:11-22). Our relationships with our spouses are different (5:22-33). Our relationships with our children are different (6:1-4). Our relationships at work are different (6:5-9). And our relationship with this world is different (6:10-24). Let us consider the Spirit's work in relationships in general and in marriage in particular.

Spirit-Filled Relationships
EPHESIANS 5:18-21

Paul opens this section by reminding us of the fountain of healthy relationships, the Spirit. Paul made a connection between the Spirit and relationships already in Ephesians (4:1-3,17-32; 5:1-17; cf. Gal 5:16–6:10). He makes another important connection here in 5:18-21. After telling us to "be filled by the Spirit," Paul gives two "one anothers"—"speaking to one another" (v. 19) and "submitting to one another" (v. 21). Here is yet another New Testament example of how a Spirit-filled believer is a person who lives in right relationship with God and right relationships within the Christian community.

In addition, Piper explains how we should also link the Spirit's work to marital relationships:

> Verses 22ff. are clearly an extension and application of the principle in verse 21. We know this mainly from the grammar of the text. The command in verse 22, "Wives be subject to your husbands," has no verb in the original. It simply says, "Wives to your own husbands." Which means it is a continuation of verse 21. The flow of thought then from verse 18 to 22 would be: "Be filled with the Spirit . . . submitting to each other out of reverence for Christ, wives to your own husbands as to the Lord." So now it should be evident where I got my main point: *Christian family life is a work of God's Spirit.* The submission of a wife to her husband and a husband's love to his wife (vv. 22-33), the obedience of children and their nurturing by parents (6:1-4), the obedience of servants and the forbearance of masters (6:5-9) all are expansions of the principle in 5:21: "submitting to each other in reverence to Christ." And this submission in verse 21 is a description of how people act when they are filled with the Holy Spirit (v. 18). Therefore, all of Christian family life is a work of God's Spirit. ("Jesus Is Precious," emphasis in original)

Be Filled by the Spirit (5:18)

The wise person (v. 17) is not intoxicated by alcohol or anything else but is filled with the Spirit (v. 18). Grammatically, Paul gives two commands: "Don't get drunk with wine . . . be filled by the Spirit" (v. 18).

But the focus seems to be primarily on the latter command (O'Brien, *Ephesians*, 390).

Following these commands are five participles—addressing, singing, making, giving, and submitting—which I take as *evidences* or *results* of the Spirit. When the Spirit fills us, these graces are present in our lives; an overflow of joy is expressed in deep thanksgiving to God and glad-hearted submission to others.

> *The fundamental meaning of being filled with the Spirit is being filled with joy that comes from God* and overflows in song. And Luke would agree with that, too, because he says in Acts 13:52, "The disciples were filled with *joy* and with the *Holy Spirit*." To be sure, one of the marks of a person filled with the Spirit is that he is made strong to witness in the face of opposition (Acts 4:8, 31; 7:55; 13:9). . . . When you are happy in God, you are a strong and brave witness to his grace. So I repeat, whatever joy or peace you find in alcohol, the Spirit of God can give you more. Even the Psalmist of the Old Testament had experienced this [Ps 4:7-8]. (Piper, "Be Filled with the Spirit," emphasis in original)

It is never God's will for a Christian to be drunk; it is sin. Drunkenness also leads to other sins because it makes a person lose control. In contrast, the Holy Spirit makes us self-controlled and filled with a deep sense of joy. The Spirit makes you like Jesus, our model for self-control and all other virtues of the Spirit.

Paul commands all believers to be filled with the Spirit. This does not refer to a deeper life or a higher life, but the normal Christian life. What a great God to command exactly what we need! Paul desires for the entire congregation to be filled with the Spirit so that worship and mutual edification and service take place. While the Holy Spirit indwells believers forever (we are "sealed"), we need constant filling. Why? Because no one lives a life of constant joy and thanksgiving and love. We need the Spirit.

Put this in the context of marriage. *The Holy Spirit makes a person loving, forgiving, peaceful, self-controlled, gentle, and servant-hearted toward his spouse.* We need His help to live like this in all relationships, including marriage. When you get married, you learn how selfish you are! Do you think the type of sacrifice described in verses 22 and 25 is possible apart from the Spirit's help? No. Everything in us wants to fight against these exhortations.

And what about conflict? Do you need the Spirit's work to reconcile? Yes. One sinner is bad enough, but now two have become one! Marriage is difficult because both fall short of the glory of God. We need the Spirit for unity, harmony, and peace in marriage.

While Paul gives no formula for being filled with the Spirit, we can point out a few things. Believe in God (Rom 15:13). Be careful not to grieve the Spirit of God (Eph 4:30). Let me also encourage you to "let the word of Christ dwell in you richly" daily (Col 3:16 ESV). The Spirit and the Word go together, as one can see by comparing Ephesians 5:18-21 with Colossians 3:16. And keep asking the Father for a fresh sense of His Spirit, for He loves to give good gifts to His children (Luke 11:13).

The Effects of the Spirit (5:19-21)

Although some see these participles in verses 19-21 as imperatives (things we must do), it seems more precise to regard them as results describing "the overflow or outworking of the Spirit's filling believers" (O'Brien, *Ephesians*, 387–88). The result of the Spirit's work in our lives is renewed worship and renewed relationships. Interestingly, the idea of being "filled with the Spirit" appeared in Exodus 31, when the craftsmen constructed the tabernacle for worship. God still fills His people to serve and worship.

Singing (5:19). We are a singing people because God is too great to merely be talked about. We are not just to think of His grace and speak of it; we are to feel it and rejoice in it.

It is difficult to know exactly what Paul meant by these three types of songs in Ephesians. He says that we should sing "psalms" (from the Psalter), "hymns" (perhaps like those in Rev 4–5), and some "spiritual songs" (perhaps spontaneous praise from the heart, like 1 Cor 14:15 implies). I think the reason for these different types of songs may be that God is "infinitely varied in his beauty and he meets us in various ways" (Piper, "Singing and Making Melody"). There are different seasons of life and different songs for the seasons.

Our singing clearly has horizontal and vertical dimensions. We sing "to one another" and "to the Lord." O'Brien is instructive here when he says Paul is not teaching two different responses of singing—to one another and to God—but rather, he "is describing the same activity from different perspectives" (*Ephesians*, 394). Remember this: When we gather for corporate worship and to sing to God, we are also ministering to one another.

Did you know that you have a responsibility in corporate worship? You encourage each other through singing. You also instruct one another through singing. Musical worship is take-home theology.

It is clear from this passage why corporate worship is important. Why not curl up on a Sunday with a box of chocolates and watch a worship service on a computer or TV? Because that does not allow you to do what this verse is teaching. Vertically, the Spirit prompts us to sing with our whole being to the Lord Jesus; we should do so horizontally, in the presence of other believers.

These two participles belong together: "singing and making music." How is this done? Paul says, "From your heart." I am glad Paul says to make melody with our hearts, not our voices! Does your heart sing? Those who are filled with the Spirit sing to Jesus because there is no one more worthy of adoration.

Regarding marriage, here is another important lesson. *Do not go looking to your spouse for something that only Christ can give you.* It is not fair to your spouse, and it is idolatry. You must answer the big questions in life—why do you exist, and who are you in Christ? When you realize God created you for His glory and your ultimate identity is in Christ, then you will not demand something from your spouse that is impossible for him to give. Sing first to the Lord. Let there be an inner music to Him. Realize He is what your heart really needs. Then out of that song, go love and delight in your spouse. If you do not make inner music to Him, you will not be happy in marriage or in singleness.

Giving thanks (5:20). The next result of the Spirit's filling is constant gratitude to God (cf. Phil 4:6-7; Col 3:16-17). Paul may have corporate worship in mind here as well (Thielman, *Ephesians*, 362). All humans are to give thanks (Rom 1:21; 2 Thess 1:3; 2:13), and thanksgiving is an essential part of corporate worship (1 Cor 14:16-17); it's particularly seen in the Lord's Supper (1 Cor 11:24).

Are you known for ongoing thanksgiving or for complaining, murmuring, and pouting? Spirit-filled believers are thankful people, not complaining people. When we consider what God has done for us in the previous chapters of Ephesians, how could we not live with constant gratitude for His amazing grace?

Submitting (5:21). The final effect of the Spirit's fullness mentioned here involves submission. This particular result is important because the idea of submission recurs in the following sections (5:22–6:9, esp. 5:22-33). Before speaking of it in marital, parental, and vocational relationships, Paul points out that we should submit to one another in the church.

This is so important because some people have sensational ideas about the Spirit's work. But here we see that the Spirit leads us into community, where practical acts of love are demonstrated (cf. Gal 6:1-5). The Spirit enables you to do what is not natural, namely, love and submit to people. A further practical note worth mentioning is this: You can be sure that if a person is acting brashly, arrogantly, or in a self-assertive way, they are not walking in the Spirit. Stott puts this well:

> The Holy Spirit is a humble Spirit, and those who are truly filled with him always display the meekness and gentleness of Christ. It is one of their most evident characteristics that they submit to one another. (*Ephesians,* 208)

The word *submit* means "to arrange under." It was used in the military to refer to the subordination of soldiers in an army to those of a superior rank (O'Brien, *Ephesians,* 399). Good soldiers surrender control. They turn loose of their selfish agendas and live in submission and for the good of others. So it is with the Christian.

Christian leaders also humbly serve others. Thielman says, "There is a sense in which even those in authority 'submit' to their subordinates" (*Ephesians,* 373). For example, Paul said that he was a "slave to everyone" (1 Cor 9:19) that he might win some. Husbands serve their wives humbly and tenderly and are even called to die for their brides. Spirit-filled leadership involves humility, as demonstrated by Jesus, the greatest of all leaders.

See the motive: Christians submit to one another "in the fear of Christ" or out of reverence for Christ. This is an indirect statement of the deity of Jesus, the Lord. We submit to others because Christ is the ultimate authority over our lives. This does not mean believers live in terror of Christ. It means they stand in awe of Christ, who is the King and Judge. Believers stand in awe not only of His holiness but also of His forgiveness (Ps 130:4).

We belong to Christ's kingdom. He is the King. Out of reverence for Him, we gladly submit to His rule and serve others with compassion.

Spirit-Filled Wives and Husbands
EPHESIANS 5:22-33

We could write an entire book on this passage of Scripture. I highly recommend Tim Keller's book *The Meaning of Marriage*, which treats this passage in great detail. I have chosen to hit the highlights of the text and magnify the need for the Spirit's work in marriage. Paul exhorts the wives (vv. 22-24) and then the husbands (vv. 25-30). He concludes with a few important summary statements and reflections on the glorious mystery of marriage (vv. 31-33).

This passage is especially important in light of our present culture. The foundation for marriage is crumbling. People are confused about gender, marriage, and family. Some are outright hostile to the historic Christian view on marriage. Köstenberger and Jones put it well:

> For the first time in its history, Western civilization is
> confronted with the need to define the meaning of the terms
> "marriage" and "family." What until now has been considered
> a "normal" family, made up of a father, mother, and a number
> of children, has in recent years begun to be viewed as one
> among several options. (*God, Marriage, and Family*, 25)

This is not simply a cultural war; it is a spiritual war. The enemy would love to confuse people and tear down the foundations of God's plan for marriage.

What is the biblical idea of marriage? Stott summarizes it well:

> Marriage is an exclusive heterosexual covenant between one
> man and one woman, ordained and sealed by God, preceded
> by the leaving of parents, consummated in sexual union, issuing
> in a permanent mutually supportive partnership, and normally
> crowned with the gift of children. (*Involvement*, 163)

In addition to affirming the goodness of marriage (and singleness, see 1 Cor 7), we need to affirm the covenant nature of marriage: it is permanent, sacred, intimate, mutual, and exclusive. We should realize that Christ, not marriage, is ultimate. Our primary loyalty must be to Jesus. While we must, by the Spirit's help, nurture our marriages, we must also remember the fleeting nature of marriage. Marriage in this life is a shadow of the ultimate marriage of Christ and His bride, as Paul illustrates in this text.

Paul does not provide an exhaustive theology of marriage here, but he does touch on the key responsibilities of husbands and wives and gives us an amazing analogy of Christ and the church. Single people do well to consider these exhortations as they prepare for marriage, and married people do well to listen prayerfully to God's Word in order that they may have a marathon marriage.

Spirit-Filled Wives (5:22-24)

Paul begins with wives. While many struggle with the idea of wives "submitting," we have already noted that the whole of Christian life is about submission. Remember that the wife is called to submit to a husband who is willing to die for her! The husband should be the first to apologize, forgive, and serve. He is to exemplify the lifestyle of Jesus to his bride. Köstenberger says,

> While some may view submitting to one's husband's authority as something negative, a more accurate way of looking at marital roles is to understand that wives are called to *follow their husband's loving leadership*. (*God, Marriage, and Family*, 73, emphasis in original)

We see a picture of the husband and wife having equal value, yet having different roles within marriage. You might compare it to a slow dance. One person leads, and one follows. One initiates, and the other responds. Both are necessary for the dance to happen. And when both fulfill their roles well, it is a beautiful thing to behold.

Further, whenever we have trouble with God's Word, we need to remember that God is infinitely wise and good. Anything He says is for our good and is the best possible plan. Many things in God's Word may cause us to react negatively, but always consider the nature of the God giving these commands.

When you think about marriage, and particularly headship, you have to remember that this is rooted in creation (Gen 1–2; Matt 19:4-6; 1 Cor 11:3-12; 1 Tim 2:11-13). Stott says, "This is not chauvinism, but creationism" (*Ephesians*, 221). Paul does not have an agenda against women. In fact, he elevated women, as Jesus did.

The instruction (5:22-24,33). What does Paul say? He says the wife must revere Christ through proper submission to and respect for her husband (vv. 22-24,33; cf. Col 3:18). The role of the wife is clear: submission and respect.

Let us take "respect" first (v. 33). The better word for this is "fear" (cf. v. 21). However, it does not mean terror but awe. Why did Paul use this term? I am not sure, but one reason surely is that the husband will give an account to God for his leading of the family. Both should stand in awe of that assignment. On a practical level the husband needs the wife's respect. Typically, women crave love; men desire respect. The wife should see the responsibility her husband has and respect him, love him, pray for him, and respect his needs.

The word *submit* creates more discussion (v. 22). This is not the only place "submission" is noted in the context of marriage. This is consistent with the New Testament's teaching (Col 3:18; 1 Pet 3:1; 1 Tim 2:11-13; Titus 2:4-5; cf. 1 Cor 11:3).

Notice Paul does not say wives submit to every man. The husband is the head of the wife (v. 23), not of all women. Also, notice that this submission is voluntary submission (see O'Brien, *Ephesians*, 411–12). This is a happy relationship. Christian wives freely and responsibly follow the loving leadership of a faithful husband, not a tyrant.

We must reject all improper caricatures of this teaching. Scripture is not talking about something akin to slavery, subservience, or of a top-down chain of command, where the subjects have to obey without question. The picture is not that of a man lying on the couch saying, "Bring me the pretzels."

One might wonder, Why are women called to "submit" and husbands called to "love"? Why not call the wives to love? I think Stott is right:

> The wife's submission is but another aspect of love. . . . What
> does it mean to "submit"? It is to give oneself up to somebody.
> What does it mean to "love"? It is to give oneself up for
> somebody. (*Ephesians*, 235)

To submit is to put the will of the other ahead of your will. To love is to put the needs of the other ahead of your needs. Paul elsewhere actually mentions both actions to wives: "So they may encourage the young women to *love their husbands* and to love their children, to be self-controlled, pure, homemakers, kind, and *submissive to their husbands*" (Titus 2:4-5, emphasis added).

Paul says the motive of godly, loving submission is this: "as to the Lord" (v. 22). Wives submit to their husbands because they want to glorify Christ (cf. 5:21; 6:8-9). The godly wife sees this duty as part of her

Christian discipleship. The motive is not to fulfill some societal role or cultural expectation. The motive is love for Christ and a desire to be conformed to His image.

What does submit "in everything" mean? It means submit in every area of life. It does not mean she follows him in matters that are sinful.

We should also point out that there is a difference in a "traditional marriage" and a biblical marriage (Köstenberger, *God, Marriage, and Family*, 74). In a traditional marriage, a certain type of division exists. Women are often responsible for cooking, cleaning, doing laundry, etc., while men are working and earning an income. While Scripture does speak of a man working outside the home as his primary responsibility and the home as the center of a woman's activity (though not limited to the home; Prov 31:10-31), "the Bible is not a law book that exacts the division of labor" (ibid.). There is freedom in Christ—freedom to work out the best way to live out the biblical guidelines. As long as Christlike headship and loving submission are practiced, it would be OK for the wife to make more money than the husband or for the wife to "bring home the bacon" while the husband is in school or injured. Further, the husband may be a better cook! A biblical marriage does not always mean a traditional marriage. The couple should simply yield to the pattern of the husband serving as the head and the wife as the helper, submitting to the loving leadership of her husband. And the two should strive to prayerfully apply this pattern faithfully in their own situation.

The illustration (5:23-24). Paul speaks of marriages as a picture of Christ's love for the church in verses 23-24, and carries it into verses 25-32. Paul shows us that marriage displays the gospel. The Old Testament also illustrated God's love for His people with a marriage. In this text it is Christ and the church specifically. In verse 32 Paul says this picture is "profound." It is awesome. In creation God had Christ and the church in mind. Consider three applications of this picture.

This illustration gives us the ultimate picture of marriage. Wives give a picture of the church to the world (v. 24). Husbands give a picture of Christ to the world (v. 23). Christ is the head, as noted in 1:22. But look what kind of head He is. Peek into the next paragraph and consider the five actions of His leadership: He loved the church (5:25); He gave Himself up for her (v. 25); He sanctified her (v. 26); He cleansed her (v. 26); He presented her (v. 27); and He "provides and cares for" the church (v. 29).

This illustration gives us the ultimate purpose of marriage, namely, the glory of Christ. Everything in this passage points us to Christ: "as to the Lord" (v. 22); "as Christ loved the church" (v. 25); "as Christ does for the church" (v. 29). Everything comes back to Christ.

While it is important for couples to work through communication problems, financial problems, personality issues, the past, and other issues, let us remember that the ultimate issue in marriage is this: Are you surrendered to the lordship of Christ? Will you submit to Him in all areas of life? If the starting point for marriage is me, then I am starting at the wrong place. Marriage exists for Christ's glory. Let your marriage be an offering of worship as you love each other, forgive each other, serve each other. Let your relationship serve as an aroma of Christ before a watching world.

This illustration provides amazing hope for marriage. Christ died for the church, which displayed her sinfulness and His saving grace. The biggest problem in marriage is sin. The ultimate solution is the grace of Jesus. Because marriage is not merely a social convention but is rooted in the lordship of Christ, who is gracious, you have great hope in marriage! Where do you turn when marriage is difficult? Alcohol, deer hunting, work, pornography? No! Those are the wrong places! Look to Christ. Marriage is intended to point us to our Redeemer.

Spirit-Filled Husbands (5:25-33)

Paul commands husbands to reflect Christ by loving their brides. We have already touched on this. We are called to love our wives as Jesus loved the church.

Sacrificial love (5:25). Christlike love is a Golgotha love. Christ's back was scourged. His hands and feet were nailed to the wood. A spear was thrust into His side. A crown of thorns was placed on His head—all because He loved the church.

Christ's sacrificial love is a foot-washing love. His headship is our model. He came to serve, though He was the head. We see in Christ authority coupled with unparalleled humility and love.

Men, marriage is a call to die. Dying to self may involve sacrificing your schedule and even good ambitions. It means giving yourself away for the good of your bride. It involves crucifying your flesh and resolving to be faithful to your bride, not yielding to the temptations of lust, anger, and pride.

Marriage is a call to serve. Christlike love takes initiative. Avoid being a passive husband. Actively love your wife (see 1 Cor 13). Christlike love involves not just service but also an appropriate Christlike attitude in serving (see Phil 2:5-11).

Sanctifying love (5:26-27). Paul says, "Cleansing her with the washing of water by the word" (v. 26). Some take this as ongoing sanctification, but I agree with O'Brien who says, "It is *positional* sanctification that is in view here, not progressive sanctification" (*Ephesians*, 422, emphasis added). That seems clear as Paul goes on to say, "He did this to present the church to Himself in splendor, without spot or wrinkle or anything like that, but holy and blameless" (v. 27).

Christ's cleansing happens by two agents: water and word. Some think "water" refers to baptism, but I do not think so. When Paul speaks of washing, he emphasizes the spiritual cleansing that takes place (cf. 1 Cor 6:11). The marriage imagery in Ezekiel 16:8-14 and the prenuptial bath in the Jewish customs may have influenced Paul. So there may be a secondary reference here to the bridal bath (O'Brien, *Ephesians*, 422). I take "the word" as the word of the gospel (see Eph 6:17). The word of the gospel is the means by which we receive spiritual cleansing. Christ cleanses His bride spiritually, and He does this through the word of the gospel (John 15:3; 17:17).

Does this have application for husbands? While a husband cannot atone for sins or cleanse anyone, there is a sense in which Christ's sanctifying work is a pattern for husbands. Practically, I think this means you should love your bride in a way to help her grow in likeness to Christ. Here is the question: "Is our wife more like Christ because she's married to us? Or, is she like Christ in spite of us?" (Hughes, *Ephesians*, 192).

Men, be concerned for her spiritual well-being. Be in the Word personally. Talk about the Word with her. Know how your wife is doing in theological knowledge, in the practice of spiritual disciplines, in her service in the local church, and in her relationships. Care for her soul. Do you know her fears, hopes, dreams, temptations, and disappointments? Shepherd her faithfully.

Satisfying love (5:28-31). After speaking of redemption as the pattern of love, Paul now refers to creation. He says husbands should love their wives "as their own bodies" (v. 28). The husband should provide, nourish, and care for his bride, just as he cares for himself (v. 29). Paul puts Genesis 2:24 underneath this directive, reminding the husband that the two have become "one flesh" (v. 30).

This directive for satisfying love may sound self-serving for the husbands or demeaning to the wives, but that is not the case. This directive makes perfect sense in light of the fact that the two have become one flesh. Just as you long to satisfy your own needs, husbands, satisfy your wife's needs. Just as you long for intimacy, joy, security, health, peace, companionship, and community, provide them for your bride also.

Husband, how are you doing at nourishing your wife (v. 29)? Are you physically nourishing her? Are you cherishing your wife (v. 30)? Are you admiring her and complimenting her?

I'll never forget one particular example of this type of love. Wayne Grudem, world-renowned theologian, was on faculty at Trinity University for 20 years. He served with scholars like D. A. Carson and Douglas Moo. They were the "Seal Team Six of Professors." But his wife suffered from fibromyalgia, a disease that causes pain to many muscle groups and for which there is no known cure. She had a difficult time walking up stairs and doing household work. They had prayed and tried everything, but there was no relief. Her pain was aggravated by cold weather and humidity. Chicago was not the most ideal place for her to live.

Some friends invited the Grudems to Mesa, Arizona, for vacation, and they learned that the warm dry climate was wonderfully helpful. They made a few trips and even rode bikes together there for first time in 12 years. Dr. Grudem told his bride, "I would like to move here, but there are no seminaries." A few days later they were flipping through the Yellow Pages and found Phoenix Seminary. Dr. Grudem called and asked if the school had any openings. The school was interested.

After much prayer and thought, Dr. Grudem began pondering the implications of Ephesians 5:28, that you should love your wife as you do your own body. He said, "If I were suffering like Margret, would I not want to move for the sake of my health?" The obvious answer was yes. But his bride did not want to move because she knew her husband had an influential role at a large, respected institution. So there they were. He wanted to move for her sake; she wanted to stay for his sake.

Finally, when Phoenix told him that they would give him a reduced teaching load with more time to write, Mrs. Grudem thought this was a wonderful incentive; the two began processing a possible move. Eventually she told her husband, "I'm going to trust you to make the decision." In the end she followed the loving leadership of her husband, who made a great sacrifice in order to nourish and care for his bride (Grudem, "Upon Leaving").

Husband, love your wife as your own body, even if it means sacrificing your career dreams. Nourish her. Cherish her.

God ordained marriage. Christ set the pattern for marriage. The Spirit empowers marriage.

The good news of the gospel is that Christ died for those who could not keep demands perfectly. And the good news is that the Spirit daily renews us and empowers us as we look to Christ for grace and mercy. This whole passage should cause us to rest and rejoice in our great groom, Jesus Christ. Spurgeon said of His love:

> This love of Christ is the most amazing thing under Heaven, if not in Heaven itself. How often have I said to you that if I had heard that Christ pitied us, I could understand it. If I had heard that Christ had mercy upon us, I could comprehend it. But when it is written that he actually *loves* us, that is quite another and a much more extraordinary thing! Love between mortal and mortal is quite natural and comprehensible, but love between the Infinite God and us poor sinful finite creatures, though conceivable in one sense, is utterly inconceivable in another. Who can grasp such an idea? Who can fully understand it? Especially when it comes in this form—"HE" (read it in large capitals) "loved *me*, and gave Himself for *me*"—this is the miracle of miracles! ("Christ's Love to His Spouse," emphasis in original)

Dwell on the love of Christ daily, as you seek to live out a Spirit-filled marriage.

Reflect and Discuss

1. Do you consider singing to be the key to worshiping together? Which is more important to you, singing from the heart or singing well? Explain your answer.
2. What are some practical ways you could submit to other Christians?
3. Why is it important to think about the role of the Spirit when discussing marriage?
4. What does it mean to "be filled with the Spirit"? What are the effects of this?
5. Why do some react negatively to Paul's instruction to wives? How would you answer their objections to the concept of "submitting"?

6. How does the illustration of marriage as a picture of Christ and the church give purpose and hope for marriage?
7. How is a husband called to love his wife?
8. How might a husband display "sacrificial love" practically?
9. How might a husband display "sanctifying love" practically?
10. Stop and pray for your own marriage or for the marriages of others.

Gospel-Centered Families

EPHESIANS 6:1-4

Main Idea: Paul provides instructions for the Christian household, covering matters of honor and discipleship.

I. **Value and Care for Children.**
II. **Set a Christ-Centered Example for Your Children.**
III. **Children, Honor and Obey Your Parents in the Lord (6:1-3).**
   A. Honor your parents.
   B. Obey your parents.
IV. **Make Disciples of Your Children (6:4).**
   A. Two challenges
      1. Do not provoke them to anger.
      2. Bring them up in the discipline and instruction of the Lord.
   B. Give them Jesus.
   C. A word of hope

I will never forget a story my friend Dr. Chuck Quarles shared at a pastors' conference a few years ago while expounding Colossians 3:18-21. A well-known biblical scholar invited Dr. Quarles to lunch one time. Dr. Quarles told this scholar he was extremely inspired by his productivity as a thinker and writer, and he went on to ask, "I'm amazed by your work. How did you manage to be so prolific?"

This theological heavyweight mumbled under his breath, "I sacrificed my son."

"I was stunned by his words," Dr. Quarles said. He thought he misunderstood him, so he asked again, "What did you say?"

The scholar replied (almost angrily), "You heard me! I said I sacrificed my son!"

Dr. Quarles said this scholar added that he had been so driven to research, write, publish, and make a name for himself in the academic world that he neglected his family. His son essentially grew up as a stranger to his father. Now, as an adult, his son was a homeless man, sleeping on the streets.

Dr. Quarles tried to comfort him: "I'm sure that's not your fault."

Even more angrily the scholar replied, "Don't you try to console me. . . . Yes, I did that! Even though people seem to be amazed by my productivity as a scholar, the fact is, I would give up every one of those books and far, far more just to have my son back!" Then this prolific writer looked across the table, straight into the eyes of Dr. Quarles, and said, "Just in case you want to walk in my footsteps, know that I pray to God you won't."

This conversation echoed in Dr. Quarles's mind for the next few weeks. He was so haunted by it that he began to take a close look at his own life as a husband and father. Dr. Quarles said, "I was blowing it." That conversation led him to consider his own priorities and adjust his lifestyle. It ultimately led him to make a change in ministry roles and a change in a place of ministry. Dr. Quarles said, "I have never once regretted that radical change."

That story had a powerful effect on my life as well. It still does. Now, obviously, kids can grow up in great homes and turn out rebellious. I understand that. The point is, parents must seek to love, nurture, and disciple their children.

Paul continues with what scholars call "Household Codes"—that is, the duties between husbands and wives (5:22-33), parents and children (6:1-4), and masters and slaves (6:5-9). The structure may reflect a similar style as other groups of codes in Paul's day. Paul, however, infuses his instruction with theology. This is more than "Be a better parent and a better child!" Paul is bringing down to earth the rich gospel instructions he has already given in the previous chapters.

For those of you who are not yet parents, remember that the whole body of Christ helps train children. Paul seems to assume children are in attendance as this letter is read, along with others who may not be parents. This instruction is for everyone. If you are single, married with no kids, or married with moved-out kids, the kids at your church are, on one level, your kids. The church is a family (see 1 Tim 5:1-2). What this means is you should love them, pray for them, teach them, and serve them—while recognizing the parents have a unique, special calling to do this.

I want to point out four truths about the discipleship of our children. The first two are general observations; the last two are direct imperatives in the text.

Value and Care for Children

The fact that Paul mentions children in such an important letter demonstrates the value the early church placed on children. Leon Morris points out that it is significant that Paul wrote "children" not just "boys" (*Expository Reflections*, 192). Snodgrass says, "Girls were valued less in ancient society, but Paul did not accept such a limitation" (*Ephesians*, 322).

The early church had high regard for children. They carried on the legacy of Jesus who said, "Leave the children alone, and don't try to keep them from coming to Me, because the kingdom of heaven is made up of people like this" (Matt 19:14; cf. Matt 18:1-6). They also reflected the values of the Old Testament, which teaches the blessing of children and the need to instruct children (Ps 127; Deut 6:4-7).

Such values were countercultural. Many in the Greco-Roman world would put kids on the trash heap for people to pick up and often turn into gladiators, slaves, or prostitutes. But the church welcomed the children. Stott notes,

> It was a radical change from the callous cruelty which prevailed in the Roman Empire, in which unwanted babies were abandoned, weak and deformed ones were killed, and even healthy children were regarded by many as a partial nuisance because they inhibited sexual promiscuity and complicated easy divorce. (*Ephesians*, 238)

We too must value everyone made in God's image—regardless of ethnicity, background, gender, or age.

The church should joyfully celebrate the birth of children. We understand that the creation of life is the work of God. We understand that parents have a holy calling to be the primary disciple-makers of their kids. Bonhoeffer said it well: "It is from God that parents receive their children, and it is to God that they in turn ought to lead them" (*Letters*, 78).

Surely there is no greater joy and responsibility than to be entrusted with these little munchkins. It is like they come with a stamp: "Yours for a limited time only." They are like wet cement. We have a short time to teach and mold them.

The church should also value children by supporting foster care and adoption. The physical act of adoption reflects the spirit of adoption that we enjoy as children of our *Abba* Father. He pursued us when we were abandoned in the trash heap and has now made us to sit in the heavens. Once we were sons of disobedience, but now we are sons and daughters of God.

Let us also welcome the functionally fatherless into our lives and our homes. Recent reports note that 80 percent of African-American children in the U.S. are being raised apart from biological fathers; 60 percent of Hispanic and 50 percent of white children are in the same situation (Chapell, *Ephesians*, 316). Many kids have fathers or mothers living, but they are nowhere to be found. Help a disadvantaged kid get through school. Care for those in need in your neighborhood. Welcome that cousin or nephew who is in need of love and support.

Let us be the church, imitating God by caring for children. Hold out the hope of the gospel and practice gospel-centered hospitality, welcoming children as Jesus welcomed us.

Set a Christ-Centered Example for Your Children

Though Paul does not say, "Set an example for your children," in 6:1-4, this point is implied based on the previous chapters of Ephesians and by the focus on "teaching children." What are children learning? They are learning basic Christian living by watching their parents.

Paul has been addressing all Christians in the church in Ephesus. Many of those Christians were parents. One of the primary places they were to live out these instructions in the previous chapters was in the home. Children are observing their parents' own relationships to the Lord. They are watching them pray, study the Bible, and worship. They know if their parents are dazzled by God's grace or not.

Children are observing how their parents value the church. They are watching how their parents are speaking truth lovingly, working honestly, giving generously, encouraging others properly, putting away bitterness and anger repentantly, and forgiving one another Christianly (4:25-32).

The first picture of God children receive is from their parents. They will get a sense of authority, love, and protection from their parents. As they see and treasure this example, it will inevitably point them away from the parents to the ultimate Father. Even when you fail to reflect God before your children, you should teach them how to repent and receive grace from God.

Your example is influential. What are they seeing? Are they learning to value mission more than money? Faithfulness to God over career success? Are they learning humility and repentance, or hypocrisy?

They are also forming their view of marriage based on their parents' marriage. Give them a compelling vision. Remember you are giving your children a picture of the gospel as well as demonstrating how husbands and wives love each other. One of the best things you can do as a parent is love your spouse and stay together.

Finally, children are learning obedience, respect, and submission as they watch their parents submit to and obey God. This point is drawn from the immediate context also. A theme of submission and obedience and respect runs through 5:21–6:9. Parents are under God's authority, both in their roles to one another and in their roles as parents. Children are watching how we obey God.

Again, we all fail as parents. This does not make us bad parents; it simply means we need grace. Do not hide your need for grace, for that is part of the teaching experience too. Kids need to know that people fail in obedience, but there is One who did not fail. He stood in our place and gives us forgiveness and empowerment. They need to know Ephesians 1–3: in Christ, we are accepted, forgiven, redeemed, and made alive.

Children, Honor and Obey Your Parents in the Lord
EPHESIANS 6:1-3

Children were made by God to glorify God. This great purpose is partly lived out by honoring and obeying their parents in the Lord. When parents are instructing children in the ways of the Lord, then the child must honor and obey them.

Honor Your Parents

How should children honor their parents? One way is through a proper attitude. Children do not honor their parents when they huff and puff, pout, or talk back to them. When children dishonor their parents like this, they dishonor God Himself. We need to teach them that.

When God introduced His written law, the first horizontal relationship was mentioned in commandment five, "Honor your father and your mother" (Exod 20:12). Physically or verbally abusing your parents was a capital offense (Exod 21:15,17).

The command to honor father and mother appears in five other places in the New Testament (Matt 15:4; 19:19; Mark 7:10; 10:19; Luke 18:20). This further highlights the importance of this command.

A child that does not grow up with honor and respect of parents will likely not honor and respect others in general.

Those of us with older parents should also honor our parents. We should show proper respect to them and give special care to them when they get older (see 1 Tim 5:4).

Obey Your Parents

How should children obey their parents? Children obey their parents by hearing and doing what their parents say. Listen to what Paul says to the Colossians: "Children, obey your parents in everything, for this pleases the Lord" (Col 3:20). If children want to please the Lord, then they must obey their parents. Obeying their parents is one way they can obey the Lord.

Children will have a difficult time obeying their parents. When they fail, they need to be reminded that Jesus died for sinners who disobey God. Make their disobedience an occasion to teach the gospel. Parents know that children do not have to be taught disobedience. They need to be taught the gospel. Remind them of Ephesians 5:18, which casts light on the previous verses and 6:1-4. Tell them the Spirit enables them to obey.

Why should children obey their parents? Paul provides some reasons. First, he says, "Because this is right" (v. 1). That seems unnecessary to state. However, I think it is worth saying because one might be tempted to think, "Should I really require obedience? Look how cute she is!" Maybe she is, but requiring obedience is still the right thing to do. Stott comments,

> Child obedience belongs to the realm which came in medieval theology to be called "natural justice." It does not depend on special revelation; it is part of the natural law which God has written on human hearts. It is not confined to Christian ethics; it is a standard of behavior in every society. Pagan moralists, both Greek and Roman, taught it. Stoic philosophers saw a son's obedience as self-evident, plainly required by reason and part of the "nature of things." (*Ephesians*, 238–39)

Second, Paul gives a motivating promise (v. 2). God promises both *blessing*: "That it may go well with you," and *safekeeping*: "That you may have long life in the land" (Chapell, *Ephesians*, 313). Paul combines Exodus 20:12 and Deuteronomy 5:16. The original promise to Israel involved a long and good life in the land of Israel. Paul omits the focus on Israel and makes the statement more general and proverbial.

Of course, this does not mean that by obedience to one's parents the child may never get sick or even tragically die. Paul is basically saying that the child is endangering himself by dishonoring his parents. Great spiritual blessings always come by obeying God's Word. Children, obey and honor your parents in the Lord.

Make Disciples of Your Children
EPHESIANS 6:4

Notice how the parents are identified throughout these verses: "Obey your *parents*" (6:1, emphasis added); "Honor your *father and mother*" (6:2, emphasis added); "*Fathers* . . . bring them up" (6:4, emphasis added). The word translated "fathers" is a word used in Hebrews 11:23 to refer to both parents. Paul could have both parents in mind, but more likely he is turning attention to fathers (Snodgrass, *Ephesians*, 322). Nevertheless, we can apply verse 4 to both parents in general, giving special attention to fathers in particular.

It is certainly best for both parents to be present in the lives of their kids. It is not the job of a day care, nannies, an institution, or grandparents to raise children. It is the parents' job. Big homes, nice cars, and long vacations are not worth neglecting your kids. This requires spiritual discipline on the part of the parents, maybe especially on the part of dads. It may call for an adjustment of one's lifestyle.

Are you conscious of your time and attention with your children? I have learned a lot from pastors because that is what I am. I read where John Piper took one of his children out to lunch every Saturday and asked the child questions. Before I had children, I noted how Pastor Mark Driscoll described having daddy-daughter dates. I try to keep these on a regular basis now. These dates normally involve good food and good conversation followed by something fun.

Both parents need to teach the kids. While the father bears primary responsibility for training and instruction, both share in the task of making children disciples of Jesus. In Proverbs, the writer says,

My son, keep your father's command,
and don't reject your mother's teaching.
Always bind them to your heart;

> *tie them around your neck.*
> *When you walk here and there, they will guide you;*
> *when you lie down, they will watch over you;*
> *when you wake up, they will talk to you.* (Prov 6:20-22; cf. Prov 1:8)

Paul told Timothy to hold fast to the instruction he received from his mother and grandmother (2 Tim 1:5; 3:14). Timothy seems to have had an unbelieving dad; fortunately, his mother and grandmother taught him.

Both parents should be united in raising the children, disciplining them, and teaching them. We should work toward sending consistent messages.

Two Challenges

Parents in general, and dads especially, have two particular challenges in raising children.

Do not provoke them to anger. In the ancient world fathers had absolute control and were sometimes harsh (Snodgrass, *Ephesians*, 32). Reports show that fathers sold their kids and could even kill them without being charged with a crime. As mentioned, many abandoned their children in the city.

Obviously, a mother can provoke a child to anger as well. But given the dominant nature of the father, it seems he has a particular tendency to do this. The father must be fair, loving, and consistent in attitude toward his child. Here are some possible causes of angering our children:

- Failing to take into account the fact that they are kids
- Comparing them to others
- Disciplining them inconsistently
- Failing to express approval, even at small accomplishments
- Failing to express our love to them
- Disciplining them for reasons other than willful disobedience and defiance
- Pressuring them to pursue our goals, not their own
- Withdrawing love from them or overprotecting them

What is the result of such actions? Children grow angry or, in the words of Colossians, discouraged. Paul says, "Fathers, do not exasperate your children, so they won't become discouraged" (Col 3:21). We should be aiming at encouragement, not discouragement!

Bring them up in the discipline and instruction of the Lord. Paul goes from a negative command to a positive command. Notice the three actions to which parents are called: bring up, discipline, and instruct.

The phrase "bring them up" does not really do justice to the notion expressed by the verb. Paul used this verb in Ephesians 5:29 in the sense of "provid[ing]," "nourish[ing]" (ESV), or "feed[ing]" (NIV). Paul basically says that dads should care for their children lovingly. Calvin said, "Let them be fondly cherished" (*Commentaries*, Eph 6:4).

Next, fathers are to "train" or "discipline" and "instruct" their children. "Instruction" carries the idea of teaching, counsel, admonition, or warning, and perhaps verbal instruction (Stott, *Ephesians*, 248). "Discipline" involves training, including punishment. Discipline is the word used in Hebrews 12 to refer to our Heavenly Father's discipline of us, which is "for our benefit" (Heb 12:5-11).

In light of what Paul has written about anger (Eph 4:26,31), such discipline must be under control. The type of instruction and discipline we are to give is "of the Lord." We are to teach Christian instruction and discipline in a way that honors the Lord.

Give Them Jesus

Earlier Paul said that "the truth is in Jesus" (4:21). Give your children Christ-centered instruction. As you walk with them, drive them places, play with them, and have meals with them, talk about Jesus! Talk about His incarnation, His death, His resurrection, and His lordship. Danny Akin advises parents well: "Have fun and talk about Jesus a lot." We are to lead our children to the truth that is in Jesus, ultimately so they may submit to the Lord Jesus. He is their highest good.

Speak to the hearts of your children as you teach them about Christ. Behavior flows from the heart (Prov 4:23; 23:26; Matt 12:34). Talk about values, beliefs, feelings, and motives. Talk about sin, repentance, grace, and the cross. Talk about becoming a new creation in Christ Jesus. Talk about the end for which they were created: to glorify God.

You will need to have dialogue, not just monologue, to do this. Ask them questions! Know what they believe or doubt. Know their fears. Discern matters of the heart (Prov 20:5). Speak to their hearts affectionately with lots of encouragement. Celebrate successes and small victories. Warn about the dangers of pride, laziness, and folly. And pray with them regularly.

When you speak to your children's hearts about the Savior, remember to teach them the biblical story line, not just biblical stories. Show them the hero of the Bible. In her amazing book *The Jesus Story Book Bible*, Sally Lloyd-Jones writes,

> Now, some people think the Bible is a book of rules, telling you what you should and shouldn't do. The Bible certainly does have some rules in it. They show you how life works best. But the Bible isn't mainly about you and what you should be doing. It's about God and what he has done.
>
> Other people think the Bible is a book of heroes, showing you people you should copy. The Bible does have some heroes in it, but (as you will soon find out) most of the people in the Bible aren't heroes at all. They make some big mistakes (sometimes on purpose). They get afraid and run away. At times, they are downright mean.
>
> No, the Bible isn't a book of rules, or a book of heroes. The Bible is most of all a Story. It's an adventure story about a young Hero who comes from a far country to win back his lost treasure. It's a love story about a brave Prince who leaves his palace, his throne—everything—to rescue the one he loves. It's like the most wonderful of fairy tales that has come true in real life!
>
> You see, the best thing about this Story is—it's true.
>
> There are lots of stories in the Bible, but all the stories are telling one Big Story. The Story of how God loves his children and comes to rescue them.
>
> It takes the whole Bible to tell this Story. And at the center of the Story, there is a baby. Every story in the Bible whispers his name. He is like the missing piece in a puzzle—the piece that makes all the other pieces fit together, and suddenly you can see a beautiful picture. (Lloyd-Jones, *Jesus*, 14–17)

A Word of Hope

Finally, in your communication and education you may feel insufficient. You are right. Parenting makes you desperate for God's help. Some days I think success equals keeping my children out of prison; on other days I think success is keeping myself out of prison!

But we take great comfort in Titus 2. Paul says the grace of God instructs us for godliness (Titus 2:12). While parents have this responsibility to train their children, God in His grace is working in their lives. Look to God for grace and strength. The psalmist reminds us of our desperate need:

> Unless the Lord builds a house,
> its builders labor over it in vain;
> unless the Lord watches over a city,
> the watchman stays alert in vain. (Ps 127:1)

Elyse Fitzpatrick quips, "The obvious difference between Paul and us is that Paul bragged about his weakness, and we try to hide it" (*Give Them Grace*, 150). Do not hide your weaknesses. Admit them. Go to God for help; His strength will be sufficient. Weak parents have a mighty Savior!

Reflect and Discuss

1. What motivation, goals, and hope do believers have when we care for children? How are they different from those of non-Christians?
2. Why is it important to set a Christlike example for your children? Pause and pray for God's help to live an exemplary life before them.
3. What does this passage teach about honoring parents? Taking into account the personalities of your children, what would be the best way to teach this principle to them?
4. How do the promises "it may go well with you" and "you may have a long life in the land" pertain to your children today?
5. Why would it be difficult to honor and obey one's parents in some situations? Describe a hypothetical or actual situation to illustrate your point.
6. What are some ways a parent might provoke his or her children to anger? How could those same situations be handled better?
7. Whose responsibility is it to disciple children? What can parents do to avoid having their authority undermined?
8. How might you teach your children the basic doctrines of the faith? Are you doing this?
9. Are you speaking the gospel to the hearts of your children? How might you do this more regularly?
10. As parents we have great hope. Explain our hope.

Transferring Masters

EPHESIANS 6:5-9

Main Idea: Paul gives instructions to slaves and masters, exhorting them to glorify Christ with proper attitudes, work ethic, and a deep awareness of Christ's lordship.

I. **Explanation: Understanding Slavery and Paul's Undermining of It (6:5-9)**
   A. The historical context for slavery
   B. Why we are opposed to slavery
   C. Paul's undermining of slavery (6:5-9)

II. **Exhortations: Paul's Christ-Centered Words to Slaves and Masters (6:5-9)**
   A. To slaves: Do your work as unto Christ (6:5-8).
      1. Glorify Christ by working respectfully (6:5a).
      2. Glorify Christ by working wholeheartedly (6:5b-6).
      3. Glorify Christ by working willingly (6:7).
      4. Glorify Christ by working expectantly (6:8).
   B. To masters: Treat your slaves as you would Christ (6:9).
      1. Practice mutuality.
      2. Avoid hostility.
      3. Live with Christ-centered accountability.
      4. Remember God's impartiality.

III. **Application: How This Passage Can Change Your Life**
   A. This passage should change the way we work.
      1. Employees: Work through Christ, like Christ, and for Christ.
      2. Employer: Lead through Christ, like Christ, and for Christ.
   B. This passage should change the way we relate to people.
   C. This passage should change the way we evaluate what is important.

What is your least favorite job of all time? I asked this question on Twitter and Facebook and received over 50 quick responses. One of my friends (and a fellow pastor) used to discard dead animals from the vet! One friend was an extermination technician, who crawled around little tight holes with snakes and other creatures. Another was a funeral home transporter, who picked up cadavers for his cousin in Norway. One friend was a portable toilet service worker; another sorted medical equipment boxes in a four-foot-high attic, scooting around in a wheel chair all day. Sewer line replacement workers, dog kennel cleaners, and excrement burners also replied.

Work is a gift from God. We should be thankful for work. But some jobs are not high on the desirability scale!

How can you find any meaning or fulfillment in your daily vocation—either for paid work or for unpaid work?

On one level you could say you work because people pay you. Right. No one has an addiction to cleaning septic systems or cleaning dog kennels. Often people pay others to do undesirable tasks. But something greater than money should motivate us.

This text shows us that we need to see Christ as the ultimate boss for whom we labor. Your job may stink, but the good news is *you can transfer masters without transferring jobs.* I do not mean that you will never have to transfer actual jobs but that in whatever job you have, the most important thing to know is that your Master is the Lord Jesus!

Paul teaches us in this section of Ephesians that the lordship of Christ should affect our view of work. We can exalt Christ through our various jobs (both paid and unpaid jobs, both awful and wonderful jobs).

One of the blessings of the Protestant Reformation was a renewed emphasis on living out one's calling or *vocatio* ("vocation") to the glory of Christ. The reformers believed that one's vocation was the person's special calling, requiring God-given talents, and God Himself is active in daily labor, family responsibilities, and social dealings.

Martin Luther said that when we pray the Lord's Prayer, we should remember how God normally provides bread: through farmers, transporters, and retailers. God does not drop Krispy Kremes down from heaven. Every part of our economic food chain is the means by which God provides for us. Luther said,

> What is our work in field and garden, in town and house,
> in battling and in ruling, to God, but the work of children,
> through which He bestows His gifts on the land, in the house,
> and everywhere? Our works are God's masks, behind which

He remains hidden, although He does all things. ("Exposition of Psalm 147")

To say it another way, there really is no separation between secular work and sacred work. It is all work done under Christ. We need to understand this. Many see little to no connection between their faith and their job. But whatever you do as a Christian, you should do it as a servant of Christ, for the glory of Christ. In the words of the often-quoted Abraham Kuyper statement, "There is not a square inch in the whole domain of human existence over which Christ, who is Sovereign over *all*, does not cry, 'Mine!'" (*Centennial Reader*, 488, emphasis in original). Because it all belongs to Jesus, everything matters.

Slaves and Masters

Before we make specific application to our places of service, we have to talk about the original context of Ephesians 6:5-9, slaves and masters. Paul has been dealing with the ancient household, what scholars call "household codes." He has dealt with wives and husbands and then children and parents. This followed his statement about submission in 5:21. In each case responsibilities are described, with the principles of reciprocity and mutuality stated.

Now Paul turns his attention to his last and most difficult of subjects in the household. It is typical for pastors to jump directly to the application and make this text about employees and employers. While I think that is an appropriate application to make, we need to remember there is not a one-to-one correlation. Slaves do not equal employees. And if we move too quickly to employers and employees, we will miss another important application.

Further, if we move too quickly, we are bypassing the most obvious elephant in this passage, namely, Why didn't Paul outlaw slavery? As a church we fight human slavery. So, what should we make of this passage? In order to understand the text and apply it, let us consider it in three parts: explanation, exhortations, and application.

Explanation:
Understanding Slavery and Paul's Undermining of It
EPHESIANS 6:5-9

The situation Paul addressed was not like slavery in American history. It was complex and massive in scope. American slavery was primarily racial and lifelong. In Paul's day it was not racial, and it was not always lifelong. There were some similarities but it was different.

The Historical Context for Slavery

Some have estimated that in the Roman Empire there were 60 million slaves (Stott, *Ephesians*, 250), or one-third of the people in a city like Ephesus. It was an accepted part of the Mediterranean world's economic life. Snodgrass reports, "In the Greco-Roman world slavery was so much a part of life that hardly anyone thought about whether it might be illegitimate" (*Ephesians*, 327). He goes on to mention the nature of slavery:

> They did not merely do menial work; they did nearly all the work, including oversight and management and most professions. Some slaves were more educated than their owners. They could own property, even slaves, and were allowed to save money to buy freedom. No slave class existed, for slaves were present in all but the highest of economic and social strata. Many gained freedom by age thirty. (Ibid.)

In Lionel Casson's excellent book *Everyday Life in Ancient Rome*, the author looks at the Roman world in the first and second centuries. In his chapter on "The Slave" he provides some firsthand accounts of slavery. He summarizes the varied nature of slavery:

> There were multitudes of Greek and Roman slaves—the gangs in the mines or on the vast ranches—who lived lives full of hardship as the slaves on the sugar plantations of Brazil or the cotton plantations in the American south. But in the days of the Roman Empire there were also many, a great many, who were able to escape from slavery and mount the steps of the social ladder, in some cases to the very top. (*Everyday Life*, 64)

Consider the upward mobility of slaves in this illustration:

> "I was no bigger than this candlestick here when I came out of Asia Minor. . . . For fourteen years I was the master's little darling. The mistress' too. . . . The gods were on my side—I became the head of the household, I took over from that pea-brain of a master. Need I say more? He made me a co-heir in his will, and I inherited a millionaire's estate."
>
> The speaker was Trimalchio, the character in Petronius's novel, *The Satyricon*, who made it from the rags of a slave to the

riches of a billionaire. A slave becoming a master's heir and inheriting an estate worth millions? It seems unbelievable. Not in the Roman world in the first century, when Petronius wrote. He was, to be sure, a novelist not a historian, but his portrait of Trimalchio is based on reality. (Casson, *Everyday Life*, 57)

Casson describes white-collar slaves:

But there also fell to them much white collar work: they were clerks, cashiers, bookkeepers of Ancient Greece and Rome. And they manned not only the lower levels of such work but the upper as well. Banks were owned by wealthy Greek or Roman families, but the officers who were in charge of them could be slaves or freedmen. (Ibid., 58)

Slaves could obtain freedom:

[S]ince they were generous in granting manumission, particularly to the slaves who worked in their offices and homes, the white collar slave worker could be fairly sure of eventually gaining it. Moreover, manumission among the Romans brought with it a precious gift—citizenship. (Ibid., 60)

Casson goes on to mention Felix, who threw Paul into prison: "Pallas's brother who was the Felix who earned everlasting notoriety for throwing St. Paul into prison; he had risen from slavery to governorship in Judea" (ibid., 61). He adds that the father of the famous poet Horace had been a slave in the civil service. He earned his freedom, bought a farm, and eventually moved so that his son could receive a great education (ibid., 63-64).

What about women? Casson writes, "There were numerous female slaves in any large household serving as maids, hairdressers, masseuses, seamstresses, nurses and the like. Many earned manumission, but upward mobility was open to them through their husbands" (ibid., 62).

This little history tour shows that slavery in the Roman world was not like slavery in our recent history. However, the question remains, How did one become a slave? Snodgrass states, "People became slaves through various avenues: birth, parental selling or abandonment, captivity in war, inability to pay debts, and voluntary attempts to better one's condition. Race was not a factor" (*Ephesians*, 327).

Slavery in America was mainly racial and executed by self-righteous people. As one can see from the history of Roman slavery, while for many slaves life was harsh and cruel, "their circumstances depended on their owners" (Snodgrass, *Ephesians*, 327). So Paul's words to "masters" were important and life altering.

Why We Are Opposed to Slavery

At first glance the apostle is silent on this cultural issue. Do the biblical writers endorse slavery? The answer is no. Neither this passage nor other passages encourage the abuse of power or the mistreatment of human beings. Quite the opposite!

However, there seems to be a bit of silence about it. Why do Paul and other New Testament writers not call for abolition? Why do they not say more?

One answer is pragmatic, namely, that Christians were at first an insignificant group in the empire. Their religion itself was still unlawful, and they were politically powerless (Stott, *Ephesians*, 255).

Additionally, the apparent silence in Scripture was because so many slaves were freed constantly and easily. Some claim that between 81 and 49 BC, 500,000 Roman slaves were freed (Ruprecht, "Slave, Slavery," 458).

Further, conditions were changing in Rome during Paul's time. Stott says that humanitarian changes had been introduced by the first century (*Ephesians*, 256).

So these are some of the reasons Paul does not spend more time on the topic here in Ephesians. He is writing to give instructions about household relationships and responsibilities within a given society. His goal is not to write a document about changing the social structure.

With that said, the Bible clearly opposes the type of cruel slavery we think of today. I base this on a few obvious biblical convictions.

First, we are called to *love* our neighbor, not *own* our neighbor (Luke 10:27). Taking people against their will is vile, sinful, and the opposite of the Great Commandment.

Second, we are to treat others the way we would want to be treated (Matt 7:12). That would preclude being ripped from our homes and transported somewhere against our will to be abused by someone. Slavery is the opposite of the Golden Rule.

Third, neither *slavery* nor *masters* are ever viewed positively in the Bible. Israel was in awful slavery in Egypt, but God freed them. Then

God gave Israel strict laws insisting that they not treat others as they had been treated in Egypt (e.g., Exod 21:16).

Fourth, one of the pictures of the gospel is that of freedom from bondage. Jesus came to let spiritual captives go free. Being a prisoner is not viewed positively. Christianity is a release-the-captives faith (Luke 4:18).

Fifth, Paul's teaching and other New Testament teachings undermine slavery. They destroy it *from within*. While you may not be able to see it, biblical writers in general, and Paul in particular, are actually *not* silent about slavery. They just deal with it differently.

How did Paul undermine slavery? For starters, Paul tells us to imitate God (Eph 5:1). Who is God? The psalmist says God is "a father of the fatherless and a champion of widows" (Ps 68:5). He is a God of justice and compassion (Ps 146:9). He stands against oppressors and cares for the vulnerable. That is quite the opposite of slavery.

Paul also calls trafficking human beings a vile sin. In 1 Timothy chapter 1 Paul lists particular sins associated with the breaking of the Ten Commandments. The breaking of the eighth commandment ("Do not steal") is represented when he mentions "kidnappers," enslavers, or slave dealers (1 Tim 1:10), a word found nowhere else in biblical Greek. This sinful act of stealing a human was also forbidden in the expansion and application of the Ten Words (Exod 21:16). Paul (like the Old Testament) forbids this particular act of slavery explicitly. Paul speaks of appropriate conduct within an *existing social state* without condoning it (as in Eph 6:5-9), and in 1 Timothy 1:10 he forbids this act of enslaving others through kidnapping or trading.

Paul also undermines slavery by teaching equality among groups. This equality is clear in our text and others (e.g., Gal 3:28; Col 3:11). In Philemon, Onesimus fled from his master Philemon, then he providentially met Paul and became a Christian. Paul urges Philemon to receive Onesimus back "no longer as a slave, but more than a slave—as a dearly loved brother" (Phlm 16). Paul was redefining the relationship in a countercultural way. It reminds me of the line in "Oh Holy Night": "Chains shall he break, for the slave is our brother. And in his name all oppression shall cease." In Christ we are equals.

Further, Paul told Corinthian believers that if they could obtain their freedom, they should (1 Cor 7:21). He recognized the benefits of freedom, demonstrating that he was not a fan of slavery.

Paul's Undermining of Slavery (6:5-9)

Here in Ephesians, *Paul plants the seeds of the destruction of slavery, beginning with the Christian community.* It was subtle but powerful. Paul focused on spreading the gospel in a society that approved of slavery, and in so doing, he planted the seeds of the destruction of slavery. Stott says, "The gospel immediately began even in the first century to undermine the institution; it lit a fuse which at long last led to the explosion which destroyed it" (*Ephesians*, 257). Snodgrass adds, "These verses are still extremely subversive" (*Ephesians*, 323).

Paul's main concern is the spread of the gospel. But he also describes the ethics required between Christian slaves and Christian masters, thereby changing typical relationships between master and slave. By changing how they related to one another, he essentially planted the seeds for slavery's destruction.

How does he tell them to relate to each other?

He admonishes both slave and master to treat each other as they would Christ. Notice in each verse either "Christ," "Master," or "Lord" are mentioned. Snodgrass is instructive here:

That masters are to treat their slaves "the same way" is cryptic but still shocking. For them to follow this instruction, they would have to treat their slaves with respect and fear and with sincerity of heart as to Christ. *That alone should have abolished slavery for Christians!* . . . The ethics move beyond the Golden Rule . . . to treating others as we would treat our Lord. (*Ephesians*, 324, emphasis added)

Paul reminds both slave and master that they are under the lordship of Christ, and "there is no favoritism with Him" (v. 9). Paul does not quote the Mosaic Law. He could have. All you have to do is go to Exodus chapters 20 through 24, and you will find laws pertaining to masters and slaves. But he does not. What does he constantly come back to? Christ! Let me ask you, if both are living under the watchful eye of Christ, how would that change the work ethic of slaves or the treatment given by masters? It would change everything. They both were to live with awareness that Christ is the ultimate Master and Judge, and with Him there is no partiality. Ligon Duncan says, "That is the recognition that both master and slave in Christ have a common Lord and that truth, that reality, that doctrine eventually undermined slavery" ("Obligations").

Paul calls masters to show justice and reciprocity toward slaves. This idea was nowhere to be found in the legal code in Paul's day. Yet Paul says so here in Ephesians: "Masters, treat your slaves the same way, without threatening them" (v. 9).

Let us move on with this understanding: neither Paul nor other biblical writers endorse slavery; they undermine it. Slavery slowly died out in antiquity because of the influence of Christianity. There were slaves in the Ephesian congregation, but they were not second-class members. They were brothers and sisters, called to unity in Christ (2:11-22; 4:1-6). Paul considers the existing structure and provides some gospel-centered instruction to both slaves and masters that we should consider carefully now.

Exhortations:
Paul's Christ-Centered Words to Slaves and Masters
EPHESIANS 6:5-9

As we consider each verse in Ephesians 6:5-9, let us apply Paul's revolutionary words about slaves and masters.

To Slaves: Do Your Work as unto Christ (6:5-8)

In each of the four verses, Jesus Christ is mentioned:

- Verse 5—"as to Christ"
- Verse 6—"as slaves of Christ"
- Verse 7—"as to the Lord"
- Verse 8—"receive this back from the Lord."

The command is clear: Live all of life for Christ. While slaves were to obey their masters, they were to see Christ as the ultimate Master.

Paul basically urged servants to transfer masters, even if they could not transfer jobs. In 1 Corinthians Paul told the one in slavery that he was actually "the Lord's freedman" (1 Cor 7:22). By calling slaves to this Christ-centered perspective, Paul gave them a higher preoccupation than serving their human masters and freed them from the mundane.

With this overarching motive in mind, how exactly were they to glorify Christ in their work? Paul mentions at least four ways this exemplary service would look.

Glorify Christ by working respectfully (6:5a). Paul says they were to obey with "fear and trembling," which probably carries the same idea as

5:21, out of "fear of Christ." They were to work seriously and reverently because they were working unto Christ.

Glorify Christ by working wholeheartedly (6:5b-6). Notice the emphasis on the *heart* in these verses: "in the sincerity of your heart" and "do God's will from your heart." Paul urged the bondservants not to be hypocrites, just working when the boss was present: "Don't work only while being watched, in order to please men." While a common temptation for the master was threatening slaves, a common temptation for the servant was being lazy or lying instead of working faithfully. Both were to remember that Christ sees all things.

Glorify Christ by working willingly (6:7). Paul says they should "Serve with a good attitude," not with a begrudging spirit. He tells them to put their heart and soul into their work because, after all, they are doing "God's will" (v. 6). Paul encourages cheerful and glad service.

Glorify Christ by working expectantly (6:8). Paul reminds them that the ultimate reward is coming: "Knowing that whatever good each one does, slave or free, he will receive this back from the Lord." No act goes unnoticed. Believers will appear before the judgment seat of Christ and be rewarded based on present faithfulness (Matt 16:27; Rom 2:6-11; 2 Cor 5:10). Think about how this perspective would change the way one could work.

The writer of Proverbs says, "A man's spirit can endure sickness, but who can survive a broken spirit?" (Prov 18:14). If a person's spirit is crushed, life can become unbearable. What lifts the spirit? Christ! Future hope!

To Masters: Treat Your Slaves as You Would Christ (6:9)

Now let us notice four words Paul gives to Christian masters in just this one verse regarding their treatment of servants. These exhortations were countercultural and life changing.

Practice mutuality. Paul says, "Treat your slaves the same way." Masters were to treat their slaves as they wanted to be treated: with integrity, respect, humility, and gentleness. They were to treat them as if they were treating Christ (cf. Matt 25:40). If masters wanted respect and service, then they should give it also.

Avoid hostility. Paul says to oversee them "without threatening." This type of exhortation to masters would have been extremely rare. But Christian masters were to be different. They were not to bully or use aggression.

Live with Christ-centered accountability. Paul says, "You know that both their Master and yours is in heaven." Masters were to live with a fear of Christ. Proverbs speaks of this equal accountability of rich and poor: "The rich and the poor have this in common: the LORD made them both" (Prov 22:2). "The poor and the oppressor have this in common: the LORD gives light to the eyes of both" (Prov 29:13). The Lord is the Judge of all the earth, of every person (Prov 15:3). An awareness of this sobering truth changes the way we live.

Remember God's impartiality. He says, "There is no favoritism with Him." Partiality was written into the Roman law. But Paul says on the last day it will not matter. The Lord Jesus is utterly impartial. Roman law was discriminatory, but heavenly justice is not.

Each of these principles shortened the distance between servant and master. This way of life was radical.

Application:
How This Passage Can Change Your Life

Perhaps you have been thinking, "I'm not a slave. I don't have slaves. Can we just move to the next passage?" Not so fast. This passage is life changing if you apply it to your life. How so?

This Passage Should Change the Way We Work

No work is merely work. It is a way to serve Christ. Think about employees and employers. Can we make this application? I think so. If these principles applied in a sometimes awful working environment of slave-master, how much more should we seek to live them out in better working conditions? You say, "My job stinks." Maybe it does. But you are not being physically threatened or abused or treated like property. Remember, your boss is Jesus.

Employees: Work through Christ, like Christ, and for Christ. Break these down for a moment. **Work through Christ.** Remember that Paul is addressing the Christian church. These are believers in Christ who have been spiritually raised from death to life (2:4-7) and saved by grace (2:8) through the atoning death of Christ (2:13). As a result, they have the indwelling presence of the Holy Spirit. They, and we, do not live our lives, love our spouses, raise our kids, or work our jobs *alone.* The living Christ abides in us. So do your work through Christ.

In the Old Testament Joseph was sold into slavery, and he ended up working for Potiphar. In Genesis 39 four times it says that "the LORD was with Joseph" (Gen 39:2,3,21,23). He was not alone! Neither are you! Remember we noted that Ephesians 5:21 leads into 6:9, and 5:21 is built on 5:18, "Be filled with the Spirit" (ESV). We are to do our jobs by depending on the Spirit's power.

Question: Do you pray before you go to work? Do you pray for the Spirit to fill you and for God to use you as a missionary where you work? You should.

Work like Christ. Jesus gives us the model work ethic. As the Suffering Servant, Jesus humbled Himself and died for sinners. He took "the form of a slave" (Phil 2:7). He left glory to seek and save the lost (Luke 19:10). He came not to be served but to serve and to give His life as a ransom for many (Mark 10:45). As a working servant, Jesus was a carpenter or stone-mason. He worked hard in the dumpy little town of Nazareth. Here is the sinless Son of God, working a job until He was 30 years old. He was doing it unto the Father.

Think about these virtues Paul just mentioned. Jesus would have exemplified them. Would Jesus have disrespected a person while working? No. Would Jesus slack when no one was watching? No. Would Jesus ever bill someone for extra time? No. Was He a begrudging servant? No. Did He minimize His job? No. If you are a follower of Christ, then you should be exemplary in your service. You should not need supervision. Besides this, your workplace is a great place to make the gospel look good to nonbelievers, not turn them off (see 1 Thess 4:11-12; Titus 2:9-10).

Work for Christ. You should do your best, as if you were doing it for Jesus. Spurgeon said,

> Did anybody thus dream of supervising Raphael and Michelangelo to keep them to their work? No, the master artist requires no eyes to urge him on. Popes and emperors came to visit the great painters in their studios, but did they paint better because these grandees gazed upon them? Certainly not! Perhaps they did all the worse in the excitement or the worry of the visit. They had regard to something better than the eyes of pompous people. ("Our Motto")

Spurgeon said this reality should lift our spirits, keep us from complaining, and keep us from becoming lazy. Stott puts it this way:

It is possible for the housewife to cook a meal as if Jesus Christ were going to eat it, or to spring-clean the house as if Jesus Christ were the honored guest. It is possible for teachers to educate children, for doctors to treat patients and nurses to care for them, for shop assistants to serve customers, accountants to audit books and secretaries to type letters as if in each case they were serving Jesus Christ. (*Ephesians*, 252)

You should also do your work for Christ now but realize that you will receive a reward from Christ later. Many Christians do not meditate on this. They think, "Our works don't matter." True, Jesus' work saves us, not our works. However, God saved us to do good works (Eph 2:10), and rewards will be given based on our faithfulness. We should anticipate the ultimate bonus: hearing the King say, "Well done." People in this life focus on the nature of one's job, but the Bible puts the focus on being faithful to your job.

Employer: Lead through Christ, like Christ, and for Christ. Now let us break this down. **Lead through Christ.** Oh, the challenge of leadership! You take on numerous responsibilities and make numerous sacrifices. You need the Spirit's power! Paul felt the pressure of leading churches (2 Cor 11:28). But he goes on to describe how in his weakness the grace of Jesus is sufficient (2 Cor 12:9). We must lead out of Christ's strength too.

Lead like Christ. Christ is not *just* the model Servant; He is the ultimate Master also! What kind of leadership did Jesus execute? Servant leadership. He displayed the attitudes those in leadership should follow. He came to serve. He took up the towel. He cared for the vulnerable. He did not seek earthly praise. He was a shepherd, not a dictator.

Lead for Christ. Paul says masters will give an account. As a leader, you may have more opportunities to bend the truth and make unethical decisions because you have less accountability and more control over your time. Remember, your audience is Christ. He is an impartial master. What this means is that you should seek to honor Him with holy leadership.

This Passage Should Change the Way We Relate to People

Our culture subtly tells us that there is a hierarchy of value among individuals, and it tells us where we fit in this value system. This text crushes that idea. Although there are different roles, in no way do these roles define one's value.

This hierarchy does not exist for the Christian. We have the same Lord, and we await the same judgment (Rom 2:6-11). Further, James tells us that showing partiality is inconsistent with the gospel of Jesus (Jas 2:1).

We should relate to people differently from the way our culture relates to people. Do not give preferential treatment to a certain class or ethnic group. Care for the rich and the powerful as well as the poor and the powerless. Be careful about your body language, your attention on others, and the way you communicate to others. Do not give the impression that you are superior or that someone is not worth your time. Do not dehumanize individuals by thinking less of them. Do not idolize any human by thinking too highly of her or him.

This Passage Should Change the Way We Evaluate What Is Important

What matters according to this text? It is your relationship with Christ. The most important thing in this life is not whether you work in a sawmill or an office building in a nice part of downtown. What matters is how you respond to Jesus Christ. Is He your Master?

Jesus said it like this: "For what does it benefit a man to gain the whole world yet lose his life?" (Mark 8:36). If you know Christ, then you are rich. Because of this, one can say with Paul, "As having nothing yet possessing everything" (2 Cor 6:10). The person who has Jesus and nothing has no less than the person who has Jesus and everything else. Do you belong to Jesus Christ? Then you have everything! Then what you do in this life matters. It matters in this life, and it will be revealed in the next life. What matters most to you? The economy? The president? Your team? Your grades? We should all long to say it like Paul: "For me, living is Christ and dying is gain" (Phil 1:21).

If you do not have Christ, then you need to receive the One who, though being the ultimate Master, became the ultimate Servant, dying for sinners like us. Jesus came to do for us what we could not do for ourselves: to free us from slavery to sin and bring us into loving relationship with the Father. He came to give us what we could not earn: spiritual life. He came to make us what we could not become: no longer slaves, but sons. He is the obedient Servant, the best Master, and the sovereign Lord. Look to Him and live.

Reflect and Discuss

1. What are some differences between slavery in Paul's context and American slavery?
2. Why should Christians oppose slavery?
3. How does Paul undermine slavery?
4. How does Paul teach slaves to work? Which of these points impacted you the most?
5. How does Paul teach masters to lead? How do you think non-Christian masters would have responded to Paul's words in the first century?
6. How should this passage change the way we work? Explain.
7. How should this passage change the way we relate to people?
8. How should this passage change the way we evaluate what's important?
9. How was Jesus the obedient Servant and the best Master?
10. Stop and pray for your own work situation. Pray for your superiors. Pray for your own heart as you seek to apply this passage.

Life Is War

EPHESIANS 6:10-24

Main Idea: Believers are called to stand firm in the midst of spiritual warfare by God's power, with God's armor, and in constant prayer.

How to Stand Strong in Spiritual Warfare

I. **Be Aware of the Battle (6:10-13).**
  A. We need the Lord's strength (6:10-11,13).
  B. We need to know our enemy (6:11-13).
II. **Be Equipped with God's Armor (6:13-17).**
  A. Belt of truth (6:14a)
  B. Breastplate of righteousness (6:14b)
  C. Gospel shoes (6:15)
  D. Shield of faith (6:16)
  E. Helmet of salvation (6:17a)
  F. Sword of the Spirit (6:17b)
III. **Be Devoted to Prayer (6:18-20).**
  A. Pray comprehensively (6:18).
  B. Pray for gospel boldness (6:19-20).
IV. **Final Remarks (6:21-24)**

My hunch is that modern readers come to this passage in one of three ways. Some love this passage. Their favorite movies may be *Braveheart, Gladiator, 300, Blackhawk Down,* and *Saving Private Ryan.* Some of them love UFC. Some probably enjoy fireworks and drive camouflage F-150s with gun racks. They get excited about gun ranges, paintball, and face paint. For these types, "the armor of God" passage is super interesting.

Others may find this text antiquated and ridiculous because of the description of ancient weaponry and warfare. A person dressed up in a tin suit does not communicate strength and vitality and security to us in the twenty-first century! We find security in soldiers with M16s, sniper rifles, grenades, laser-guided weapons, and tanks. Even better would be some soldiers with attack helicopters and stealth bombers (or perhaps a few drones). For modern adults—and even today's kids who grow up playing video games that rarely have men in tin suits—this picture may seem a bit ridiculous.

Another group might find this militaristic language fanatical and unenlightened. Have we not had enough of religious holy war talk? Is not all Paul's talk about "the Spirit" and "evil" simply the product of an uninformed, superstitious writer? Are not the real problems in the world simply psychological, physiological, relational, economical, and/or political?

How should we respond to such questions? Allow me to make four introductory points.

This passage is not antiquated; it is ageless. While it may seem old-fashioned, it could not be more relevant. We cannot replace the items of armor with contemporary items—"the bazooka of righteousness" or "the drone of truth"—not only because it would be silly but because it would lose the metaphorical point. Part of the point has to do with the part of the body these pieces cover, so a tank or a drone would simply not apply.

This passage is ageless because humanity has not changed. Our spiritual needs have not changed, and the evil one is still active. He is just as active now as he was in the garden. Believers in Ephesus, and believers in every city, have the same need for Christ and His mighty power.

In addition, this passage is not ridiculous; it is rooted in the Old Testament. While Paul is certainly aware of Roman soldiers, and was maybe even looking at them at the time of writing, his language is more influenced by the majestic warfare imagery of the Old Testament, especially from Isaiah. The Old Testament often refers to God (and His Messiah) as a warrior and His people as "troops" who are in need of God's strength. Here are a few:

> *The Lord is a warrior;*
> *Yahweh is His name.* (Exod 15:3)

> *You have clothed me with strength for battle;*
> *You subdue my adversaries beneath me.* (Ps 18:39)

> *Contend, O Lord, with those who contend with me;*
> *fight against those who fight against me!*
> *Take hold of shield and buckler*
> *and rise for my help!*
> *Draw the spear and javelin against my pursuers!*
> *Say to my soul, "I am your salvation!"* (Ps 35:1-3 ESV)

The LORD advances like a warrior;
He stirs up His zeal like a soldier.
He shouts, He roars aloud,
He prevails over His enemies. (Isa 42:13)

How beautiful on the mountains
are the feet of the herald,
who proclaims peace,
who brings news of good things,
who proclaims salvation,
who says to Zion, "Your God reigns!" (Isa 52:7)

Even more significantly, God and His Messiah also wear these items mentioned in Ephesians 6.

Righteousness will be a belt around His loins;
faithfulness will be a belt around His waist. (Isa 11:5)

He made my words like a sharp sword;
He hid me in the shadow of His hand.
He made me like a sharpened arrow;
He hid me in His quiver. (Isa 49:2)

Paul is picking up these allusions. Paul's readers resonate with this background, and so should we. This passage is rooted in the Old Testament imagery of the King of kings. It points us to the nature of the Messiah and His mighty works.

Next, this passage is not bizarre; it is a brilliant conclusion. It serves as a climactic conclusion to an amazing letter. The armor of God does not come out of nowhere. Paul alludes to several key ideas that were already mentioned in the letter:

- *Divine power*—The call to "be strengthened . . . by His vast strength" (6:10) draws our minds back to the earlier prayers (1:19-20; 3:16,20).
- *Already/not yet*—This passage reminds us that Christ has already triumphed over the powers of darkness (1:21; 3:10; 4:8), giving us new life and freeing us from the fear of these powers (2:2); but we have *not yet* experienced the full fruits of Christ's victory, for their powers still exist (though they are defeated!—4:27; 5:16). Ephesians 6 reminds us that a battle still rages.

- *Christlike virtues*—The virtues connected with the pieces of armor have already been mentioned: truth (1:13; 4:15,21,24-25; 5:9), righteousness (4:24; 5:9), peace (2:14-18; 4:3), the gospel (1:13; 3:6), the Word of God (1:13; 5:26), salvation (1:13; 2:5,8; 5:23), and faith (1:13,15,19; 2:8; 3:12,17; 4:5,13).
- *Prayer*—The summons to prayer in 6:18-20 also reflects previous language like "all the saints" (3:18), "the mystery" (1:9; 3:3-4,9; 5:32), and "boldness" (3:12), as well as Paul's imprisonment (3:1; 4:1).
- *"Put on"*—Earlier Paul said we should "put on the new self, created according to God's likeness" (4:24) and "be imitators of God" (5:1). Now he says we should "put on the full armor of God" (6:11). The armor given to us is God's own armor. To put on the armor of God is to put on the Messiah Himself. It means to be identified with Him and to fight with His strength, displaying His character.

Therefore, what we have here is a carefully put-together conclusion that recaps and motivates the hearer.

We must remember a few things about this passage, like the fact that the critical battle has already been won! There is just a mop-up operation going on. Christ is Lord, and we are in Him.

Remember also that the emphasis is not on us memorizing each piece of armor and "praying it on." It is more about putting on the characteristics and virtues that are ours through our union with Jesus Christ. We are to put on Christ, which simply means, as in 4:24, to recognize who we are in Christ and to live consistently with that identity with the spiritual resources that are ours. Because of this emphasis we have confidence and hope! We do not have to live in bondage and in fear.

Finally, this passage is not uninformed; it is truly informed. Paul has been speaking of the *ethical and relational* challenge we have in 4:1–6:9. Now he points out with more emphasis the *cosmic and spiritual* battle that exists. We should note that Paul has already mentioned life in the Spirit. However, here he addresses it with greater, more sustained, cosmic emphasis. He shows us that more is going on than meets the eye. We cannot simply say that our relational challenges in the church, our behavioral challenges in the home, or our ethical challenges in society are the results of everything *except* spiritual problems. They may surely involve physical and psychological challenges, but we are complex beings; and many of our problems are spiritual warfare issues. Paul takes us from a moral perspective to a cosmic perspective. As Stott says, "Beneath the surface, an unseen spiritual battle is raging" (*Ephesians*, 261).

In our culture everyone wants to talk about problems without talking about evil, faith, or the Spirit. Anyone who proposes a spiritual cause to a problem is labeled as a *fanatic*, or *naïve, silly, unenlightened*, or *uninformed* about the real issues. Some may give a sentimental value to those of faith but nothing more. In their hearts they believe such talk is inane.

We think we are so advanced, and yet the streets still run with blood; humans are being oppressed, treated like animals; families are breaking down everywhere, and so on. We are in a broken world that is influenced by the "god of this age" (2 Cor 4:4). The Bible will not allow for a simplistic answer to the problems of this world. Clearly there are some answers in the fields of sociology, biology, etc., but they cannot and will not provide all the answers. You must take into account sin and Satan when you try to assess the problems of this world. Paul, as a trustworthy and inspired apostle, is not uninformed about the real problems; he is informing us about the real, unseen battle beneath these visible problems. Let us now consider his words.

How to Stand Strong in Spiritual Warfare

In Ephesians 6:10-17 Paul exhorts the Ephesians (and us) to stand firm, by God's strength, in God's armor, in the midst of spiritual warfare. The three imperatives are "be strengthened," "put on the full armor of God," and "stand." These imperatives "dominate the text, the rest of the verses are explanatory" (Snodgrass, *Ephesians*, 337). Notice the lead sentence in verse 10: "Be strengthened by the Lord and by His vast strength." The next verse shows how this strength is appropriated: "Put on the full armor of God"; and why it is necessary: "So that you can stand against the tactics of the Devil." Again the point is to stand in God's strength with God's armor in the midst of spiritual warfare.

Notice the repetition: "stand" (v. 11), "withstand" (v. 13 ESV), "take your stand" (v. 13), and "stand, therefore." In verse 14 "stand" is issued as an imperative, and according to O'Brien it "is the chief admonition of the passage" (*Ephesians*, 472).

Observe a defensive element here. We must "resist" the Devil's temptations. It calls to my mind James's words, "Resist the Devil, and he will flee from you" (Jas 4:7). Stand, holding your ground, not giving in an inch. Say, "I will not yield to your temptation. I will not listen to your lies. I will not budge."

But there is also an offensive element in the text. We are to take up the sword of the Spirit (v. 17) and speak the gospel in the face of opposition (vv. 19-20).

Paul also highlights a corporate element in the text. Together, we must put on the armor of God (cf. Phil 1:27-28). If you are familiar with the Battle of Thermopylae, that is the picture I get. It was one of the most famous last stands. In 480 BC, though outnumbered, the Greeks held back the mighty Persians for three days. Like the three hundred Spartans, we too take our stand, fighting our enemies in God's power. We fight together clothed in the armor of God, which allows us to extinguish the arrows of our enemies.

We may apply this all-important text in three parts: be aware of the battle, be equipped with God's armor, and be devoted to prayer. This is how we stand firm against the enemy's attacks and how we advance the gospel in the midst of opposition.

Be Aware of the Battle
EPHESIANS 6:10-13

We Need the Lord's Strength (6:10-11,13)

Paul begins with "finally, be strengthened by the Lord and in and by His vast strength." We must be strengthened by the mighty power of the Lord because we do not want to crumble when the evil one tempts us. Do not look in the wrong place for strength. Our strength is not in our resources and ability, in how long we have been Christians, in how much we know about the Bible, or in how long we have been in ministry. Our strength is in our union with Jesus Christ and His mighty power (1:19). In another passage that alludes to being a soldier, Paul says, "Be strong in the grace that is in Christ Jesus" (2 Tim 2:1). We are called to look in the right place, to the right person: Jesus. Say, "Yes, I'm weak, but I don't have to remain weak. I will find my strength in the Lord" (see 1 Sam 30:6; Heb 11:32-34).

We must remember who we are and what is ours in Christ. The strength that is mentioned in verses 10-11, and 13 implies that the Devil can be resisted as we walk in the Lord's strength.

We Need to Know Our Enemy (6:11-13)

Paul has already mentioned "the Devil" in Ephesians (4:27). His Greek title, *Diabolos*, means "slanderer." He opposes. He accuses. "Satan" in Hebrew means "adversary." Consider some other titles:

- "The Devil" (Matt 4:1; 13:39; 25:41; Rev 12:9; 20:2)
- Satan is head of the demons and his minions (Eph 6:12; also Job 1:6; Luke 11:18).
- "The serpent" (Gen 3:1,14; 2 Cor 11:3; Rev 12:9; 20:2)
- "Beelzebul" (Matt 10:25; 12:24,27; Luke 11:15)
- "The ruler of this world" (John 12:31; 14:30; 16:11)
- "The god of this age" (2 Cor 4:4)
- "The evil one" (Matt 13:19; 1 John 2:13)
- "The dragon" (Rev 12:9)

His various names display the fact that he is wicked, powerful, and cunning.

Consider how Paul describes the enemy. He tells us that the Devil is *evil*. We need God's armor because we are facing one who opposes God. Paul mentions "the spiritual forces of evil" (v. 12) and "the evil day" (v. 13).

Further, the evil one is also *strategic*. In verse 11 Paul tells us to be aware of the Devil's "schemes" (ESV) or "tactics." Satan is wily, subtle, and devious. Paul has pointed out some of the ways he works already. He tries to gain a foothold by tempting us to speak falsehood (4:25), have uncontrolled anger (4:26), steal (4:28), or share unwholesome talk (4:29). These are all former ways of life, the ways we once walked before God made us alive with Christ (2:1-5). Satan can make things look attractive and desirable and distort the truth, camouflaging the evil.

Next the evil one *wrestles*. In verse 12 Paul says we "battle" or "wrestle" (ESV) not against flesh and blood but against spiritual forces of evil. The word used to describe the battle is not used elsewhere in the New Testament but was commonly used for the sport of wrestling in the first century (O'Brien, *Ephesians*, 465). The context of the match is between soldiers. It is a close, intense battle, filled with manipulation and strategy. The Devil is not firing laser guided missiles from a distance; he is upon us. Jesus told Peter, "Satan has asked to sift you like wheat. But I have prayed for you that your faith may not fail" (Luke 22:31-32).

One might have wondered, "What do you mean we don't wrestle with flesh and blood, Paul? You have been beaten with rods, imprisoned, left for dead, shipwrecked, endangered countless times, and more. What do you mean your battle isn't physical?" We know from the apostle that behind these battles is another battle. There is an unseen, cosmic, and spiritual battle in which we are engaged.

Some think these "authorities" and "world powers" are political entities. They think Paul is speaking about cultural and societal systems. Even though Satan surely can and does work through such systems, I do not think Paul is referring to that here. He seems to be speaking of the powers that work with the evil one in general.

We must also remember that the Devil has been *defeated*. We can have confidence because Jesus has already won the victory for us (1:19-22; 4:8). Paul does not urge us to win the battle here but to stand. The authority of the powers has been broken, and their final defeat is coming soon. Just like a defeated enemy, Satan is mad about it! When you study historical battles, you see this trend. When an army is defeated, they do not easily surrender. They get even more intense and vicious. We are not called into this battle as if the victory is in doubt. The decisive victory has been won. We fight with confidence because all things will ultimately be put under Christ's feet!

In verse 13 Paul mentions "the evil day." There are various interpretations of this phrase, but I hold the view that this is a combination of the present evil age we are in (5:16) and of particularly tempting occasions. Consider Matthew 4:11 and the phrase "then the Devil left Him." This presupposes that the Devil had come in force to tempt and destroy. While the evil one wanted to attack Jesus all the time, he came with particular force at certain times.

We must stand against his schemes in our own days in which the battle is particularly intense. I have personally found I often meet serious spiritual opposition on Sundays or on my "days off." In these moments I must run to God's Word and prayer so I can experience the grace of Jesus to empower me to take a stand. And because there is a corporate dimension to this text, congregations should also be aware of particularly evil days in the church. Congregations must also immerse themselves in God's Word and seek God in fervent prayer in order to take their stand against the evil one. We are all in a battle—let us be aware of it.

Be Equipped with God's Armor
EPHESIANS 6:13-17

After telling us to put on the armor, Paul now describes it. The first thing to recognize is the armor is "of God" (v. 13). As mentioned, in the Old Testament God is a warrior (Isa 11:1-5; 59:17). The same armor the Messiah wears in battle is also our battle gear. There is no reason to yield one inch to Satan if we have put on the full armor of God. Nevertheless, we must be ready and equipped. We don't wear swimsuits or pajamas; we wear battle gear.

Belt of Truth (6:14a)

Truth is important in Ephesians. It is revealed in the gospel (1:13; 4:15), and believers must be truth-speaking people (4:24-25; 5:9). As we buckle on this piece of the Messiah's armor, we live in His truth and speak His truth, displaying the characteristics of our victorious King. Do not give the Devil a foothold by neglecting to be a person of truth in your language, behavior, and attitude.

Paul summarizes the source of truth in 4:21: "The truth is in Jesus." Coming to Jesus, believing in Jesus, resting in Jesus is coming to the truth. Put the truth of Christ on every day. Preach the truth of the gospel to yourself, and live in that truth throughout the day.

Breastplate of Righteousness (6:14b)

For the Roman soldier the breastplate covered the chest to protect it against assaults and arrows. Paul draws this language from Isaiah 59:17, where Yahweh puts on "righteousness like a breastplate." Once again we are to put on the virtues of our Messiah.

This does not refer to *imputed* righteousness—that is, our right standing before God. I never have to put on that righteousness because Christ has given it to believers permanently. Rather, this seems to refer to *practical righteousness*—that is, right living, as in Ephesians 4:24 and 5:9. Put on those righteous qualities associated with your new life in Christ, the same righteous qualities reflected in the life of Jesus.

Put on the breastplate of righteousness so you do not give an inch to Satan in the areas of impurity, lust, greed, or injustice. Realize who you are in Christ, and live out that new identity in righteous living.

Gospel Shoes (6:15)

Paul says, "As shoes for your feet, having put on the readiness given by the gospel of peace" (6:15 ESV). Soldiers must have the right kind of footwear. Shoes are important. Go to a shoe store today, and you might find Crocs, boots, biking shoes, hiking shoes, tennis shoes, basketball shoes, running shoes, baseball cleats, football cleats, sandals, flip-flops, and Manolo Blahniks. The message conveyed is, "Shoes are really important, and you need different types for different activities."

Paul actually does not refer to shoes specifically (though it is implied). His words are translated in different ways:

And with your feet fitted with the readiness that comes from the gospel of peace. (NIV)

And having shod your feet with the preparation of the gospel of peace. (NASB)

And your feet sandaled with readiness for the gospel of peace.

Without diving into all the interpretive issues, Paul is basically saying believers should always be ready to share the gospel. Be ready to herald the good news of Christ (cf. Isa 52:7).

Historians tell us that the Roman soldiers were issued great footwear. Their studded half boots enabled them to travel great distances. They covered a lot of ground in a short amount of time, pursuing the enemy into every nook and cranny. They went into hard places. We need to go to every nook and cranny also as we take the gospel to faraway places, even hard places.

Remember, Paul tells us to take up the whole armor. Paul does not say one guy can put on the breastplate (because he is all about holiness), another can put on the belt (because he likes truth). No, each of us must take up the whole armor, the whole character of Christ.

What are we announcing? Paul says it is the "gospel of peace" (v. 15). Isaiah says, "How beautiful on the mountains are the feet of the herald, who proclaims peace, who brings news of good things, who proclaims salvation, who says to Zion, 'Your God reigns!'" (52:7b). Earlier in the book Paul told us that through the blood of Christ, we are brought near to God (Eph 2:11-22). In 2:14 Paul says of Jesus, "He is our peace." We are reconciled to God and enjoy the peace of God through the death of Jesus (cf. Rom 5:1). Paul also says of Jesus, "He proclaimed the good news of peace" (Eph 2:17).

Jesus was the ultimate One with beautiful feet, who came with His gospel shoes, announcing peace to Jews and Gentiles. Those who know Christ have His peace and have this same mission.

In the midst of this passage on warfare is a message of peace. This is the difference with our mission and other religious missions. We are not taking life; we are offering life. We are willing even to lay our lives down because Christ laid His down for us, and we know He will raise us up.

Shield of Faith (6:16)

The word Paul uses for "shield" is not the small one, the size of a Frisbee, that left the body exposed, but the big one, the size of a door, that covered the whole body. Biblical writers often refer to God as a shield (Pss 18:30; 28:7; Prov 30:5). We have a shield to protect us from the darts of the enemy when we put on Christ, believing the promises of God. As we believe what He says about us, what He says is ours.

Helmet of Salvation (6:17a)

Roman helmets were made of tough iron or bronze with cheek guards and with an inside lining of sponge that made the weight bearable (O'Brien, *Ephesians*, 480–81). Some of us do not have the neck muscles to hold them up. Nothing short of an ax could penetrate these helmets.

Here again the language from Isaiah 59:17 comes to mind. Yahweh, the victorious warrior, wears the "helmet of salvation." In Thessalonians Paul calls it "a helmet of the hope of salvation" (1 Thess 5:8). God's people are to put on the hope they have in Christ. To resist the Devil, we must be assured of our salvation. Go to God daily and be reminded of the great object of your faith: Christ. Our hope is in Him. If you are trusting in Him, then do not listen to the Devil's lies. Say to the evil one, "I have been saved from sin's penalty, I am being saved from sin's power, and I will one day be saved from sin's presence." Say to him, "I am alive with Christ, redeemed, forgiven, reconciled, raised with Christ, and seated with Christ." Put your helmet on, and do not let the evil one get to your head.

Sword of the Spirit (6:17b)

The final piece of equipment is an offensive weapon. The believer must take up the sword and engage the enemy. The term refers to a short sword or dagger used in personal combat. It is the sword "of the Spirit," meaning the Spirit makes the sword powerful and effective. Paul identifies it with "God's word," a term Paul often uses for the gospel. However,

Paul normally uses *logos, but here he uses *rhema*, which usually refers to the spoken word. If that is the case here, then he is referring to speaking the gospel, which is powerful and effective by the Spirit of God (O'Brien, *Ephesians*, 482).

Again, one hears echoes from Isaiah about the Messiah here (Isa 11:4; 49:2; cf. Rev 19:15). We are given access to the weaponry of the Messiah for battle when we are united with Him. We are to speak the gospel in the realm of darkness so that those who are held captive by the evil one may go free.

I always enjoy visiting places that have old weapons, especially swords. Sometimes you can see the really big swords in the museums. Some of them weigh more than I do. What many think, as they hold or look on these massive swords, is that they are interesting but practically useless for modern warfare. No one would recommend them to be issued to troops today. How similar this is to their opinion of the Bible. Many people admire the Bible and may put the Bible on display in their homes somewhere (normally a huge Bible), but some of these same people never use the Bible. Why? They deem it like an ancient sword, useless for modern warfare.

This should not surprise us. In the garden the evil one raised doubt and suspicion about God's word. But do not be deceived. You can trust God's Word. You need God's Word. Do not go into battle without a sword. Read it. Meditate on it. Pray it. Proclaim it.

What about the soldier's back? Paul mentions no equipment for the backside. I find it interesting that in *Pilgrim's Progress* Bunyan says because Christian had no armor for his back, the best option was to stand his ground. Let us hold our ground against the evil one, with our armor on, as we advance the gospel into the world.

Be Devoted to Prayer
EPHESIANS 6:18-20

Paul does not begin a new sentence in verse 18. It is a continuation of thought. We stand firm against the enemy's schemes through prayer. We are to take up the sword of the Spirit prayerfully.

Unlike the other items previously mentioned, prayer is not associated with a piece of armor or equipment. However, a modern piece of equipment does comes to mind: a walkie-talkie. Piper uses this picture in describing prayer:

We cannot know what prayer is for until we know that life is
war. Life is war. That's not all it is. But it is certainly that. Our
weakness in prayer is owing largely to our neglect of this truth.
Prayer is primarily a wartime walkie-talkie for the mission of
the church as it advances against the powers of darkness and
unbelief. It is not surprising that prayer malfunctions when
we try to make it a domestic intercom to call upstairs for more
comforts in the den. God has given us prayer as a wartime
walkie-talkie so that we can call headquarters for everything we
need as the kingdom of Christ advances in the world. (Piper,
Let the Nations Be Glad, 41)

While such a device is not in Paul's mind, prayer is the means by which
we call on God to help us in our battle. What a gift it is to be able to
communicate with our God.

When Paul says, "Pray at all times in the Spirit," I do not think he is
referring to "speaking in tongues." We should understand Paul's words
in light of the rest of Ephesians. We should simply take it as a fact that
all true prayer is by the Spirit. We come to the Father, through Christ, by
the Spirit. And because of the gift of the Spirit, the Christian warrior has
constant access to God in the midst of the war (2:18; cf. 3:16; Jude 20;
Rom 8:26).

Let me mention just two parts of this Spirit-enabled prayer.

Pray Comprehensively (6:18)

Paul mentions four universals (four "alls") to express the comprehen-
siveness of prayer. We pray "at all times." So everywhere, all the time, we
can pray.

We pray "with all prayer and supplication" (ESV). I doubt a sharp
distinction is intended here with these two words. Paul is simply emphasizing faithful prayer.

We should stay alert "with all perseverance." Like good soldiers, we
need to keep alert and not fall asleep. This idea appeared in the ministry of Jesus, who encouraged His disciples to "stay awake and pray" in
light of temptation and the weakness of the flesh (Mark 14:38) and in
view of the return of Christ (Mark 13:32-38; cf. 1 Pet 4:7). We read about
persistence and perseverance in prayer elsewhere in the New Testament
(Acts 2:42; 4:23-31; 6:4; 12:5; Rom 12:12; Col 4:2). We need to persist
in prayer to overcome fatigue, discouragement, and hardship, and for
boldness in our witness.

The last "all" is making intercession "for all the saints." The unity of the church has been a major concern in the letter. Now Paul says we should pray for all other Christians. When you become a Christian, you get a new family, which means a new responsibility to pray for them.

The focus on "all" emphasizes the fact that because all of life is war, all of life must be lived in prayer. Since there is a war, pray. Pray all the time. Pray with all perseverance and supplication. Pray alertly and persistently. Pray for all the saints.

Pray for Gospel Boldness (6:19-20)

Paul, the prisoner in chains, humbly requests prayer from others because he wants to communicate the good news boldly and effectively. The greatest theologian-missionary of all times is asking for prayer! That should encourage you! He has the position (as do we) of being an "ambassador," a representative of Jesus; but, he knows he does not have sufficient resources to communicate the gospel effectively, so he calls on the church to pray for him. Instead of feeling self-pity or resentment, he asks for prayer for the mission!

Pray for others as they share the gospel. Why? Satan does not want us to have the right words to say or to be bold in the face of conflict. Evangelism is spiritual warfare. The culture opposes it. So we need God's power to do it faithfully. Paul experienced the Lord's presence in his own imprisonment. He writes,

> At my first defense, no one stood by me, but everyone deserted me.
> May it not be counted against them. But the Lord stood with me and
> strengthened me, so that the proclamation might be fully made through
> me and all the Gentiles might hear. So I was rescued from the lion's
> mouth. (2 Tim 4:16-17)

Final Remarks
EPHESIANS 6:21-24

After speaking of his need for God's power to speak the word and of his imprisonment, Paul closes with a reminder about his particular situation. Here we see that Paul was not just a theologian-missionary-church planter. He was a lover of people. In his letters he thanks people.

Tychicus is one of the brothers that made up the family of God. He served with Paul for some time (Acts 20:4; Col 4:7; 2 Tim 4:12;

Titus 3:12). Tychicus may have delivered the letter to Ephesus (as well as the letter to the Colossians). Can you imagine that task?

Paul sends him to "encourage your hearts" (v. 22). What a great ministry! In many ways Tychicus does what every missionary-preacher-evangelist does. He spreads the Word and encourages the saints.

In the benediction (vv. 23-24) Paul concludes by using the words with which he began his letter: peace and grace (cf. 1:2). He also mentions faith and love. It is appropriate to mention love three times in a letter that emphasizes the unfathomable love of God. This love, faith, grace, and peace all flow from God, the Father of our Lord Jesus Christ.

But notice that Paul adds something here that he has not mentioned in regard to love explicitly (though it has been implied), namely, their love *for* Christ. He closes with a statement about their personal relationship with Christ. Paul has told them of God's great love, but now I must ask, Do you love Christ? Do you love Him? Are you a Christian? Have you turned from sin and placed faith in the Lord Jesus Christ? Do you love Him with an "undying love" that will go on into eternity?

What a great question to end such a letter. Let us love Jesus! Soon we will see Him, and then we will put our weapons down. Then we will not regret having put all our trust in His perfect work, and we will not regret having been faithful soldiers engaged in His mission.

Reflect and Discuss

1. Why might some scoff at this passage about warfare? How would you respond?
2. How does Paul summarize many ideas from the previous chapters with this final section on the armor of God?
3. How is "standing" significant in literal warfare? What does Paul's frequent use of "stand" signify in spiritual warfare?
4. From where do Christians derive strength? How do we do so?
5. Explain the nature and work of the enemy, based on this passage.
6. Explain the pieces of armor. What does it mean to "take up the armor of God"?
7. Explain how you can use the "sword of the Spirit."
8. What does this passage say about praying comprehensively?
9. How does it encourage you that Paul asked others to pray for him as he proclaimed the gospel?
10. What encourages and challenges you most in Paul's "final remarks" (6:21-24)?

WORKS CITED

Akin, Daniel L. "Invading Satan's Territory." *danielakin.com*. Accessed November 15, 2013. http://www.danielakin.com/wp-content /uploads/old/Resource_201/Exposition%20of%20Ephesians%20 -%201.pdf.

Arnold, Clinton E. *Ephesians*. Zondervan Exegetical Commentary on the New Testament. Grand Rapids, MI: Zondervan, 2010.

Baker, Mark, and Joel Green. *Recovering the Scandal of the Cross : Atonement in New Testament and Contemporary Contexts*. 2nd ed. Downers Grove, IL: InterVarsity, 2011.

"Baptist Faith and Message 2000, The." *Southern Baptist Convention*. Accessed November 15, 2013. http://www.sbc.net/bfm/bfm2000.asp.

Barth, Markus. *Ephesians 4–6*. Anchor Bible. Garden City, NY: Doubleday, 1974.

Bonhoeffer, Dietrich. *Letters and Papers from Prison*. Dietrich Bonhoeffer Works, vol. 8. Edited by John W. de Gruchy. Translated by Isabel Best, et al. Minneapolis, MN: Fortress, 2009.

Bruce, F. F. *The Epistle to the Colossians, to Philemon, and to the Ephesians*. The New International Commentary on the New Testament. Grand Rapids, MI: Eerdmans, 1984.

Burke, Trevor J. *Adopted into God's Family*. Downers Grove, IL: InterVarsity, 2006.

Calvin, John. *Calvin's Commentaries*. Bible Hub. Accessed April 2, 2014. http://biblehub.com/commentaries/calvin/ephesians/6.htm.

Carson, D. A. *A Call to Spiritual Reformation: Priorities from Paul and His Prayers*. Grand Rapids, MI: Baker, 1992.

Casson, Lionel. *Everyday Life in Ancient Rome*. Revised and expanded. Baltimore: The Johns Hopkins University Press, 1998.

Chapell, Bryan. *Ephesians*. Reformed Expository Commentary. Philipsburg, NJ: P&R Publishing, 2009.

Chester, Tim, and Steve Timmis. *Total Church: A Radical Reshaping Around Gospel and Community*. Wheaton, IL: Crossway, 2008.

Christian Spectator, The. Volume 3. New Haven: Converse, 1821.

Crabtree, Sam. *Practicing Affirmation: God-Centered Praise of Those Who Are Not God*. Wheaton, IL: Crossway, 2011.

Duncan, J. Ligon. "The Obligations of Householders and Servants." *First Presbyterian Church Jackson, Mississippi*. Accessed November 19, 2013. http://www.fpcjackson.org/resource-library/sermons/god-s-new-family-an-exposition-of-ephesians-lvi-god-s-household-rules-marriage-and-family-11-the-obligations-of-householders-and-servants.

Dunn, John. "The Great Evangelical Awakening of the 18th Century." *New Creation Library*. Accessed November 20, 2013. http://www.newcreationlibrary.net/books/pdf/072_GreatAwakening.pdf.

Eddy, Sherwood. *Pathfinders of the World Missionary Crusade*. New York: Abingdon-Cokesbury Press, 1945.

Finlan, Stephen. *Problems with Atonement: The Origins of, and Controversy about, the Atonement Doctrine*. Collegeville, MN: Liturgical Press, 2005.

Fitzpatrick, Elyse, and Jessica Thompson. *Give Them Grace: Dazzling Your Kids with the Love of Jesus*. Wheaton, IL: Crossway, 2011.

Grudem, Wayne. "Upon Leaving: Thoughts on Marriage and Ministry." *Trinity Magazine* (Summer 2001): 20–21.

Hodge, Charles. *A Commentary on the Epistle to the Ephesians*. New York: Robert Carter and Bros., 1860.

Hughes, R. Kent. *Ephesians: The Mystery of the Body of Christ*. Preaching the Word. Wheaton, IL: Crossway, 1990.

Keller, Tim. *The Freedom of Self-Forgetfulness: The Path to Christian Joy*. Lancashire, UK: 10 Publishing, 2012. Kindle edition.

———. *The Meaning of Marriage: Facing the Complexities of Commitment with the Wisdom of God*. New York: Dutton, 2011.

Köstenberger, Andreas, with David Jones. *God, Marriage, and Family: Rebuilding the Biblical Foundation*. Wheaton, IL: Crossway, 2004.

Kuyper, Abraham. *A Centennial Reader*. Edited by James Bratt. Grand Rapids, MI: Eerdmans, 1988.

Lloyd-Jones, Sally. *The Jesus Storybook Bible: Every Story Whispers His Name*. Grand Rapids, MI: Zondervan, 2007.

Luther, Martin. *Commentary on Romans*. Translated by J. Theodore Mueller. Grand Rapids, MI: Kregel, 1954.

————. "Exposition on Psalm 147." Pages 107–35 in *Luther's Works: Volume 14: Selected Psalms III*. Edited by Jaroslav Pelikan. Translated by Edward Sittler. St. Louis: Concordia, 1958.

MacArthur, John. *Ephesians*. The MacArthur New Testament Commentary. Chicago: Moody, 1986.

Mahaney, C. J. *Living the Cross Centered Life: Keeping the Gospel the Main Thing*. Colorado Springs, CO: Multnomah, 2006.

Mitton, C. L. *The Epistle to the Ephesians*. Oxford: Clarendon, 1951.

Moore, Russell. *Adopted for Life: The Priority of Adoption for Christian Families and Churches*. Wheaton, IL: Crossway, 2009.

Morris, Leon. *Expository Reflections on the Letter to the Ephesians*. Grand Rapids, MI: Baker, 1994.

Moule, H. C. G. *Charles Simeon: Pastor of a Generation*. London: Methuen & Company, 1892.

O'Brien, Peter T. *The Letter to the Ephesians*. Pillar New Testament Commentary. Grand Rapids, MI: Eerdmans, 1999.

Packer, J. I. *Knowing God*. Downers Grove, IL: InterVarsity, 1973.

Packer, J. I., and Mark Dever. *In My Place Condemned He Stood: Celebrating the Glory of the Atonement*. Wheaton, IL: Crossway, 2007.

Piper, John. "Be Filled with the Spirit." *Desiring God*. Accessed November 7, 2013. http://www.desiringgod.org/resource-library/sermons/be-filled-with-the-spirit.

————. "Jesus Is Precious as the Foundation for the Family." *Desiring God*. Accessed November 11, 2013. http://www.desiringgod.org/resource-library/sermons/jesus-is-precious-as-the-foundation-of-the-family.

————. *Let the Nations Be Glad: The Supremacy of God in Missions*. Grand Rapids, MI: Baker, 1993.

————. "The Purpose of Prosperity." *Desiring God*. Accessed November 8, 2013. http://solidjoys.desiringgod.org/en/devotionals/the-purpose-of-prosperity.

————. "Race and Cross." *Desiring God*. Accessed November 1, 2013. http://www.desiringgod.org/resource-library/sermons/race-and-cross.

————. "Satan Seeks a Gap Called Grudge." *Desiring God*. Accessed December 9, 2013. http://www.desiringgod.org/resource-library/sermons/satan-seeks-a-gap-called-grudge.

————. "Singing and Making Melody to the Lord." *Desiring God.* Accessed November 7, 2013. http://www.desiringgod.org/resource-library /sermons/singing-and-making-melody-to-the-lord.

Rice, Wayne. *More Hot Illustrations for Youth Talks.* Grand Rapids, MI: Zondervan/Youth Specialties, 1996. Kindle edition.

Ruprecht, A. "Slave, Slavery." *The Zondervan Pictorial Encyclopedia of the Bible, Volume 5.* Edited by Merrill C. Tenney. Grand Rapids, MI: Zondervan, 1975.

Snodgrass, Klyne. *Ephesians.* The NIV Application Commentary. Grand Rapids, MI: Zondervan, 1996.

Spurgeon, C. H. *An All-Around Ministry.* Reprint. Carlisle: The Banner of Truth Trust, 2000.

————. "Christ's Love to His Spouse." *The Spurgeon Archive.* Accessed November 15, 2013. http://www.spurgeongems.org/vols40-42 /chs2488.pdf.

————. "The Great Change," *The Spurgeon Archive.* Accessed April 1, 2014. http://www.spurgeon.org/sermons/2474.htm.

————. "Jacob and Esau," *The Spurgeon Archive.* Accessed April 1, 2014. http://www.spurgeon.org/sermons/0239.htm.

————. "Our Motto," *The Spurgeon Archive.* Accessed September 15, 2013. http://www.spurgeongems.org/vols25-27/chs1484.pdf.

————. "A Sermon and a Reminiscence." *The Spurgeon Archive.* Accessed September 1, 2012. http://www.spurgeon.org/s_and_t/srmn1873 .htm.

Stott, John. *Involvement: Social and Sexual Relationships in the Modern World, Volume 2.* Old Tappan, NJ: Fleming H. Revell, 1978.

————. *The Living Church: Convictions of a Lifelong Pastor.* Downers Grove, IL: InterVarsity, 2007.

————. *The Message of Ephesians.* The Bible Speaks Today. Downers Grove, IL: InterVarsity, 1979.

Thielman, Frank. *Ephesians.* Baker Exegetical Commentary on the New Testament. Grand Rapids, MI: Baker, 2010.

Townend, Stuart. "How Deep the Father's Love for Us." Thankyou Music, 1995.

Tripp, Paul David. *Instruments in the Redeemer's Hands: People in Need of Change Helping People in Need of Change.* Resources for Changing Lives. Philipsburg, NJ: P&R, 2002.

SCRIPTURE INDEX

Genesis
1–2 *137*
1:26 *109*
2:24 *141*
3:1,14 *177*
8:21 *121*
12:1-3 *22*
15:7-21 *57*
17:1-21 *57*
26:2-5 *57*
28:13-15 *57*
37:3,23 *78*
39:2,3,21,23 *167*
49:24 *99*

Exodus
3:19-22 *98*
15 *27*
15:3 *172*
19:5-6 *13*
20:3 *123*
20:7 *123*
20:9 *113*
20:12 *149–50*
20–24 *163*
21:15,17 *149*
21:16 *162*
24:1-8 *57*
31 *133*

Numbers
12:3 *95*
31:7-9 *98*

Deuteronomy
4:20 *29*
5:16 *150*

6:4 *97*
6:4-7 *147*
7:6-8 *22*
14:2 *22*
29:29 *23*

1 Samuel
16:7 *86*
30:6 *176*

2 Samuel
5:2 *99*
7 *57*
12:29-31 *98*

Job
1:6 *177*
5:9 *76*
9:10 *76*
29:14 *104, 115*
40:10 *104, 115*

Psalms
4:4 *111*
4:7-8 *132*
18:30 *181*
18:39 *172*
23:1 *99*
28:7 *181*
33:12 *29*
35:1-3 *172*
68 *98*
68:5 *162*
68:18 *98*
78:71-72 *99*
80:1 *99*
90:2 *21*

93:1 *104, 115*
95:6-7 *83*
103:8 *47*
103:11-12 *89*
104:1 *104, 115*
110:1 *40*
115:3 *23*
119:18 *36*
119:34 *36*
119:53 *112*
119:135 *36*
127 *147*
127:1 *155*
130:3-4 *28, 115*
130:4 *135*
132:9 *104, 115*
135:4 *29*
143:8 *88*
145:8 *115*
146:9 *162*

Proverbs
1:7 *128*
1:8 *152*
2:1-5 *128*
2:6 *128*
3:34 *95*
4:23 *153*
6:16-17 *111*
6:20-22 *152*
9:10 *128*
10:1 *128*
11:2 *95*
12:15 *128*

12:19 *111*
12:22 *111*
13:16,20 *128*
13:20 *128*
14:16 *128*
15:3 *166*
18:14 *165*
20:5 *153*
20:17 *111*
21:6 *111*
22:2 *166*
23:26 *153*
25:11 *114*
28:19 *113*
28:26 *128*
29:13 *166*
30:5 *181*
31:10-31 *139*
31:30 *86*

Isaiah
9:6 *59*
11:1-5 *179*
11:4 *182*
11:5 *173*
26:19 *127*
28:16 *64*
40 *39*
40:11 *99*
42:6-8 *22*
42:13 *173*
49:2 *173, 182*
52:7 *61, 173, 180*
57:19 *61*
59:17 *179, 181*

60:1 *127*
66:2 *95*

Jeremiah
10:14 *111*
13:25 *111*
17:9 *46*
23:2 *99*
31:3 *89*

Ezekiel
16:8-14 *141*
34:10 *99*
36:27 *31*

Joel
2:28 *31*

Jonah
1:6 *127*

Micah
5:5 *59*
7:18 *47*

Zechariah
8:16 *111*

Mattheww
4:1 *177*
4:11 *178*
5:12 *126*
5:14 *126*
5:16 *52, 126*
5:27-30 *122*
6:12 *61*
6:12,14-15
 115
7:12 *161*
7:17-18 *113*
7:22-23 *37*
7:24-27 *128*
9:34 *46*
10:25 *177*
11:28-29 *95*
12:24 *46*
12:24,27 *177*

12:34 *153*
12:36 *114*
13:19 *177*
13:39 177
13:48-49 *113*
15:4 *149*
16:27 *165*
18:1-6 *147*
18:15-17 *66*
18:21-35 *115*
19:4-6 *137*
19:14 *147*
19:19 *149*
25:40 *74, 165*
25:41 *177*
26:64 *40*

Mark
1 *112*
1:11 *26*
2:5 *28*
3:5 *112*
3:22 *46*
7:10 *149*
8:36 *125, 169*
9:7 *26*
10:19 *149*
10:45 *167*
12:36 *40*
13:32-38 *183*
14:36 *26*
14:38 *183*

Luke
1:79 *59*
2:1 *26*
2:14 *59*
4:18 *162*
6:36 *115, 119*
7 *28*
9:35 *25*
10:27 *161*
11:11-13 *85*
11:13 *133*

11:15 *46, 177*
11:18 *177*
12:15-21 *123*
12:32-34 *124*
15 *45*
15:23-24 *45*
18:20 *149*
19:1-10 *113*
19:10 *167*
19:42 *59*
20:41-44 *40*
22:31-32 *177*
23:35 *25*
24:31-32,45
 35

John
1:14 *75*
3 *49*
3:3 *48*
8:44 *111*
10:11-18 *99*
12:31 *46, 177*
13:34-35 *67,
 120*
13:35 *34*
14:6 *12, 108*
14:9 *119*
14:15-17 *86*
14–16 *31*
14:18 *31*
14:27 *59*
14:30 *46, 177*
15:3 *141*
15:5 *84*
15:8 *51*
15:16 *22*
15:20 *71*
16:7 *31*
16:11 *46, 177*
16:26-27 *85*
17:3 *37, 107*
17:17 *141*
17:21 *97*

17:26 *90*
20:19-21 *61*
21:16 *99*

Acts
2:33 *31*
2:41 *66*
2:42 *7, 64,
 183*
3:16 *84*
4:8, 31 *132*
4:23-31 *183*
6 *66*
6:4 *183*
7:55 *132*
7:60 *84*
9 *18*
9:1-2 *6*
9:2 *11*
9:15-16 *71*
11:27-28 *99*
12:5 *183*
13 *66*
13:1 *99*
13:9 *132*
13:48 *22, 51*
13:52 *132*
14:23 *99*
15:32 *99*
16:14 *35*
17:6 *11*
18:3 *113*
18:9-10 *24*
18:19-20 *10*
18:23–21:17
 7
18:24-27 *13*
18:27 *51*
19 *18*
19:8,10,22 *8*
19:9 *11*
19:9-10 *10*
19:9-20 *10*
19:10 *8–9*

19:11-20 *11*
19:22-23 *11*
19:23-41 *10*
19:25-27 *12*
20 *17*
20:4 *184*
20:17,28 *99*
20:18-19 *8*
20:19 *12*
20:19,31,37
 84
20:27 *8*
20:28 *99*
20:28-29 *99*
20:28-41 *12*
20:31 *12*
20:36 *84*
21:8 *99*
21:9 *99*
22:4 *11*

Romans
1:5 *75*
1:9 *34*
1:18-23 *57*
1:18-32 *106,*
 123
1:20 *52*
1:21 *134*
1:25 *111*
2:4 *115*
2:6-11 *165,*
 169
4:2 *51*
5:1 *59, 180*
5:2 *38*
5:5 *118*
5:8 *48, 95,*
 120
6:4 *36*
8:8 *46*
8:9 *30*
8:11 *39*

8:15 *26*
8:15,23 *26*
8:16 *30*
8:19-23 *29*
8:26 *183*
8:29 *128*
8:29-30 *25*
8:31-39 *89*
9:1-3 *25*
9:4 *26, 57*
9:4-5 *56*
9–11 *22, 25*
9:15 *47*
9:20 *25*
9:32 *64*
10:1 *25*
10:11 *64*
10:14-17 *25*
10:15 *61*
11:6 *24*
11:13 *6*
11:33 *76*
12:2 *110*
12:3 *75*
12:3-8 *95*
12:4-8 *97*
12:12 *183*
12:13 *113,*
 119
13:12,14 *104,*
 115
15:5 *75*
15:13 *133*

1 Corinthians
1:4 *35*
1:27-30 *25*
1:28-29 *22*
1:31 *51*
2:1-5 *76*
2:2 *58*
3:5 *74*
3:10 *75*

3:16-17 *64*
4:1 *72*
4:4 *175*
4:7 *51*
4:16 *118*
5:9-13 *66*
6:9-10 *124*
6:9-11 *122*
6:11 *125, 141*
6:14 *36*
6:18 *123*
6:19 *64*
6:20 *28*
7 *136*
7:21 *162*
7:22 *164*
9:15,18 *113*
9:17 *72*
9:19 *135*
11:1 *71, 118*
11:3 *138*
11:3-12 *137*
11:24 *134*
11:26 *67*
12:7,11 *100*
12–14 *97*
12:28-29 *99*
13 *102, 141*
13:4 *96*
14:15 *133*
14:16-17 *134*
14:32 *99*
15:3-5 *58*
15:9-10 *74*
15:19,52-55
 38
15:32 *8*
15:58 *39*
16:8-9 *8*

2 Corinthians
2:6 *66*
3:18 *110*

4:4 *46, 177*
4:5 *96*
4:6 *36*
4:16 *86, 110*
4:17 *72*
5:10 *165*
5:17 *48*
5:21 *52, 120*
6:10 *169*
6:14 *125*
6:16 *64*
8–9 *67*
11:3 *177*
11:23 *74*
11:28 *168*
12:9 *75, 168*

Galatians
1:4 *45, 128*
1:6 *48*
1:15 *48*
1:15-16 *74*
1:16 *6*
2:19-20 *88,*
 120
3:13 *28, 120*
3:27 *105, 115*
3:28 *60, 162*
4:5 *26*
4:6 *26, 119*
5:5 *38*
5:16–6:10
 131
5:16-21 *46,*
 106
5:19 *122*
5:19-21 *124*
5:22 *118*
5:23 *95*
6:1 *95*
6:1-5 *135*
6:2 *67*
6:6 *99*

6:10 *119*
6:15 *52, 56*

Ephesians
1:1 *5, 7*
1–2 *83, 89*
1:2 *14, 185*
1–3 *149*
1:3 *19–20, 94*
1:3–2:10 *15*
1:3–3:21 *15*
1:3-6 *21–22,*
  89
1:3-10 *21*
1:3-14 *5, 19,*
  32–33
1:3,17 *118*
1:4 *21,*
  22–23,
  25–26
1:4-5 *23*
1:4-6 *15*
1:4-14 *21*
1:5 *22–23,*
  26–27, 63,
  97, 119,
  129
1:5,9 *23*
1:5,9,11 *23*
1:5,10 *23*
1:5,11 *23*
1:6 *21, 26,*
  48, 119
1:6-8 *14, 23*
1:6,12,14 *22*
1:7 *27*
1:7-8 *21,*
  27–28
1:7-10 *27*
1:7-12 *15, 21*
1:8 *23, 28*
1:9 *28, 174*
1:9-10 *28, 60,*
  78

1:10 *21, 23,*
  78
1:11 *23, 29,*
  38
1:11-12 *30*
1:11-14 *21,*
  29
1:11,14 *29*
1:12 *30*
1:12-13 *30*
1:12,14 *21*
1:12,18 34
1:13 *13, 24,*
  30, 32, 51,
  108, 174,
  179
1:13-14 *15,*
  21
1:13,15,19
  174
1:14 *20,*
  30–31
1:15-16
  33–35
1:15,18 *13*
1:15-23 *5, 15,*
  33
1:17 *14,*
  35–36, 85
1:17-19 *33*
1:17-20 *35*
1:17-23 *82*
1:18 *35,*
  37–38, 77
1:18-20 *37*
1:19 *15,*
  37–39,
  176
1:19-20 *38,*
  44, 75,
  173
1:19-22 *178*
1:20 *39–40,*
  82

1:20-23 *33,*
  37–39
1:21 *173*
1:21-22 *9, 40*
1:22 *139*
1:22-23 *41*
1:23 *41, 90*
2:1 *44, 106*
2:1-2 *89*
2:1-3 *44–45,*
  47, 50, 53,
  56
2:1-5 *6, 177*
2:1-7 *44*
2:1-10 *5, 15,*
  105
2:2 *45–46,*
  52, 173
2:2-3 *45*
2:3 *44, 46*
2:4 *14, 44,*
  47–48, 57
2:4-5 *89*
2:4-7 *40, 47,*
  50, 166
2:4-9 *14*
2:5 *44, 48–49*
2:5-6 *62*
2:5-7 *13–15,*
  48
2:5,8 *48, 174*
2:6 *49–50*
2:7 *48, 50*
2:8 *49, 51,*
  166, 174
2:8-9 *50*
2:8-10 *14, 44,*
  50
2:9 *51*
2:10 *15,*
  51–53,
  100, 126,
  168

2:11 *55–56,*
  105
2:11–3:21 *15*
2:11-12 *56,*
  68
2:11-22 *5, 16,*
  30, 55, 77,
  90, 120,
  130, 164,
  180
2:12 *56–57,*
  96
2:12,17,19 *68*
2:13 *14, 55,*
  57–58,
  166
2:13-14 *55*
2:13-18 *55,*
  57
2:13,19-22 *68*
2:14 *14, 55,*
  59, 95,
  180
2:14-15 *16*
2:14-16 *59*
2:14-18 *174*
2:15 *59–60*
2:16 *55, 60*
2:17 *14, 61,*
  180
2:18 *61, 63,*
  68, 79, 82,
  85, 183
2:19 *14, 16,*
  57, 63, 73
2:19-22 *62,*
  68
2:20 *7, 64,*
  98–99
2:20-22 *64*
3:1 *5–6,*
  70–71, 82,
  94, 174
3:1,6,8 *70*

3:1-13 *5, 70*
3:1,13 *71*
3:2 *70*
3:2-6 *72, 77*
3:2-13 *82*
3:3-4,9 *174*
3:4 *72–73*
3:4-6 *70*
3:5 *73, 99*
3:5-6 *73*
3:6 *174*
3:7 *74–75*
3:7-8 *6, 74*
3:8 *4, 70,
    74–76, 97*
3:8-9 *75*
3:8-10 *75*
3:8,18 *13*
3:9 *73, 76*
3:10 *4, 173*
3:10-11 *77*
3:11 *78*
3:12 *61, 79,
    85*
3:12,17 *174*
3:13 *71–72*
3:14 *69, 82*
3:14-15 *83,
    118*
3:14-16 *82*
3:14-21 *5, 79,
    82*
3:16 *30,
    85–86,
    183*
3:16-17 *86*
3:16-19 *85*
3:16,20 *173*
3:17 *85–86,
    89*
3:17-19 *87*
3:18 *86, 89,
    174*

3:19 *85–86,
    89–90, 95*
3:20 *85–86,
    91*
3:20-21
    91–92
3:21 *77, 91– 92*
4 *93*
4:1 *6, 94,
    105, 174*
4:1-2 *16*
4:1-3,17-32
    131
4:1–5:14 *16*
4:1-6 *77, 94,
    164*
4:1–6:9 *174*
4:1–6:24 *16*
4:1-16 *5*
4:2 *120*
4:2-3 *90, 94,
    101*
4:3 *14, 16,
    174*
4:4-6 *16, 96*
4:5,13 *174*
4–6 *26, 52*
4:6 *14, 85,
    118*
4:7 *14, 97*
4:7-10 *97*
4:7-12 *97*
4:7-14 *16*
4:8 *97–98,
    173, 178*
4:9-10 *98*
4:11 *98*
4:11-12 *77,
    98*
4:12 *13, 52,
    100–101*
4:13 *90, 101*
4:13-14 *101*

4:13-16 *90,
    101, 103*
4:14 *101*
4:15 *102,
    126, 179*
4:15-16 *16,
    102*
4:15,21,24
    111
4:15,21,24-25
    174
4:15,25 *5*
4:16 *102*
4:17 *17, 105*
4:17–5:14 *17*
4:17-19 *38,
    105, 109*
4:17-24 *105,
    110*
4:17-32 *5,
    105, 118*
4:18 *44, 56,
    106*
4:19 *106, 122*
4:20 *107*
4:20-21
    106–7
4:20-24 *14,
    105–6*
4:21 *107–8,
    153, 179*
4:22 *104, 109*
4:22-24 *106,
    108*
4:23-24 *109*
4:24 *104,
    106, 109,
    118, 126,
    174, 179*
4:24-25 *179*
4:25 *110–11,
    177*

4:25-32 *105,
    110, 115,
    148*
4:26 *111–12,
    120, 177*
4:26-27 *111*
4:27 *45, 111,
    173, 177*
4:28 *111–13,
    119, 177*
4:29 *14, 106,
    114, 120,
    177*
4:29-30 *111,
    113*
4:29,31-32
    116
4:30 *31, 114*
4:31 *112–13*
4:31-32 *111,
    114*
4:32 *61,
    89–90,
    115–16,
    119–20*
5:1 *27, 63,
    100, 118,
    129, 162,
    174*
5:1-2 *118*
5:1-14 *5*
5:1-17 *118,
    131*
5:2 *88,
    118–20,
    129*
5:2,8 *17*
5:3 *13,
    122–23*
5:3-6 *122*
5:3-12 *106*
5:3-14 *121*
5:4 *113, 122,
    124*

5:5 *123*
5:5-6 *124*
5:6 *46, 125*
5:7 *125*
5:7-10 *125*
5:7-14 *127*
5:8 *14, 118,*
    125
5:9 *126, 174,*
    179
5:10 *126*
5:11 *129*
5:11-14 *126*
5:14–6:9 *17*
5:15 *118,*
    128–29
5:15–6:24 *17*
5:15-17 *127*
5:15-33 *5*
5:16 *128–29,*
    173, 178
5:17 *128, 131*
5:18 *90, 106,*
    131, 150,
    167
5:18-21 *124,*
    131, 133
5:18-22 *131*
5:19 *131, 133*
5:19-21 *133*
5:20 *134*
5:21 *131,*
    135, 138,
    158, 165,
    167
5:21–6:9 *149*
5:22 *131–32,*
    138, 140
5:22–6:9 *135*
5:22-24
    136–37
5:22-24,33
    137

5:22-33
    130–31,
    135–36,
    146
5:23 *138–39,*
    174
5:23-24 *139*
5:24 *139*
5:25 *77,*
    120, 132,
    139–40
5:25-30 *136*
5:25-32
    139–40
5:26 *13, 139,*
    141, 174
5:26-27 *141*
5:27 *139, 141*
5:28 *141–42*
5:28-31 *141*
5:29 *139,*
    140–42,
    153
5:30 *141–42*
5:31-33 *136*
5:32 *139, 174*
5:33 *138*
6 *38*
6:1 *150–51*
6:1-3 *149*
6:1-4 *5,*
    130–31,
    146, 150
6:2 *150–51*
6:4 *151, 153*
6:5 *164*
6:5-6 *165*
6:5-8 *164*
6:5-9 *5,*
    130–31,
    146, 158,
    162–64
6:6 *164–65*
6:7 *164–65*

6:8 *164–65*
6:8-9 *138*
6:9 *163–65,*
    167
6:10 *173, 175*
6:10-11,13
    176
6:10-13 *176*
6:10-17 *175*
6:10-20 *17*
6:10-24 *5,*
    130
6:11 *174–75,*
    177
6:11-13 *177*
6:11,16 *45*
6:12 *177*
6:13 *175,*
    177–78
6:13-17 *179*
6:14 *175, 179*
6:15 *14, 61,*
    180
6:16 *181*
6:17 *141,*
    176, 181
6:18 *13,*
    182–83
6:18-20 *174,*
    182
6:19-20 *176,*
    184
6:20 *6, 71*
6:21-24 *185*
6:22 *185*
6:23-24 *14,*
    17, 185
Eph 4:26,31
    153

Philippians
1:1 *74*
1:21 *169*
1:27-28 *176*

1:29 *51*
2:1-11 *95*
2:3 *95*
2:5 *110*
2:5-8 *98*
2:5-11 *95,*
    141
2:6-11 *40*
2:7 *167*
2:9-11 *98*
3:10 *37, 101*
3:17 *118*
3:20 *63*
4:6-7 *134*
4:8 *110*
4:18 *121*
4:19 *85*

Colossians
1:4 *34*
1:5 *38*
1:9-10 *37*
1:12 *29, 38*
1:13 *26*
1:13-14 *27*
1:17-22 *78*
1:19 *90*
1:20 *59*
1:24 *70–72*
1:24-29 *70*
1:25 *70, 72*
1:26-27 *70*
1:27-28 *70*
1:28 *70, 76*
1:29 *75*
2:3 *128*
2:6-7 *89*
2:7 *89*
2:9-10 *90*
2:11,16-21 *59*
2:12 *49*
2:14 *60*
3:1 *49*
3:1-3 *110*

3:5 *122–23*
3:6 *125*
3:8 *124*
3:8-9 *108*
3:8-10 *108*
3:9-10 1*04,
115*
3:10 *109*
3:11 *60, 162*
3:12-15 *95*
3:15 *59*
3:15-16 *87*
3:16 *67, 133*
3:16-17 *134*
3:18 *137–38*
3:18-21 *145*
3:20 *150*
3:21 *152*
4:2 *183*
4:5 *128*
4:6 *128*
4:7 *184*
4:16 *14*
9-10 *108*

1 Thessalonians
1:2 *34*
1:3 *34*
1:6 *118*
2:9 *113*
2:14 *118*
4:3 *123*
4:11-12 *167*
5:8 *38, 181*
5:11 *67*
5:12 *99*
5:12-13 *99*
5:18 *124*

2 Thessalonians
1:3 *34, 134*
2:13 *134*

3:7,9 *118*
3:10-12 *113*

1 Timothy
1:10 *162*
1:14-15 *74*
1:15 *6, 96*
1:16 *95*
2:11-13
137–38
3:3 *95*
3:15 *63, 102*
4:1-4 *9*
4:14 *99*
5:1-2 *63, 146*
5:4 *150*
5:9 *66*
5:17 *99*
5:17,19 *99*
6:6 *124*
6:9-10 *124*
6:17 *124*

2 Timothy
1:3 *34*
1:5 *152*
1:9 *24*
2:1 *176*
2:2 *73*
2:9 *71*
3:1-5 *45*
3:14 *152*
4:5 *99*
4:12 *184*
4:16-17 *184*

Titus
1:1 *22*
1:2 *38*
1:5,7 *99*
2:4-5 *138*
2:9-10 *167*

2:12 *154*
2:14 *51*
3:4-5 *115*
3:5 *110*
3:7 *38*
3:12 *185*

Philemon
3 *34*
16 *162*

Hebrews
1:3 *40*
4:14-16 *79*
5:11-14 *102*
10:24-25 *67*
10:31 *47*
11:23 *151*
11:32-34 *176*
12:5-11 *153*
13:7 *100*
13:17 *66, 99*
13:20 *99*

James
1:5 *128*
1:27 *119*
2:1 *169*
4:7 *175*
5:17-18 *91*

1 Peter
1:1 *22*
1:3-4 *29*
1:8 *88*
1:12 *78*
1:16 *122*
2:1-3 *102*
2:4-8 *64*
2:5 *64*
2:9 *122*
2:9-10 *38*

3:1 *138*
3:13 *71*
4:7 *183*
4:8 *96*
4:10 *100*
4:10-11 *98*
5:1-4 *99*
5:2 *99*
5:2-3 *99*
5:4 *99*
5:8-10 *71*

2 Peter
1:10 *22*
3:9 *96*
3:12 *71*

1 John
1:1-5 *122*
2:13 *177*
2:15-17 *45*
3:2 *37*
3:16 *34*
3:18 *120*

Jude
20 *183*

Revelation
1:5 *27*
2:1-7 *17*
4–5 *133*
12:9 *177*
19:15 *182*
20:2 *177*